Divorcing a Narcissist

The lure, the loss and the law

Dr Supriya McKenna (MBBS)

Karin Walker (LLB MCIArb)

BATH PUBLISHING

Published February 2021

ISBN 978-1-9163023-6-5

Bath Publishing Limited
27 Charmouth Road
Bath
BA1 3LJ
Tel: 01225 577810
email: info@bathpublishing.co.uk
www.bathpublishing.co.uk

Bath Publishing is a company registered in England: 5209173

Registered Office: As above

Dedications

Supriya

For Michelle Coleman, for 35 years of unparalleled hilarity and friendship.

Also for Querinthophorez

and

In loving memory of my mother, Shashi Kanta Nahan.

Karin

For my family and friends.

"There is no greater joy, nor greater reward than to make a fundamental
difference in someone's life."
(*Mary Rose McGeady*)

"One person can make a difference, and everyone should try."
(*John F. Kennedy*)

Also from Bath Publishing

Narcissism and Family Law

A Practitioner's Guide

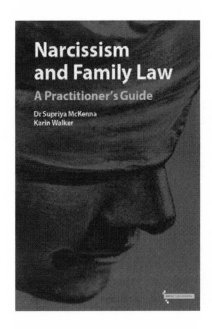

Order the companion guide for practitioners from bathpublishing.com/collections/family.

Narcissism and Family Law: A Practitioner's Guide will help lawyers spot when they are dealing with a narcissist, whether they are their client or on the other side, and sets out innumerable practical insights and tips for how lawyers can moderate the effects of their behaviour. Divorce cases involving narcissists get messy, combative and costly so the advice set out in these pages could save the lawyer and their client months of angst and unrewarding effort and help to keep costs proportionate.

About the authors

Dr Supriya McKenna

Supriya started her career as a family doctor (GP) and magazine health writer in the UK. Having developed an interest in the field of narcissism, she now works as an educator, writer, coach and mentor in this area. She advises professionals dealing with clients who have been affected by narcissistic individuals, and also works directly with those who have fallen victim to narcissistic abuse, including in the area of separation and divorce. She has hands-on experience of the UK Family Court system, and is committed to raising awareness of personality disordered individuals in society at large, in order to minimise the adverse impact they can have on those around them, and to empower victims to break the generational chains of narcissistic abuse.

Supriya is a moderately accomplished singer, an amateur poet, a dog lover and proud mother. She adores the great British countryside, beautiful landscapes and excellent architecture.

Karin Walker

Karin is a solicitor, mediator, arbitrator (finance and children) and a collaborative practitioner. She founded KGW Family Law, based in Woking, UK, in 2012, where her objective remains to guide clients towards the best possible solution that places family first.

Karin is recognised by both the Legal 500 and Chambers and Partners as a leader in her field. She regularly writes on the subject of family law, speaks nationally and internationally on all aspects of family law and has made appearances in the national press and on television. She was an elected member of the Resolution National Committee and chair of the Resolution DR committee from 2014 to 2017.

Karin is married with two children and two grandchildren. She is a Liveryman of the Worshipful Company of Arbitrators and a Trustee of Guildford Shakespeare Company. She enjoys gardening, running, walking her dog and spending time with her family and friends.

Supriya and Karin have also co-written a companion book for legal practitioners – *Narcissism and Family Law: A Practitioner's Guide*.

Contents

Chapter 3: Why me?

Chapter 4: The narcissist and their children

Chapter 5: Deciding to leave   133

Chapter 6: Practical early steps to take   145

Chapter 7: Early legal considerations   163

Introduction

Divorcing a narcissist may well be one of the most traumatic processes a person can experience. It is fraught with difficulties. At a time when you are dealing with the trauma of the breakdown of your relationship, and coming to terms with the sad realities of what that relationship really was, you are also being subjected to the most horrific, seemingly relentless, abuse at the hands of the narcissist through the divorce process itself.

The person you truly believed loved you, and who you loved (and perhaps still do), will turn on you with alarming venom. You will be left reeling in shock at how anyone, let alone someone with whom you shared a relationship and maybe even children, could be so cruel. You may be waiting for the punishment to end, for your narcissistic ex-partner to finally see the error of their ways, and become more reasonable. Perhaps even for them to become your friend, once the dust has settled. But there is little point trying to sugarcoat this – you will be waiting indefinitely. In cases involving a narcissist, acceptance of the situation rather than hope that it will change, is the only way to move forward.

You may not have heard of Narcissistic Personality Disorder until recently. Perhaps a confused internet search, as a result of the odd behaviours or abuse you were enduring, first brought up the term. Maybe it was a friend, a therapist, or even your divorce lawyer who tentatively made the suggestion to you. If so, please understand that even just grappling to come to terms with the fact that your partner is a narcissist is a huge struggle. But doing it whilst separating or divorcing can be incomprehensibly difficult. And, frankly, it is made much worse by the fact that hardly anyone you know will believe what you are experiencing. Narcissists, by their very definition, are charming, affable and plausible; but these traits, although highly convincing to those who don't know them well, are merely skin deep.

1

If you are divorcing a narcissist, you will need to be prepared for what is to come. You will feel isolated. You will be shamed for your over the top reaction to the split. You will be blamed for the acrimony. You will be told by well meaning but ignorant people that you are just upset, that you should not label others, that there are always two sides to every story. You will be badmouthed by your narcissistic ex to all who will listen, including work colleagues, and maybe even your own children. You will be stunned at how low the narcissistic individual will stoop with baseless accusations and frank lies. You will lose friends, and even family, as people side with your narcissistic former partner, taken in by stories of victimhood, with you painted as the perpetrator. You may be stalked, bugged, or receive threats of financial and social ruin (threats which may turn out not to be empty). When you need support the most, you will be abandoned, by all but your truest friends. And, to add to the confusion, you may then be sucked back into the relationship as the narcissistic individual turns on the charm and lays themselves at your feet once more, with shallow promises of change and undying love. Sad to say, this is merely run of the mill in divorces involving narcissists.

Here in the UK, as in much of the world, we are led by the US in terms of concept recognition. Narcissistic Personality Disorder (NPD) is only now properly becoming recognised in the UK as a personality disorder, and we still have a long way to go. Even doctors, psychiatrists and psychologists may be untrained in this particular personality disorder and unaware of the profoundly negative impact it has on the lives of those who orbit the narcissist and on society at large. If these mental health professionals don't yet fully grasp the concept, what hope do the general public have of understanding it? And, indeed, what hope does your divorce lawyer have?

Narcissistic personality disorder results, ultimately, in unsatisfactory relationships. Divorce rates are very high in this group, but although some narcissistic relationships are short term, it can also take decades for the spouse of the narcissist to finally see the limitations of their marriage and pluck up the courage to leave. Most importantly, a good percentage of cases which may be seen as simply 'high conflict' by divorce lawyers actually involve a narcissistically disordered person. Understanding the mindset of the narcissist enables you, as their former partner, to predict challenging behaviours, and therefore pre-empt them with effective strategies, in conjunction with a lawyer who is similarly well informed.

All narcissists have the same fundamental core issues and, although those with the disorder are infinitely different, as all humans are, they all behave in the same ways in certain situations. And the good news for you is that divorce is one such situation. Your narcissistic spouse will behave badly – very badly indeed, in fact. But they will behave *predictably* badly. And, in the words of Louis Pasteur, "Chance favours the prepared mind".

The purpose of this book is to get you through the process of separation and divorce with a narcissist with the least possible fallout. We help you navigate the legal system, with sound, practical information. We put you in the driving seat of your divorce, as far as possible, and prepare you for what may well be the biggest battle of your life. We wish to pre-empt for you what is to come, and to explain it, so that you are empowered to act in your own interests and in the interests of your children. We hope to remove the fear that the narcissist will instil in you, and help you to make rational decisions from a calm and logical place. We will try to manage your expectations of what can be achieved and how, and teach you how best to communicate with your narcissistic ex partner, both through the divorce and afterwards, if that is necessary at all. We hope to help you understand what lies at the root of Narcissistic Personality Disorder, so that you can understand the behaviours of the narcissist and what it is that you went through in your relationship. And lastly, we hope to take you onwards to the next chapter of your life – which, right now, may seem frighteningly blank – with hope, optimism, strong boundaries and fortitude.

But what if you are completely new to this strange world of personality disorders, and are wondering whether this book is even relevant to your situation? We aim to help you with that confusion and guide you, step by step, towards understanding narcissism, so that you can decide whether it applies to your spouse or not.

This book is designed as a companion guide to *Narcissism and Family Law – A Practitioner's Guide* for legal practitioners. It is absolutely critical that your legal team understands what they are dealing with if they are to avoid unwittingly becoming the instruments of your narcissistic partner's abuse. If they are not already very well versed in the specifics of NPD (and at the time of writing, most are not), please do lead them to this companion book. And if they are not willing to learn about what you are up against, in their *own* time (you should not be paying an hourly rate for your lawyer to be educated on this matter), then find one who is.

In cases like these, your lawyer needs to be your closest ally. They need to have empathy. They need to believe you. And they need to have the humility to be willing to learn. This cannot be emphasised enough. In this book, we give you tips to help you to find the right lawyer for you.

If this is the first you've heard of NPD, you may be wondering why NPD is not well recognised in the UK and why we lag behind our American counterparts in this area, both in the medical profession and in the law.

The International Classification of Diseases and Related Health Problems, Tenth Edition (ICD-10) is a large tome. In healthcare settings, this is the book used as the gold standard for medical diagnoses in the UK. At this point in time, what the Americans separately categorise as 'Narcissistic Personality Disorder (NPD)' only gets a brief mention in ICD-10. It falls into the 'Other Specific Personality Disorders' section, mentioned in only one word. So it's there, named, and nodded to for completeness, but without any detail. NPD is potentially further lost in translation in the upcoming new edition, ICD-11 (which comes into force in 2022). Here, *all* personality disorders are re-classified into a single diagnosis of 'Personality Disorder' which may be mild, moderate or severe. In other words, NPD is not specifically defined in ICD-11, although it fits the criteria as a personality disorder. The real world impact of this remains to be seen.

> " **Your lawyer needs to be your closest ally. They need to have empathy. They need to believe you. And they need to have the humility to be willing to learn.** "

However, over in the USA, the DSM-5 (the American Psychiatric Association's Diagnostic and Statistical Manual of Mental Disorders, Fifth Edition) is the authoritative guide to the diagnosis of mental disorders. In this manual, Narcissistic Personality Disorder is described in some detail as one of ten distinct diagnosable personality disorders.

It is clear that 'narcissists' (correctly meaning those exhibiting behaviours consistent with Narcissistic Personality Disorder) exist on our shores as well as in the USA – and recognising their well defined patterns of behaviour will be of great help in your divorce if you are married to one.

Of course, it is not your job nor your lawyer's job to 'diagnose' NPD, and nor should it be. Many people, understandably, also feel uncomfortable with the concept of 'labelling' when it comes to situations such as these. However, those with NPD exhibit exact, clear, repeatable, defined behaviours which are consistent and predictable. These behaviours, particularly through divorce proceedings and child residency issues, cause mayhem. By their adversarial nature, family courts are a playground for those with NPD, providing fuel for such behaviours.

Whether one feels comfortable using a label of NPD or not, the behaviours are occurring regardless. It is not necessary to acknowledge the label of NPD, if you feel it is unhelpful. But we do suggest that by acknowledging the patterns of behaviour, you will be able to approach resulting issues with helpful targeted precision. We also respectfully request that you accept that we will be using the medical terminology of 'Narcissistic Personality Disorder' as well as the terms 'narcissist', 'narcissistic adaptation' and 'narcissism' throughout this book as shorthand for the behaviours we ask you to recognise. For us, there is no judgement implied in using these terms.

Put another way, in spite of the shorthand, we are not confining people to a label. Individuals are as richly infinite in personality as the number of ways musical notes can be combined to form a symphony; we are simply pointing out recurring behaviours, in much the same way as a musician would recognise repeating themes that occur within different musical works. Every person is a symphony, uniquely original, narcissistic or not.

It's also worth being aware that as mere humans, people who encounter these types will invariably find them infuriating, especially in the context of divorce or separation. We are all guilty of labelling people in these circumstances; it is easy in our minds to label them as 'difficult', 'mad', 'nasty', or worse. We suggest that rather than reflexly making these unflattering judgements, it would fairer, more accurate and infinitely more helpful to all involved to use the correct terminology.

We wish you all the best in navigating these tricky waters if you are divorcing a narcissist. Although we cannot be with you in person, we want you to know that we are with you in spirit, all the way. We hope this book brings you information, courage and strength.

Dr Supriya McKenna

Karin Walker

A Narcissist's Prayer

That didn't happen.

And if it did, it wasn't that bad.

And if it was, that's not a big deal.

And if it is, it's not my fault.

And if it was, I didn't mean it.

And if I did,

You deserved it.

Anonymous

Is my partner a narcissist?

1

"*The acknowledgement of a single possibility can change everything.*"
(Aberjhani)

This book is written for those divorcing or separating from narcissists, so it stands to reason that, first, you have to be sure that it is actually a narcissist that you are dealing with. But recognising that you have been narcissistically abused may not be quite as easy as it sounds. Narcissistic abuse is mostly *covert* emotional abuse – subjectively difficult to spot and hard to quantify. Physical abuse, which may also be a feature of narcissistic behaviours is, at least, pretty easy to label by friends and relatives as being wrong, even if it's hard for the victim to be objective.

But before we talk about narcissists and how to identify them, we need to briefly focus on *you*, something which many victims of narcissistic abuse aren't so good at doing, as they've been so focused instead on meeting the needs of their narcissistic partner.

First, let's talk about you

If you are dealing with a breakdown of a narcissistic relationship, you will have been subjected to abuse for some time, the full extent of which you may not realise to begin with. Narcissists don't look like your average cartoon villain, nor the devil incarnate, and they are not always easy to spot. Abuse usually starts slowly, perhaps with small jibes or put downs, and the volume is turned up little by little – so slowly, in fact, that you do not notice it. A victim of narcissistic abuse is the proverbial frog in the pot of hot water, staying in the water as the temperature is slowly increased, becoming tolerant of the heat, and so not jumping out, even when the water starts to boil.

You will have to look deeply into your history with your partner, and view it objectively. And you will have to be aware that any abuse you have endured will have affected you in ways that make it difficult to accurately objectively assess your situation. It is usual for victims of narcissistic abuse to be surprised when they realise that their partner is a narcissist – but inevitably, when they are able to look back in the cold light of day, they see that the warning signs had been there all along. It can take a long time to reconcile the two different versions of your reality that you may have been recently starting to notice.

Why is it so difficult to know whether you've been in a relationship with a narcissist?

1. Cognitive dissonance

If you have been in a relationship with a narcissist, you will have experienced a psychological phenomenon called cognitive dissonance, and may well still be experiencing it now. This cognitive dissonance is another big reason why you may find yourself confused about what you have been through, and unsure if your other half is a narcissist. Essentially, cognitive dissonance is when the brain is trying to hold two opposing beliefs at the same time. For example, "My partner loves me because they buy me flowers every week and tells me that I am the only one they could ever love" would be Belief A. But if this person was also being cheated on by their spouse, then Belief B, "My partner keeps having affairs and so cannot really love me", would be competing with Belief A. The brain finds this very uncomfortable to deal with, and it looks for ways to resolve the psychological discomfort. It has a few options to choose from:

Denial. Here the brain simply tunes out from the belief it doesn't like, by denying that it ever happened ("He didn't really ever cheat on me – I believe what he says. He loves me"). Here Belief A has won.

Minimising. ("He cheated on me, but that's not so bad – all men cheat. He loves me"). Again, Belief A has won.

Justification. Here the brain accepts that the unwanted thing happened, but justifies it, so that it is not an issue and it doesn't compete with the other belief ("He cheated on me, but it was my fault, because I had been distant due to my mother's illness. He still loves me"). Belief A has won again.

Acceptance/powerlessness. ("He has cheated on me and he doesn't love me, but I am powerless to leave because the children are young"). Here Belief B has won. Note that the brain still feels relatively comfortable here, because it has chosen just one Belief.

In practical terms, this means that the brain of a partner of a narcissist does a very good job of convincing itself that nothing is wrong or of accepting bad behaviour – and does this outside of the person's awareness. It does it *subconsciously*. It looks for ways to feel okay about the way they are being treated. It wants to maintain a positive attitude towards their narcissist partner because it cannot imagine life without them. And the reason for *this* is the next reason why you may be finding it so difficult to view the situation objectively, if your partner is indeed a narcissist. This is known as Trauma Bonding.

2. Trauma bonding

The abusive behaviours of the narcissist (most likely to be stealthy and covert to start with) actually lead to their victims *becoming addicted* to the narcissist, losing their autonomy and becoming trapped in the relationship. They are therefore kept exactly where the narcissist wants them, as a reliable and steady source of attention, too invested to break free.

But how do the abusive behaviours lead to the victims becoming addicted to the narcissist? Narcissists use 'intermittent reinforcement' to keep their victims hooked to them. This works due to the brain being flooded with certain brain chemicals (neurotransmitters) during the initial honeymoon phase of the relationship.

If you have been in a relationship with a narcissist, you will always have been 'love-bombed' at the beginning. You will have been showered with attention, with over the top professions of love and grand gestures, and communication will have been constant. This is an important time for your brain chemicals, when they first start to be produced in huge quantities.

But what starts as the 'perfect' relationship, with the narcissist being loving and caring, then turns ever so slightly sour with subtle abuse. The victim, with a sinking heart, absorbs the blame and becomes desperate to get back the feelings of the initial phase of the relationship (related to the high levels of neurotransmitters in their brain). They find themselves jumping through hoops to placate or win over the narcissist, who gives out varying wins (big or small) at unpredictable times. Perhaps a tiny bit of attention here and there, interspersed with an unexpectedly lavish meal or profession of everlasting love, followed by a silent treatment and then mild humiliation.

This throws the brain chemicals into havoc – they are sometimes depleted (when they become craved for) and sometimes sky high. From a neurochemical perspective, this is an addictive cycle, similar to the one employed by slot machines, and it's precisely the varying unpredictable nature of the wins that keeps the victim 'in the game', chemically hooked to it.

The victim begins chasing their tail, eventually, perhaps over years, becoming grateful for the smallest crumbs of good behaviour or attention from the narcissist. Sometimes just the absence of abuse, name calling or silent treatments (if these are in your particular narcissist's repertoire) becomes enough to make them feel at peace.

With slot machines, the initial payout keeps the gambler playing, sinking more and more cash into the machine, hoping that the next win is around the corner. Just as they are about to tire of the game, a small win occurs, re-igniting their desire to continue playing for the jackpot. More money is lost, but another neurochemical releasing win follows, as they hoped. It is no accident that these machines are designed to be profitable. The gambler is never really the winner. And in exactly the same way, nor is the victim of narcissistic abuse.

This chemical addiction to the narcissist, as a result of their intermittent reinforcement schedule of rewards, is trauma bonding. It leads to false hope that things can get better, and a pattern of rumination in the victim about how they can get back to that place of loving calm. It teaches them to try harder. To be better. To give more. To ask for less. To want less. To dance to the narcissist's tune, and all the while, to be grateful for any scraps tossed their way, and to scrabble on the floor for them, starving and needy. These are the exact same tactics that cult leaders use to ensnare their victims, and they are all known to be pathologically narcissistic in personality. Addicts of any sort are driven by their addictions, and do not view them with objectivity. It's no wonder victims find it hard to see the narcissist for who they are.

3. The pain of separation

Whether your partner has left or whether their behaviour has finally caused you to leave, or to be considering leaving, you will be in pain. Bear in mind that the same areas of the brain light up in the emotional pain of separation as in severe physical pain. If your partner was indeed a narcissist, the 'trauma bonding', which you will be trying to overcome, makes this pain much more acute than in a 'normal' break up. It *literally hurts* – and no one functions well when in agonising pain. Again, seeing your partner objectively, whether narcissistic or not, is difficult when in this state.

Grief is big part of the end of a significant relationship, and it is divided up into several phases. These phases are not linear and the grieving person can oscillate between them, slowly inching forwards but taking backward steps every now and then. Denial that the relationship is over is followed by anger. Bargaining, where the person tries to 'make a deal' in order to avoid the grief (perhaps going back to their partner and trying to be 'better' or 'negotiating with God') is the next stage. Depression is described as the next stage, and eventually, acceptance that the relationship is over will come, as the final stage. If you are in any of these stages, except acceptance, it is obvious that it will be difficult to assess the situation with clarity. And, if you do eventually come to the conclusion that your marriage was indeed with a narcissist, then you will have the added complication of feeling as though you are grieving the loss of something that wasn't even real. Many people then add 'guilt' to the list of emotions they are experiencing, as they don't feel they even have the right to grieve. It's very complicated indeed, and hardly conducive to rational thought.

4. Episodes of 'hoovering'

If the narcissist does not want the separation, they will employ the hoovering tactic; seeking to persuade the other to change their mind and continue the relationship. This is often done through love-bombing (showering you with 'love'), promising to change and even threatening suicide. Often, this will lead to you, as the victim, repeatedly changing your mind about whether you want to issue divorce proceedings. You may find yourself having a petition drafted a number of times, or even issued but not served, or withdrawn. Narcissistic individuals are great at sucking their victims back in – especially if they have located their spouse's Achilles heels over a long marriage or relationship. They will play on your sympathy, your love and your sadness. It's confusing to say the least, and is guaranteed to throw you off balance.

5. Anxiety

You may be experiencing intense anxiety as a result of your unsatisfactory relationship, and especially if you have been experiencing narcissistic behaviours. But anxiety isn't just an emotion – it has physical manifestations too, as the brain tries to get your attention. We've all experienced anxiety in some form, perhaps before a tricky interview, or at an exam. Sweaty palms, shaking, shortness of breath, palpitations. But anxiety can be debilitating too – you can be crippled by episodes of chest pain, convinced that you are having a heart attack. You may suffer from diarrhoea that is so profuse that you cannot go to work. You may be doubled over with abdominal pain, or feel constantly sick. Panic attacks may affect how you live your life. Your sleep may be affected, and you may find yourself regularly waking in the middle of the night unable to get back to sleep, wrecking your ability to function in the following days. Back pain, neck pain, headaches, and every other type of ache, are common. They are not 'in your head' – they are real, but the brain is interpreting your emotional pain as being physical, misinterpreting the nerve signals as coming from a physical source. Distracting symptoms of anxiety are hardly going to help you in your quest to understand your situation.

6. Hope

If you are or have been in a relationship with a narcissist, hope that things will go back to how they were when they were perfect is a huge factor. If you do not realise that 'how things were' was merely the narcissistic individual reflecting *your* adoration of them back to you, you will believe that your relationship was real. You will believe that their love for you was deep. You will be trapped by images of their romantic gestures, not only during the initial 'love-bombing' phase of the relationship, but also in the subsequent intermittent phases where they sought to draw you back in after they had withdrawn, or criticised you and made you feel bad. Hope can prevent you from seeing the relationship as it really was. It has to be left outside the door, whilst you scrutinise your past to see if the patterns of narcissism were a feature of your relationship. 'Euphoric recall', which is the tendency to only remember the fantastic times, is a pronounced feature in narcissistic abuse, and keeps unrealistic hope in the picture.

7. Guilt

A big feature, particularly when you are the party leaving the relationship, is guilt, and a real narcissist will play on this with reckless abandon. As if you don't already feel guilty enough, you will be made to feel as though you have destroyed your narcissistic partner's life by considering leaving. Perhaps they will make you feel as though you have used them. That you lied to them when you made your wedding vows. That you are ruining the lives of your children by depriving them of a two parent household. Many people worry that their narcissistic partner's behaviour may actually be caused by a brain tumour, or any stress that they are under, or some other type of illness. They believe that they may be abandoning them in their hour of need, contrary to their vows of 'in sickness and in health'. Guilt is another emotion that muddies the waters of objectivity and makes it difficult for you to see your partner's behaviour as being narcissistic.

> "As if you don't already feel guilty enough, you will be made to feel as though you have destroyed your narcissistic partner's life by considering leaving."

8. Isolation

Many people who have been in a relationship with a narcissist have found themselves socially isolated as a result. This may be because the narcissist's embarrassing or self-centred behaviours have turned friends and family away, or because the narcissist themselves have deliberately isolated you from those you love, by their disapproval of them, or their insistence that you focus on them instead. It may be that you have no one to confide in, or no one who can give you their opinion regarding your partner. This can leave you questioning your own reality, with no 'anchor' to keep things real. Again, this leaves you confused about the realities of your relationship.

9. The after-effects of narcissistic abuse

If you have been in a long-term relationship with a narcissist, you may be experiencing unexpected, intrusive flashbacks which can throw you off balance. You may have become a 'co-dependent' as a result of the relationship, unable to prioritise your needs ahead of the narcissist's, or anyone else's. This inevitably makes it difficult for you to advocate for yourself, or to consider what would be in your own best interests – not ideal in a divorce. You may have developed the phenomenon of 'learned helplessness', where you feel unable to stand up for yourself, and you accept other people stepping over your boundaries, or treating you badly, as a matter of course. And you may be so used to being controlled by your narcissistic partner that you struggle to take back the control for yourself, and find yourself waiting to be told what to do. All of these factors can make looking out for yourself, and the process of working out and coming to terms with the reality of a narcissistic relationship, seem like an uphill struggle.

The overriding message here is that none of this is easy. Be kind to yourself. You have every reason to be confused. That said, let's now try to help with that confusion by presenting the facts as we delve into the world of narcissism and the features of those with narcissistic personality disorder.

What is a narcissist?

The term 'narcissist' conjures up a variety of images. Some think of the selfie-taking social media addict, expertly pouting at the camera. Others may suspect the mirror watcher, staring dreamily at their own reflection. You might guess that it is the combination of selfishness and vanity that makes up the essence of a narcissist. Power crazy politicians may spring to mind, or difficult bosses. You could be forgiven for thinking of drivers of flashy sports cars, or compulsive wearers of designer labels. Mildly irritating. Occasionally infuriating. Difficult at times, even. But relatively benign. Others may think of megalomaniacs or dictators; genocidal generals or crazed murderous lunatics. Cult leaders. Evil villains. People most of us are never likely to meet. Many more may think of 'narcissism' as simply a buzzword, trendy and overused; bandied about, here in the UK, for conversational effect. And a few will believe that, as everyone is a little bit narcissistic (this is correct, by the way), they should discard the term entirely.

But, as we will explain in detail, these stereotypes are not always helpful. The narcissist you know may have been flying under the radar for many years, without you, or others, having a clue.

We will delve much more deeply into the behaviours exhibited by those with NPD after a brief look at the textbook definition, below, which is a good starting point.

DSM-5 definition of NPD

In the American Psychiatric Association's Diagnostic and Statistical Manual of Mental Disorders, Fifth Edition (DSM-5), NPD is defined in two different ways.

The first is as follows:

- A pervasive pattern of grandiosity (in fantasy or behaviour)

- A constant need for admiration

- A lack of empathy

beginning by early adulthood and present in a variety of contexts.

A person with NPD will have at least five of the following nine criteria:

- A grandiose sense of self-importance

- A preoccupation with fantasies of unlimited success, power, brilliance, beauty or ideal love

- A belief that he or she is special and unique and can only be understood by, or should associate with, other special or high-status people or institutions

- A need for excessive admiration

- A sense of entitlement

- Interpersonally exploitive behaviour

- A lack of empathy

- Envy of others or a belief that others are envious of him or her

- A demonstration of arrogant and haughty behaviours or attitudes

The second, more modern, alternative model for diagnosing NPD is described in a new section of DSM-5 (Section III); the '*Emerging Measures and Models*' section.

In this new model, paraphrased below, NPD is characterised by difficulties in two or more of the following four areas:

- **Identity**. Those with NPD excessively refer to others for their own self-definition and self-esteem regulation. In other words, their own self-esteem and how they see themselves is overly dependent on how others view them. Their appraisal of themselves is either overly inflated or overly deflated, and they may vacillate between the two extremes. These fluctuations in self-esteem directly affect their emotions at any time.

- **Self-direction**. Those with NPD set goals in order to gain approval from others. They have personal standards that are either unreasonably high (in order to see oneself as exceptional) or too low (from a sense of entitlement from others). They are frequently unaware of their own motivations in relation to this. Because of this, they can be high achievers, or the exact opposite, expecting others to provide for them.

- **Empathy**. Those with NPD have impaired ability to recognise or identify with the feelings and needs of others. However, they are excessively attuned to the reactions of others, but only if these are perceived as relevant to the self. They over or under estimate their own effect on others.

- **Intimacy**. Those with NPD have relationships that are largely superficial. Relationships exist to regulate their own self-esteem. Relationships are not fully mutual, as those with NPD have little genuine interest in others' experiences and are driven by a need for personal gain.

In addition to the areas above, NPD is characterised by the presence of both of the following pathological personality traits:

- **Grandiosity**. Feelings of entitlement, either overt or covert; self-centeredness; firm attachment to the belief that one is better than others; condescension toward others.

- **Attention seeking**. Excessive attempts to attract and be the focus of the attention of others; admiration seeking.

Narcissists are therefore not 'evil' or 'bad'. Nor are they 'mentally ill' (unless they have some coexisting mental illness, such as depression). NPD is actually what is known as an 'adaptation'. In other words, this particular personality type became hardwired into their brains as a result of how they reacted to an adverse environment and to their upbringing in their formative years. *It was the way they adapted to their childhood circumstances that brought about their personality.*

Those with NPD cannot appreciate (other than intellectually) that others are distinct from themselves, and have needs, wishes, thoughts and feelings separate from their own. It is as if they are stuck in the toddler stage or adolescent stage of emotional development, in which the world revolves around themselves. If you take another quick look at the listed DSM features of NPD you may be struck by this. And if you have been in a relationship with a narcissist, this analogy is highly likely to resonate with you – partners of narcissists often feel that they have to look after them as if they are children, or put up with toddler style tantrums.

Although those with NPD cannot really be considered as intrinsically 'bad', some of the behaviours which they exhibit and the traumatic effect these have on those around them are certainly not 'nice' or 'desirable'. They may be acceptable in a three year old, and understandable in a 15 year old, but in adulthood they are abusive – and this is a simple fact. Little wonder, then, that divorce is rife in this group.

As the spouse of a narcissist, you need to know that NPD cannot be treated with medication. The only treatment is specialist psychotherapy, which can take between five and ten years to have an effect. The vast majority of people with NPD will not wish to be formally diagnosed as they either will have no insight into their personality disorder, or, if they do, they will not see it as a problem. This is a personality adaptation which serves most narcissists well in life, as they are able to exploit others without a guilty conscience (due to the combination of a fundamental lack of empathy and a need to see themselves as superior). Only a very very tiny minority (usually the highly intelligent, high functioning variety) will be motivated enough to undergo specialist psychotherapy. Of those that do present to professionals, it is often family members at their wit's end who have instigated the process of diagnosis, often as an ultimatum ("Either you go to therapy or we get a divorce"). Of these, most will drop out of treatment, as it involves a deeply honest look within, which is often too hard to bear.

Put plainly, the vast majority of narcissists will therefore never be 'cured' or 'changed', and to hope that they will be is a false hope. Accepting this fact is crucial for your own future well-being, but difficult.

Interestingly, a study conducted at Queen's University, Belfast, showed that the more obvious type of narcissist, the 'Exhibitionist Narcissist', is actually happier in life than most people. They are mentally tougher, and perceive less stress. For them, there is nothing to fix, as the exploitative nature of the disorder largely works to their benefit. It's not hard to see how this could have an effect on the numbers that present for diagnosis and treatment – to them it's a case of "If it ain't broke, why fix it?"

> **"The vast majority of narcissists will never be 'cured' or 'changed', and to hope that they will be is a false hope. Accepting this fact is crucial for your own future well-being. "**

How common is NPD?

The lifetime incidence of NPD in the USA is quoted as being between 0.5% and 6.2%, depending on the study and methods used. Clearly more standardised studies need to be carried out on this. What seems to be consistent, though, is that NPD is more common in males, overall men accounting for around 75% of those diagnosed.

The figures are higher in prison and military populations.

Is narcissism on the increase?

Many speak of an epidemic in NPD, with cases on the rise. This may or may not be true, but it seems that many of the traits associated with NPD are increasingly seen as positive attributes, to be aspired to, such as the ruthless pursuit of wealth, power, status and fame. It may be that narcissistic traits are being culturally embedded in our societies and being normalised as a result. Some psychologists postulate that the modern way in which we build our children's self-esteem may be contributing to a rise in narcissism, with educators and parents telling their children how special and unique they are to make them feel more confident, rather than encouraging them to achieve self-esteem through hard work ("My clever little princess...").

Many believe that social media has a part to play, with numbers of 'friends' and 'likes' conferring an addictive and misplaced sense of self-worth to those with narcissistic tendencies. Carefully curated, photo-shopped and filtered images, posted with idealised stories, give a sense of the perfect life, none of which bears any resemblance to the messy truth that goes along with being human. People can construct whole new identities, glittering online personas for the world to comment on, and to be jealous of. Being an 'influencer' is an actual job, and real life relationships and connections may be waning as superficiality increases.

Even online dating results in people being seen as commodities, not humans with real feelings. Empathy in this arena seems to be on the decline, with ghosting and breadcrumbing being the norm, and hook-ups are easy to find in this new digital age. All of this is fuel to a narcissistically disordered person. An excellent way to distract oneself from the chronic boredom and emptiness that lies at the core of this condition, and to bolster one's fragile ego with approval and validation from multiple sources. Perhaps these environmental factors are also making more people narcissistic, or perhaps they are simply just new ways for those who already have narcissistic personality adaptations to outwardly express their narcissistic behaviours. Only time will tell.

How does one 'get' Narcissistic Personality Disorder?

In order to get to grips with the confusing and abusive behaviours displayed by the narcissist, it helps to consider what led to this personality adaptation in the first place. Even though NPD is handed down through the generations, the consensus is that narcissists are made, not born – narcissism is not genetic.

> **"Narcissists are made, not born – narcissism is not genetic."**

As a result of their upbringing, the narcissist is deeply lacking in self-esteem, and has little sense of a true identity. It's crucial to understand that this is the core wound which leads them to behave in the abusive ways that they do. Almost everything that the narcissist does is done to avoid feeling the emptiness and low self-worth within them.

There are a variety of parenting styles that can lead to Narcissistic Personality Disorder. Many are as a result of being brought up by narcissistic parents, but this is not always the case. These styles can also overlap. You may well recognise one of these scenarios as having taken place in the childhood of your narcissistic partner. If you ever met your partner's parents, have a think about their personalities, and their likely expectations of their children as they were growing up. The clues will be there.

1. Conditional love

Children in these households may be brought up to believe that they are only worthy of love and attention when they achieve greatly. When they come first in the music competition or get into the national swimming team, they are showered with praise. When they get 99% in an exam, their parents may still ask if anyone else did better than them. They are not valued by their parents unless they are perfect and the very best in many arenas – the scholarship winner, the most polite child in the room and also the prettiest. Status and specialness is everything, and they are a huge disappointment if they fail.

They are not seen or heard for who they truly are by their parents, and are forced to have only hobbies and interests that their parents see as worthy, rather than being encouraged to explore their own likes and interests. Any attempt to show their real selves is met with humiliation, derision, withdrawal or disapproval. These children work incredibly hard to please their parents, desperate to win their approval and love, caught in a never-ending upward spiral of achievement. They develop a sense of self based on external validation, and a sense of emptiness within. The child comes to believe that they are only lovable if they are flawless, and becomes deeply ashamed of any areas where they are less than perfect. They have an important role to play for their parents, whether they like it or not. Parental approval and, later, the approval of the outside world become pillars essential for propping up their low intrinsic self-esteem and the image of themselves that they present to the world. Interestingly, as adults, they may describe their childhood as having been ideal and loving, and their parents as good. Does this sound like your partner's childhood to you?

2. The belittling parent

This parent, often a narcissist, may be explosive and easily angered. They ridicule and humiliate their children and partner, put them down and invalidate their feelings. They devalue and demean their family and others as a way of inflating their own shaky sense of self-worth, but of course, no child could possibly know this. They may alternate victims within the family unit, so no one is sure where they stand at any one time. These children tiptoe around the parent's moods, and may try to avoid them or placate them where possible. "You are useless" may be a common refrain, and the child may internalise this message but outwardly have the need to prove to the world and themselves that they are special, and that the parent was wrong. These children may grow up feeling driven to be wealthy, powerful or famous, as a way of justifying their own existences and finding external validation. They may learn that power is an effective tool to use in their own relationships. Alternatively, as adults, they may become afraid of seeking the spotlight, and seek to affirm their sense of specialness by basking in the glow of another. It's easy to see how NPD can be passed down the generations in this way. Do you recognise this belittling personality in your mother-in-law or father-in-law?

3. Using children as admirers

In these households an Exhibitionist Narcissistic parent uses their children as their fan club. The children are brought up to idealise the parent, placing them on a pedestal, and worshipping them. They are taught not to out-do the parent or seek admiration for themselves, and they are demeaned, criticised and de-valued if they do. In return for this adoration, the narcissistic parent rewards them with attention, praise and conditional love. These children can grow up to become so called 'Closet Narcissists'. They have been unwittingly taught narcis-sistic values and beliefs (and the associated abuse tactics), but tend to shy away from the spotlight, achieving their own sense of specialness or importance by associating with those who they admire. They find may themselves re-enacting their childhood role in their adult life as the supporting actress or actor in an-other Exhibitionist Narcissist's show, possibly with their boss or partner. If your partner is a narcissist, they may still, even as an adult, fawn over the brilliance of their mother or father, having never developed appropriate boundaries and behaviours. Do they constantly still defer to their parent? Does it feel uncom-fortable, watching this dynamic?

4. The overvaluing parent

These parents, possibly in a misguided attempt to raise their child's healthy self-esteem (maybe as a result of the so-called 'self-esteem movement'), see their child as unique and extraordinary. These parents idealise the child, in-flating their achievements and bragging about them, holding up the child as being flawless. They over-estimate the child's qualities, and over-praise them, lavishing them with applause even when the child doesn't perform well. They believe their child to be cleverer than they actually are. It may be that the child internalises their parents' inflated view of them and comes to believe that they are unique, extraordinary, superior to others and entitled to privileges. Could this be your partner's upbringing? Do your in-laws still brag about your partner, disproportionately?

The crux of the matter – narcissistic supply and the False Self

If there's only one concept you take from this book regarding understanding narcis-sists, the concept of Narcissistic Supply should be it – because this underpins every single thing that a narcissist does.

Those with Narcissistic Personality Disorder do not *look* as if they have low self-esteem – in fact, in most types, quite the reverse is true. They outwardly project to the world a 'False Self', which is an outward image (or a 'mask'). This False Self often appears grandiose or self-assured, and is so convincing and so at odds with the underlying emptiness within that a casual onlooker would find it difficult to see what lies beneath. This 'mask' can temporarily drop when the narcissist feels threatened, or abandoned. *And this self-assured outward image cannot be maintained without attention from others.*

The False Self has an important job to do. It shields the narcissistic individual from facing the truth about themselves – that they are vulnerable, afraid and un-happy – and it defends them against anxiety, depression, panic and emptiness. (Of course, you may feel sympathy at this point, but before you read on, you have to know this: it's sad, but all the jumping through hoops in the world from you won't change a narcissist's inner void).

Essentially, narcissists require validation from external sources, and this val-idation must be constant. Think of their False Self as a suit of armour which, although impressive, is constantly rusting in lots of different places. It needs continual repair, patching up and polishing from the outside, from multiple sources. No one source (or person) will ever be enough to keep the narcissist's armour intact. If your partner is indeed a narcissist, you may well recognise this feeling of 'not being enough' for them, and you may be aware of others, apart from you, who they also use to obtain this external validation.

In other words, narcissists need 'feeding' attention in some form or other to maintain the fragile image that they present to the world. This, in turn, props up their lacking sense of worthiness and self-esteem. They need to see themselves reflected positively in the eyes of others, and if that is not available, conflict, drama or attention in any other form will do.

This external validation is what is termed 'Narcissistic Supply'. Without narcis-sistic supply those with NPD are forced to feel their own sense of unworthiness and shame – this feels like an existential crisis to a narcissist, to be avoided at all costs. Narcissistic supply is the narcissist's oxygen. To a narcissist, the words of Oscar Wilde may ring true: "There is only one thing in life worse than being talked about, and that is not being talked about".

This plays out in the divorce process, a feeding ground for narcissistic supply, where the narcissist obtains it from their own lawyer as well as from the spouse, and, often through sympathy, from those around them.

To summarise, a narcissist is always on the lookout for narcissistic supply – at-tention, which comes in four forms: adoration, admiration, drama and conflict.

Without it, their false self crumbles and they are forced to face their own feelings of inadequacy, of shame and of low self-esteem. Look at those four words again – adoration, admiration, drama and conflict. Could obtaining these be the key motivators that drive *your* partner?

"**There is only one thing in life worse than being talked about, and that is not being talked about.** "

Oscar Wilde

What does a narcissist look like in daily life?

It is commonly accepted that there are four major ways in which those with NPD present themselves to the outside world; as the Exhibitionist Narcissist, the Closet Narcissist, the Devaluing Narcissist and the Communal Narcissist.

Whilst some with NPD will present predominantly in just one of these ways, some overlap is possible, depending on the situation the narcissist finds themselves in, and what works well for them in that situation. It seems that in some narcissists, one type comes to the fore in times of stress, but then recedes into the background when the stress subsides, leaving the narcissist to go back to their default type. There are also subtypes, which reveal themselves in the narcissist's behaviour. Some use sexuality and looks as their means of getting attention (the somatic subtype). Others use their intellect (the cerebral subtype). And some use all of these at various times, in varying proportions.

It's also important to realise that those with narcissistic adaptations, like all people, have a range of individual personality traits. They can be nice at times. They come in many different shapes and sizes. There are as many different outward appearances as there are narcissists. What is consistent between types, however, is their desperate need to cling to feeling special. It's just *how* they do this that differs.

We said earlier that NPD is more common in men (the ratio of males to females estimated at around 3:1), but this is actually only true in the Exhibitionist Narcissist category. This might be because brashness, loudness and being overtly competitive are traits which society finds more acceptable in men, whereas female narcissists tend to express their narcissism in different ways, falling into one of the other categories. Closet Narcissists and Communal Narcissists are thought to be equally represented by both genders.

Let's take a closer look, to see whether you recognise your partner in any of these.

The Exhibitionist Narcissist

Dennis

The Exhibitionist Narcissist (also known as the 'Grandiose' or 'Overt' Narcissist) is the typically extroverted type. They are superficially charming in whatever way works best for them, and on the surface there are unlimited different outward appearances. They may present themselves as the affable buffoon, or the magnanimous entrepreneur. The altruistic pastor, with a dedicated following. The hardworking doctor, the dentist, or the strong, powerful CEO. The housewife, with over-achieving children and the perfect home. The childless housewife engaging in Twitter rants. The failed actress, or the famous actor. Many are financially successful in their chosen fields, but many are not, preferring instead to exploit others financially, as a result of the sense of entitlement which is part and parcel of the disorder.

The Exhibitionist Narcissist

► superficially charming

► the affable buffoon

► magnanimous entrepreneur

► big personalities

► winning smiles

► sense of entitlement

What is common to all narcissists of this type, though, is their ability to deploy devastating charisma at the drop of a hat. At first they are very likeable indeed, with big personalities and winning smiles.

25

The recipient of their charms often feels flattered that such a person could be shining their light on them. The high functioning narcissists might be able to keep up the charm offensive for years, but lower functioning types will often let other behaviours come to the fore more quickly.

Traits of the Exhibitionist Narcissist tend to stand out less in younger narcissists (think of the arrogance of youth, for example), but as the narcissist ages, they can seem more pronounced and incongruent with reality. (Note that there are cases in which narcissistic traits become less pronounced with age too – it seems very much to be an individual outcome).

Dennis

Sixty year old Dennis is larger than life. Gregarious. Charismatic. Funny, even. He describes himself as a 'property magnate', although he is actually an estate agent, employed by a small local firm.

If you'd ever met him, even in his younger days, you would probably have found it difficult to get a word in edgeways. He has a tendency to shout people down if they try to speak, and he interrupts constantly. Dennis's conversation is purely based upon stories about his life, which he tells in minute detail, holding court for hours around a dinner table. He will talk about people you have never met, and about his job, which he explains in grand terms. And, if he is unfortunate enough to lose control of the conversation at the table, he will start quoting limericks and one liners in a voice so loud that he will actually be shouting, until everyone has to stop their conversations and listen.

Dennis will brag throughout his anecdotes what an excellent memory he has for detail. In fact, one of his favourite phrases, delivered as he taps his forehead with his forefinger, is: "I'm as sharp as they come – absolutely *nothing* passes me by. I'm one clever cookie." He's always been vain too – his locks are the result of expensive anti-balding treatments, and he'll regularly catch sight of himself in the mirror and say: "God Dennis, you're one handsome fella." It's all done with a big smile though, as if he's being ironic. It's disarming. At first.

Dennis might, at some stage, ask you a token question about your life, if you happened to be at one of these soirees. But if your answer lasted more than a sentence, he would start jiggling his hands and legs impatiently, and even humming

Dennis

tunelessly over you, before finally cutting you off. He would not listen to your answer, and certainly would not be able to talk to you further about it. Dennis doesn't do real two-way conversation. He talks at you, not with you.

At these events, his long-suffering wife, Jane, is silent, until asked to confirm something in his stories, which she will jump to immediately with the girly giggle that is expected of her, and which has become automatic over 30 years of marriage. The rest of the time she looks bored, empty, and utterly disengaged. A once vivacious woman, she hasn't felt as if she has been heard or seen for decades. Even her hair is styled the way Dennis likes – long and blonde, when she prefers a short bob. She loves red roses, but Dennis has never bought her flowers, often quoting 'a Chinese proverb' if she ever hints: "The man who truly loves a woman *never* buys her flowers", he would say grandly, making her feel that she should be grateful for this romantic non-gesture.

When she first met Dennis she was in her late twenties, paralysed with grief at the early death of her fiancé. He told her that he'd been sent to her by God to cure her of her grief. That their love was special, unique, perfect. He was dashing, clever and full of life, and her parents were charmed, and happily gave them their blessing to marry. At long last her pain was taken away and she felt lucky as he whisked her away from her parents. But she barely saw them again after that – Dennis made her feel guilty when she went to visit (he would never accompany her) and would punish her with silent treatments that lasted for days, until she came to learn that it just wasn't worth it. He was so lovely to her most of the rest of the time, after all. The same went for her friends – one by one she lost touch with them, and her circle contracted to just Dennis. "It's just you and me against the world", he would tell her. The ultimate romance.

These days, in restaurants, Dennis orders for his wife, without consulting with her, in an upper class accent that bears no resemblance whatsoever to his normal voice. He'll always customise his order somehow – a special side order that's not on the menu, a separate plate of basil leaves perhaps. He's slightly cold and aloof to the waiting staff, but not openly rude, not like you hear narcissists are supposed to be, although Jane cringes at his aggression and impatience when he orders a takeaway

Dennis

over the phone. Dennis always manages to look unimpressed with the food when it arrives, and if there happens to be an overweight person in the restaurant, Dennis will be sure to mention it later, and say how the sight of them eating put him off his food. No one would dare point out that Dennis is rather on the rotund side himself, of course.

When it comes to control, Dennis has taken over most of Jane's roles in the house, except for the most menial tasks, and is also in charge of all the finances and bills. Any changes to the house are decided by him, and all interior design and furniture buying decisions are exclusively his realm. He took control so gradually that she barely noticed, and when she did, she felt she should be grateful to him for trying to reduce the burden on her. A few years ago, Jane was disappointed that when he re-did the kitchen he did not install a new dishwasher in place of the old one, but she did not make a fuss. She just got on with the washing-up as expected, quietly resentful. She doesn't know how she'd cope without him, although she has fantasised about leaving for many years. But she knows that Dennis would try to destroy her if she left, both financially and emotionally – he has made that abundantly clear, with threats to burn down the house if she so much as thought about it. It's too late to leave. Besides, Dennis has convinced her in no uncertain terms that "no one else could ever love her".

Dennis has even stopped Jane, who once loved to cook, from planning and cooking the meals, wearing her down with years of 'good humoured' critiques of her offerings, and she's been downgraded to just cleaning up the mess he makes whilst cooking. She feels she should be grateful, but can't quite artic-ulate why she just feels angry. Dennis's meals are pretty poor, but delivered with such great fanfare that no one would ever dare tell him. He's convinced that he is a superior chef.

Dennis sold Jane's car many years ago, and insists that he does all the driving. Every car journey with him is a white knuckle ride, with blind corners being taken at breakneck speed, and terrifyingly risky overtaking. Dennis accelerates past horses, saying they should not be on the road, and ploughs through puddles, soaking any unfortunate pedestrian who might hap-pen to be nearby, completely unremorseful.

Jane has learned to zone out and dissociate from the experience, closing her eyes and trying to accept that Dennis is an expert driver. He's only written off a few cars, after all. She tries not to remember the time he drove the car through a three foot deep river, and got stuck in it, nor his seeming confusion at not getting to the other side. It was as if he thought he could defy the rules of nature – as if the water should have parted for him. But then again, the rules never do seem to apply to Dennis.

The painful neck she experiences from her head being repeatedly thrown back into the headrest after every journey with him is now something she has simply chosen to accept, as are the points that she has had put on her driving licence for speeding when Dennis had, in fact, been the driver. It would seem exploitation, risk taking, lack of empathy and a belief that the law does not apply to him are particularly prominent when Dennis gets behind the wheel.

Jane's world now revolves exclusively around Dennis's plans and wants. Her only family, her parents, are now dead, but Dennis's family, who have never approved of his wife, have always been in the picture. She had enjoyed working before and, briefly, during her marriage, but Dennis made it clear that he wanted her to be at home, so she gave up a job she loved, even though they desperately needed the money. When Dennis or any of her children are out of earshot and so free to speak, she will tell you, as the outsider, wistful stories of her days at work in hushed tones so that the family does not hear. But as soon as they reappear, you'll be struck by how abruptly and guiltily she changes the subject, and reverts back to her default subservience.

Jane has been accused of having affairs more times that she can remember, with almost any male that comes to the house. Plumbers, electricians, postmen, neighbours – Dennis believes she's been with them all, and if she can convince him that she hasn't had a physical affair, then he will accuse her of being emotionally involved. It's got to the point where she actually feels guilty when he rages at her, and finds herself apologising, reflexly. She's even questioned herself at times, unsure whether she's got it wrong, and she is, in fact, the one behaving badly. Even though she knows about Dennis's propensity for watching pornography on his computer late at night, she still

Dennis

believes that he has higher moral standards than her, because he tells her so. It doesn't even occur to her that he is projecting. That he is the one having serial affairs with younger women he's met at work or online.

When the children were little, money had been extremely tight, but Dennis had insisted upon buying a large house on the very best estate in the area, because image is important to Dennis. He justified it in financial terms, in his usual over-bearing, know-it-all way. It seemed to make sense to his wife at the time, and she bowed to his superior intellect.

But the house was a wreck, needing years of work doing on it, and Dennis put his young family to work on it with him, as they could not afford tradesmen. All the work done on the house had to be absolutely perfect – not even the slightest bump in the walls. It was extremely slow going, and the young children would spend endless hours sanding down woodwork to get it ready for Dennis's painting. It took decades for the house to be finished, and the children spent their entire child-hoods living in a building site. And when the lounge was fi-nally finished to perfection, with a flawless white carpet and a glittering chandelier, the room was locked by Dennis, and opened only occasionally for visitors, his own children having to occupy even less of the house than before.

The family struggled financially as the mortgage payments were huge – they actually went hungry at times and were poorly clothed. But, as the breadwinner, Dennis would always find enough for a couple of pints of beer in the pub, and would sometimes tantalise his young children by returning to the house with an Indian takeaway for just himself. His wife, his enabler, never said a word about her rising resentment.

Many years later, upon the death of her parents, Jane's inher-itance got them out of the financial hole they had been in. There was no question what it would be used for – paying off some of the mortgage and an eye-wateringly expensive holi-day to the Seychelles. It wasn't her cup of tea at all, but Dennis insisted. He spent the fortnight asking her to cover up and leaving her alone in the room at night whilst he 'talked prop-erty' with the wealthy holiday makers whose approval he se-cretly sought.

Dennis

In the early days, Dennis was prone to terrifying rages, and would smash things up. He would throw their wedding dinner china at the wall, jump up and down on the glass coffee table that used to be Jane's beloved grandmother's, and slash furniture with a knife, threatening suicide as he did so. The children would huddle with their mother as he raged violently, and they never knew what kind of mood he would be in. They did notice, however, that during these uncontrollable outbursts he was able to avoid damaging the antique harpsichord that he had managed to procure. Dennis knew better then to damage such a status symbol, and no one was allowed to touch it, let alone play it. Dennis himself can't play a note but he will tell you that he has a fine singing voice and is a natural musician.

In spite of it all, Dennis's two sons grew up desperate for his approval. At times he would cut all contact with them if they did not succumb to his will – sometimes for years. But in spite of this, their desperate need for his approval and conditional love continued into their adulthoods, even when they became parents themselves. With Dennis, even now, there is always a golden child, although who that is at any one time varies, depending on who aligns with him in the latest invented family drama. For his sons, their wives and their own children, one minute you are flavour of the month; the next, a huge disappointment, or someone who is 'too big for their boots'. There is no in between. His family's successes are either over-celebrated or resentfully downplayed by Dennis and backstabbing and badmouthing is the norm in this family. Under the surface, someone is always getting the silent treatment although, in public, it is always hugs, giant smiles and over the top professions of love. The image of a perfect happy family, to be maintained at all costs. Notably, no one ever dares criticise Dennis though, not even behind closed doors.

And in spite of all of this, Dennis genuinely sees himself as the ultimate family man – a loving father and husband, and his eyes will suddenly well up as he tells you this, for just a second or two. Still moved by and believing these shallow displays of emotion, his adult sons orbit around him to this day, unaware of their roles as mere bit parts in his show. They probably even agree with his own assessment of his fine, upstanding character, so enmeshed are they in his world and in their own dysfunctional upbringing.

Although he might sound like a fictional cartoon villain, there are many real versions of Dennis in homes everywhere. Of course, not all narcissists are as clichéd as Dennis, and most are nowhere near as easy to spot. But even those overt narcissists like Dennis seem to go unnoticed. They simply wreak havoc on the lives of those around them, with controlling abuse, until the day, if it ever arrives, when someone finally plucks up the courage to break free.

And when that happens, the so-called 'narcissistic injury' experienced by the abandoned narcissist leads to even more rage, wrath and abuse. "Hell has no fury like a narcissist scorned", to misquote the proverb. These are the divorces that go well beyond simple acrimony.

The Closet Narcissist

Susan

The Closet Narcissist (also called the 'Vulnerable', 'Introverted' or 'Covert' Narcissist) is very much harder to spot than the exhibitionist type. The difficulty lies in the outward appearance that the Closet Narcissist projects to the world, which is not immediately recognisable as arising from NPD. They generally appear, on the surface, mild mannered and meek, a little insecure but warm. It can take years to figure out that you have been in a relationship with a Closet Narcissist, and you may find that hardly anyone else will believe you.

The Closet Narcissist looks very different from the Exhibitionist type of narcissist because, deep down, although they need to feel special, have a sense of entitlement, are preoccupied with status and have all the other features associated with NPD, they are *afraid to be the centre of attention because they fear being exposed as being inadequate and false.*

Closet Narcissists were taught in childhood that they were not allowed to act as if they were special or seek attention, and they were punished harshly for doing so, often by a narcissistic parent, who wanted them to admire them and cater to their needs instead. Like the Exhibitionists, they desperately need external validation to crush their core feelings of low self-esteem and inadequacy, but they have to go about getting this feeling of specialness using covert tactics.

Most often they try to feel special *by association*, by attaching themselves to a person, cause or object that they hold up as being special. Then, rather than asking people to admire them directly, they divert attention away to this third party, asking people to admire it instead, whilst basking in the reflected glory, soaking up its perfection, wonderfulness, uniqueness and entitlement to special treatment. They often consider themselves as 'the wind beneath the wings' of another.

The problem with this is that they have made an emotional investment in whatever it is they have idealised, so when that person, cause or object falls off its pedestal, there is no more glory in which to bask. This is when they find their true feelings of inadequacy are exposed, and depression hits. Depression is more common than in the Exhibitionist Narcissists, who are not emotionally invested in people and objects in the same way as the Closets, as they use them merely as mirrors to reflect back their own perceived greatness rather than as the *source* of their own importance.

Closet Narcissists can be manipulative, talking behind others people's backs, and resentful and envious of others who do get noticed. They tend to play the victim in order to secure attention, and may work hard at their jobs to covertly get noticed. Compared to their Exhibitionist cousins, they can be more defensive and might view others as being more hostile.

The Closet Narcissist

► mild mannered and meek

► insecure but warm

► plays the victim

► need to feel special by association

► preoccupied with status

► afraid to be the centre of attention

► sense of entitlement

Susan is 55. She's quietly spoken, with a gentle manner. Susan comes across as articulate and thoughtful, and she dresses her plumpish figure in tasteful, reasonable quality clothes.

She goes through cycles – at times you won't find Susan out of doors without full, expertly applied makeup, even just for a trip to the supermarket, and her hair will be nicely styled any time she leaves the house. But at other times she will make no effort at all, hoping to just slip by unnoticed. She's just a perfectly decent woman, who listens to Radio 4, never misses her favourite soap opera, reads every Booker prize nominated novel, and enjoys following people on Facebook. Even though she's in her fifties, she still talks about all the games she played with her perfect baby son when she was a stay at home mum. She seems kind. Giving. A little shy. A little put upon perhaps. But otherwise the very image of a devoted mother, step-grandmother and wife.

Susan came from a working class background. Her father was a brutish man who undermined her confidence at every turn, telling her that she was "no bloody good" and yet expecting her to idolise him. Secretly she knew she wanted greater things, and decided from an early age to escape into a better social class.

Susan can't remember ever having spoken like the rest of her family, and her voice never bore a trace of the Yorkshire accent she was surrounded by. In fact, so different was her accent to all those her around her, including her three siblings, that her nickname was 'Duchess'.

Susan left school at 16 with a few basic qualifications, but she wanted more for her life than just to stay in the town where she grew up. She applied herself to diligently learning typing and secretarial skills and, a few years later, secured a job as a secretary in a small solicitor's firm in the South of England, miles away from her family.

Within weeks, Susan had become enthralled with her boss, Roger. To her Roger was perfect. A high earning lawyer, who was clever, sophisticated and debonair. She stayed late at the office and worked as hard as she could to get his attention. She would live for the occasions that Roger would buy her

Susan

lunch as a thank you for all her hard work, and eventually her adoration paid off. Within a year Roger had left his wife and children to be with Susan, twenty years his junior. It was a whirlwind romance, and Susan made sure she was to Roger everything his wife was not, throwing herself 100% into her role as the perfect partner for him. The fact that he was special, and had chosen her, made her feel special too, and she believed she was the envy of her peers and family.

She delighted in buying Wedgewood china for their new flat and made sure Roger's wardrobe had all the accoutrements befitting of such a high status man. Designer silk ties, expensive cufflinks, handmade shoes – all the things his wife hadn't deemed him important enough to have.

She didn't object when Roger bought her a new top-of-the-range car, but she would quietly tell other people that she was embarrassed about driving it as it felt like she was showing off. This became a pattern, Susan always managing to subtly find fault with things, albeit in her gentle, self-effacing, 'I'm not good enough' sort of way. He should have given the flowers he bought her to his mother as they were her favourite blooms; she felt too self-conscious to wear the stunning diamond necklace he'd bought (although she casually dropped it into conversation with others); the surprise pamper day at the spa was a lovely treat but not her sort of thing, and so on.

Susan's cooking skills quickly made her the 'hostess with the mostest', initially winning favour with Roger's friends, but she never seemed to make any meaningful friendships of her own. When one of his friends' wives, who was much older than her, did not invite her to her daughter's hen party, Susan took it personally and cried for hours on end about how humiliated she felt at her insensitivity. "That's the last time I invite *her* for dinner," she fumed to herself, once her tears had subsided, and she resolved to give the wife in question the cold shoulder from that day on. She couldn't help but spread a little malicious gossip amongst the wives about the woman in question too, suggesting that she was worried about her mental health.

After a year or so, Roger started trying to encourage Susan to take up a hobby in order to make some friends, but Susan resisted, making up excuse after excuse. Unknown to him, Susan would moan to her family about how desperate she was to take an evening art class and join a book club, but how she felt that Roger would be upset with her if she went out, especially as he worked such long hours. Susan was an expert at playing the victim, telling others how she was missing out under the guise of putting someone else's needs above her own. This was a pattern that continued throughout her life and interactions with others.

The reality was that it was Susan who didn't like Roger going out in the evenings or weekends. Whilst initially she supported his interests, telling him how much she admired him for them, and cheering at the finish lines of his running and cycling races, once she felt secure in their relationship, she grew tired of them. She would go quiet when it was time for him to go out, and would barely speak to him for 24 hours afterwards, although she would tell him, monosyllabically that it was fine, and that nothing was wrong. Susan hated being left on her own.

Roger, a sensitive soul, couldn't stand these silent treatments, and slowly gave up his hobbies, including his longstanding poker night with pals. Susan was delighted, and rewarded him with wonderful romantic dinners and passionate nights on the evenings when he would have previously been out. Roger's young partner had him hooked, and he ignored his gut instinct that something was wrong. He even found himself cutting himself off from any of his friends who tried to broach the subject of Susan's isolating behaviour. In time, Roger became drawn into Susan's romantic notion that they didn't need anyone else in their lives.

The wedding was a tiny affair – just a few close family members were invited, as Susan said she didn't want to be in the spotlight. She fell pregnant very quickly, and the birth itself was long and traumatic. Susan still revels in telling stories about it, referring to it as the best day of her life. She carries the baby's hospital wristband around with her in her handbag to this day, even though Sebastian is now grown up – a clear token of her commitment to her family and motherhood.

Roger and Susan decided to take it in turns to bottle feed the baby at night, but when it was Roger's turn, she would stay awake anyway, not really trusting him to do it right. On her nights she would become cross with Roger if he fell asleep,

Susan

expecting him to be on standby for her if she needed anything, even though by this time Roger was back at work. Contrary to her version of events, Susan did not cope well with motherhood, and Roger wondered whether she had postnatal depression. He felt that he couldn't do anything right, from the way he cooked, to the vacuuming, to even the way he made her coffee. She told her family, behind his back, that Roger was never home and was unsupportive, in spite of his hard work in the home and the increasing number of chores that she considered to be 'blue jobs'. By the time Sebastian was a year old she was out of control – she would start arguments in the car about Roger's driving and would regularly pull at the wheel or try to stop the car by pulling on the handbrake.

Roger and her mother encouraged her to visit her GP at this point, but Roger was confused when she came back from the surgery with a note for him, telling him that the doctor had signed *him* off work for two weeks, on the grounds that *he* was behaving oddly, and that he needed to see the doctor to be assessed for depression.

Susan was sure from the day that Sebastian was born that he was destined for great things and would one day follow in his father's footsteps as a great lawyer. Even as a baby she dressed him up in little suits. But when Sebastian had been at school for a few years, it became clear to his teachers that he was behind on his reading, and they asked Susan and Roger if they would consider having him tested for dyslexia. Susan was disgusted at the suggestion, and felt that the school were shaming Sebastian, and her. She moved him to a fee-paying school, on the understanding that dyslexia was never brought up again by the teachers. Roger just went along with it, as he now often found himself doing, bowing to her wisdom in such matters.

Susan, for all her quiet proclamations of Sebastian's brilliance to others, would put Sebastian down in private, criticising the way he spoke, stood and interacted with others, and telling him that he was slower than all the other children. When he didn't get the lead in the nativity play she was be deeply resentful of the mother of the child who did, and quietly suggested to the biggest gossip amongst the other mums that she had heard someone say that bribery had been involved.

Susan was to be disappointed at every turn by Sebastian's academic difficulties, but she insisted that if he worked harder he would still be able to become a lawyer. Sebastian grew up resenting his mother more and more and, aged 16, begged her to allow him to have a test for dyslexia. She refused, saying that it was unnecessary.

It became clear to Sebastian over time that his mother could not accept him as being anything less than perfect, as it reflected badly on her. He never did achieve academically and left school to start an apprenticeship as a builder, much to Susan's disdain and embarrassment, especially as Roger's children from his previous marriage had gone on to have high flying careers. Sebastian felt like his 'failures' were seen as a deliberate and personal affront to his mother, something others might criticise *her* for.

Susan was outraged by other people's immoral behaviour, judging them harshly for anything that didn't measure up to her high moral standards, even though she herself had met Roger when he was married.

If Roger was even mildly friendly to a waitress or any other woman, Susan's jealousy would surface, and her mood would spiral downwards. Feeling abandoned and rejected she would accuse Roger of not loving her, with much quiet sobbing. She would move into the spare room for days on these occasions, whilst licking her wounds. Her double standards were never noticed by Roger, and Susan would tell him that as he had been unfaithful to his wife with her, he couldn't be trusted. She would sink into depressions at these times, and many others too.

From her thirties onwards, poor Susan suffered from a variety of ailments. Her sore fingers, which she was sure was arthritis, were due to her mother teaching her to type when she was young. Her chronic back pain was due to the hours she would spend in her childhood, bent over an ironing board. Her knee pain was caused by her mother neglecting the injury she sustained whilst playing hockey aged 15. When Roger actually required an operation on his knee, Susan, exaggerating wildly, posted on Facebook that she had been told that he might need an amputation. Flurries of sympathetic comments came flooding in, and Roger, who valued his privacy at the best of

Susan

times, was quietly embarrassed. Roger was dismayed to find her cold and unhelpful after his knee replacement operation, and dismissive of his pain, focusing instead on how miserable she felt about a perceived slight from some superficial acquaintance or other.

In the early days, when Roger's older children from his first marriage visited, Susan would perfectly play her role of caring, friendly stepmother, whilst digging for details of their home, holidays and lives.

Once they had left Susan would quietly express her concerns and worries about how their mother was bringing them up and spoiling them, whilst making a big show of clearing up the house after them, scrubbing every surface excessively, huffing and puffing. She was particularly aggrieved if they kept any of their belongings at her house, making little comments about the 'inconvenience' every now and then. When Roger came upon a notebook in which Susan had detailed all the things that his children had left at the house, and for how long, he realised just how much Susan felt that everyone was taking advantage of her hospitality and generous nature.

When her step-children had their own partners and children, Susan would beg them to allow her to babysit, and would send numerous lonely sounding text messages saying how much she missed them. But when the day came for her to babysit her step-grandchildren, she would always complain to anyone else who would listen about how put upon, used and unappreciated she was.

She would make comments about her step daughter-in-laws' child-rearing methods to Roger, always under the guise of concern, and she took great delight in 'worrying' about the grandchildren's diet and her daughter-in-law's post-baby weight. She would be perturbed about the size of their houses, and would constantly be asking when they would be moving, to give the step-grandchildren more space.

It seemed to Susan that she had the weight of the world on her shoulders with all her worry. If you talk to her now, after serving you tea and cake, she will sigh and admit to you how difficult her life is, having to look after her ailing elderly parents (who live many miles away, and are actually being cared for by her sister), her babysitting duties regarding her grandchildren (who she only actually now sees once a month, and now never to babysit) and looking after Roger (who, although he is now nearly 75, is very physically fit).

Susan quietly complains that Roger doesn't like to drive as much as he used to, and seems resentful of the fact that she is now married to an old man. Susan doesn't like to drive in the dark, on unfamiliar roads, at rush hour or on the motorway. She even plans all her drives so that she doesn't have make any right turns, and avoids roundabouts if at all possible. She insists that Roger continues to do most of the driving, even though his eyesight is failing, he is worried that he might crash, and despite the fact that even his children won't let him drive the grandchildren.

Roger has been miserable for years, but cannot put his finger on exactly why he feels so emotionally disconnected from Susan. Susan continues to go silent when hurt, to play the victim, and to make comments about him and his children behind his back. When his children do visit, she will always start an argument at the dinner table, by expertly pressing somebody's buttons, and then leaving the table to go to bed, whilst a heated argument ensues. No one has noticed the pattern yet.

Softly spoken, but passive aggressive, controlling and manipulative. Superficially self-effacing. Playing one person off another, and being quietly judgemental. Creating tension, stealthily. Offering only conditional love and unable to empathise with another's pain. The long-suffering daughter, mother, grandmother and wife, who puts the best interests of others above all else. Believing in the fantasy of perfect romantic love with Roger, and being painfully wounded when he fails to deliver. Projecting an image of the perfect happy family to the outside world, but secretly jealous of others. Easily offended and highly sensitive to criticism. Prone to bouts of depression, shame and worthlessness. Secretly needing to believe she is morally and intellectually superior to others, although with no real evidence. And all the while, presenting a quietly charming exterior to the world, contradicted by the fact that she has hardly any real friendships at all.

The Devaluing Narcissist

Anton

The Devaluing Narcissist is also called the 'Toxic' or 'Malignant' Narcissist.

These narcissists use grandiosity as a defence (e.g. claiming they are the best at something), but when this grandiosity is punctured, and their defences are brought down, they turn on others to bring them down. They exhibit many of the other more general narcissistic behaviours too, but what is more prominent in this type of narcissist is that they *devalue, criticise, and demean others in order to inflate themselves.* In reality, they are jealous and envious of others but, rather than express this, they put down the other party. They can be sadistic and have a strong sense of schadenfreude. Donald Trump, US President at the time of writing, demonstrates devaluation beautifully, putting down anyone who does not agree with him with public name calling, criticisms, badmouthing and ridiculing.

Those with higher intellect do this more stealthily. They either devalue the person behind their back to someone else: "He thinks his job is so difficult, but really a monkey could do it …" or they tell the person they are devaluing that someone else has made the comments about them, for example, "My sister is worried that you are pregnant because of your weight gain …" (meaning "you are fat").

Some believe that these Devaluing Narcissists are actually Exhibitionist Narcissists who aren't clever, talented, funny or charming enough to maintain their image of outer grandiosity, and so turn to devaluing others to maintain their false sense of superiority.

Some narcissists flit between the two types. On good days they are Exhibitionist Narcissists, on bad days, Devaluing. You may find them magnanimous and charming on one day and corrosive on another (when they will coldly or angrily point out your flaws). They will always know better than you.

Anton

Anton is 49, and bisexual.

He used to be married to Michelle, with whom he had a child, but after ten years of marriage he left her for Peter, a successful IT architect who works at a big firm in London. Michelle will tell you that, in his wedding speech, the only thing Anton said about her was: "As you can all see, Michelle scrubs up well." She thought it was just his quirky sense of humour at the time, and smiled along with the wedding guests; but this was a pattern that was to continue throughout their marriage.

Anton is a dapper looking chap, always well presented in expensive jeans and perfectly ironed shirts. He has pearly-white teeth, and will flash you a huge winning smile when you see him; initially you cannot help but be drawn in by his friendliness.

Anton will tell you that he's had a variety of successful careers over his lifetime, and explain to you that he has many areas of expertise. You'd be forgiven for thinking that he was the primary earner, if you didn't know better. Most recently he described himself as a designer, but really he had just dabbled in designing expensive things for the large house he shared with Peter. Just two years ago he designed a metal and glass staircase for the house (a bit of a monstrosity, in Peter's view) but Peter had spent thousands on having it made just to keep Anton happy. Anton had seen something similar at a rich American friend's house, and decided that he needed to outdo it.

One thing is for sure; Anton is an excellent blagger. When married to his former wife, he lied on his CV about his qualifications, and was able to get two mediocre sales positions. But Anton lost both jobs after the six month probation periods,

Anton

for reasons he could not convincingly explain away; but it was clear that his cocky arrogance would have been apparent to his bosses. Amongst other things, his CV tells you that he has been an entrepreneur, a web designer, a copywriter and, in his youth, a surfing instructor. (The truth is that he can barely surf at all, although his brother had been a big name in this sport). In reality, he spent most of the marriage as a house husband, but not a terribly effective one.

On meeting Anton, particularly if you are reasonably presentable, he might look you up and down and suggest alternative looks for you, even if he doesn't know you very well. "Why do you wear so much grey? It's depressing, darling. Try injecting some colour here and there." Or, "Have you thought about going blonde? You look like everybody else with your hair that way. It's so hard to tell people apart these days ..." You might just think he's a bit opinionated, at first. Or you might think he's genuinely trying to help. But over time you'll get used to that sinking feeling at his subtle (and not so subtle) put downs.

Anton is a bit of a show-off. He'll drop impressive things into conversations, and name drop where possible. He enjoys occasions where he can lean back expansively in his chair, his hands behind his head, and talk knowledgeably to an audience about things he considers himself to be an expert in, which is most things. He loves to play 'devil's advocate' when anyone expresses an opinion, but this is now wearing thin, and he has driven away most of their friends. If you want to send your child to private school, Anton will tell you why they should be state educated, or vice versa. If you want to buy a Mercedes, Anton will tell you that what you need is a BMW. If you want to get a dog, Anton will give reasons why a cat would be better. It took Peter years

The Devaluing Narcissist

- ▶ devalues, criticises, and demeans others in order to inflate themselves

- ▶ jealous and envious of others

- ▶ puts down the other party

- ▶ name calling, criticisms, badmouthing and ridiculing

Anton

to realise that Anton had no *real* opinions, other than when he felt slighted by another, when his low opinions of them were very real indeed.

In the absence of many deep friendships, Anton began to thrive on Twitter, creating full blown arguments about politics with anyone who would engage, and propagating conspiracy theories as if they were fact. He ranted and raged in the digital space about anyone who disagreed with him, alternately calling them 'hotshots' or 'stupid'. He did have a few people who thought he was great though, mostly younger gay men who he met through the internet, who were impressed with his worldly ways, maturity and wealth. Peter didn't like this at all, but Anton happily took him to their parties, to show him that he was being silly, and they were nothing more than friends. Peter wasn't sure, but knew that he would just have to trust him.

Whenever Anton met someone impressive or new, he would tell Peter how marvellous they were, ad nauseum, dropping them into any conversation that he could with the slightest excuse. He'd text them late into the night, whilst sitting next to Peter on the sofa, and chuckle loudly at their messages, especially when he knew that Peter was feeling a little insecure about them, or they were supposed to be sharing quality time together. If Peter said anything, Anton would accuse him of being paranoid and jealous, although it was Anton who would regularly go through Peter's phone messages and emails.

It was also Anton who would ring Peter constantly if he was at an evening work do, or had a late work finish, and then accuse him of having affairs when he got home. Again, it was Anton who would take Peter's pulse, comment on his breathing pattern, and snarl at him that he could read his mind, whilst accusing him of these affairs. And sadly, it was also Anton who would then refuse to speak to Peter for weeks after these late working nights, coldly blanking him, but he was still able to laugh at whatever sitcom he was watching on the TV. On one level Peter knew this was abuse, but when Anton turned on the charm a few weeks later, acting loving and warm, he would forgive it all, grateful to be loved once more, and anxious to do whatever it took to stop these jealous episodes from recurring.

Anton had made a bit of money on a couple of flats in the early days at the start of the property boom, more by luck than design, but he still believes this qualifies him as an expert in all things property related.

After a few years together Peter learned to avoid taking him to friends' and colleagues' homes, finding his know-it-all attitude cringeworthy. And the more lovely the home, the more critical Anton would be. "But why did you buy a house with a north facing garden?" "I know you've finished doing up the house, but have you thought of knocking down this wall and this wall, and going for something more open plan?" "I'm surprised you have so much bedroom space, when you only have one reception room." "What you need is to dig out the floor and build a conversation pit." "You haven't put in a wine cellar?" "Oh, such a shame it's grade 2 listed – you can't replace the whole of the back of it with glass, and it's so very dark inside." "You don't have a larder?" he once said to the owner of a modest house on an estate, whose friendship was very important to Peter. "But where do you store your food?"

These visits would be followed by a journey home during which Anton would launch into an angry tirade about how Peter obviously preferred the other person's house to their own and that if he earned as much as he should, they'd also be able to buy a much better house themselves. He'd then spend days planning another modification to their own home – a bar, a cinema, remote controlled garden fountains. The building work was never ending, but no builder would ever stay for long after dealing with Anton's indecision, rudeness, perfectionism and know-it-all attitude. Peter kept haemorrhaging money on builder after builder, for years, just to try to steer clear of Anton's wrath. He didn't know for a long time that Anton had for years also been viewing houses for sale that were well out of their price range, nor that he'd put down so many false offers that the local estate agents had blacklisted him.

When Peter and Anton first met, Anton lavished attention upon Peter. He insisted that they spent almost every waking moment together, and they were barely out of each other's sight. He proclaimed his love for Peter within days, and spoke of their soulmate connection. Peter fell head over heels in love, and although he felt guilty about breaking up Anton's marriage, he also felt that he had finally found 'The One'. Anton

Anton

had all the same interests as him, was a great listener and validated his deepest darkest fears and vulnerabilities. He felt heard, understood and adored like never before, but more than this, he felt valued and respected. Anton would take him out for him lovely meals, insist upon pressing his shirts for him, and would gaze adoringly at him as Peter serenaded him on his classical guitar. Peter felt lucky. Appreciated.

But over the years, Anton's criticisms of Peter grew and grew, and Peter found himself walking on eggshells. It got to the point where he never knew what kind of mood Anton would be in when he returned home from work, and he got used to walking through the door to be met with chaos and mess. It often took him 15 minutes to steel himself to get out of the car, once parked on the driveway. Dirty dishes and bowls were left around the house, chest hair shavings were clinging to the bathroom floor, and wet towels would be thrown on to Peter's side of the bed, leaving it damp. Boxer shorts and clothes would be all over the bedroom floor – Anton would empty drawers on to the floor whilst searching for an item, and then just walk away, expecting Peter to sort it all out. Even the cleaner they had twice a week could not keep on top of the mess, and Peter would find himself launching into the housework as soon as he got home, often having stopped en-route at the supermarket to buy food to cook, as he knew Anton would have been 'too busy' to do it. Most days he had to vacuum the cat hair from the sofa just for somewhere to sit. He tried for years explaining to Anton how this made him feel, but Anton would just look coldly at him and suggest he pay for a full time housekeeper if he didn't like it.

Peter was a keen gardener in his spare time when they met, so Anton developed an interest in this area too. Peter thought this was lovely, as it would be something they could do together, and he was thrilled when Anton decided to commence a gardening course which would lead to an impressive gardening qualification. Although Anton never got around to taking the exams, he started to consider himself to be the expert, and would return from the garden centre with a boot full of plants which he would place and leave in position for Peter to plant, whilst he reclined on the decking, barking orders, and complaining about how long the digging was taking Peter. If it wasn't fun, he didn't feel he should have to do it, although he was happy to reap the rewards of, and take the credit for, someone else's hard work.

Over the years, everything became either a power struggle or a competition. Peter was an accomplished amateur classical guitarist, and so Anton took lessons. When he realised he would never be as good at playing classical guitar as Peter, he began to openly wince at Peter's playing, or try to drown out the sound by turning the TV on to its loudest volume. Once, at a dinner party they had thrown, he even stuck his fingers in his ears and walked out of the room to go to bed, saying he had a migraine, when their guests had asked Peter to play something. And dinner parties became a bone of contention for other reasons too. Anton would leave most of the cooking and house tidying to Peter and then apologise to their guests about the food: "Oh dear, so sorry that Peter's chicken is dry." Peter even caught him stealthily turning up the stove and oven on one occasion, and when confronted he actually smirked. He'd always make a point of leaving the house just before the guests were due to arrive too, under the guise of picking up more wine, and then make his grand smiling entrance once they were there, seemingly oblivious to Peter's stress at being left in the lurch. And then he'd present his own offering, usually a dessert, with such feigned coy modesty, that his guests felt obliged to ooh and ahh in delight.

Anton also seemed to love being late. He was late to everything he could be. He'd arrive at weddings as the bride was walking down the aisle. He would prevaricate about what to pack for holidays, leaving it all until the last minute so that they would miss flights, or end up not seated next to each other on the plane due to late check-ins. He would never manage to make it on time to work, even when he had had a paying job. And they would always miss the first ten minutes of the show any time they went to the theatre, as he would insist upon taking his time getting ready, or having a last minute shower beforehand. He would even make Peter late for work on occasions, forcing him to apologise to his boss, and when Peter tried to discuss it, he showed no remorse, instead making a big show of looking bemused as to what all the fuss was about, calling Peter 'square' and 'boring' for wanting to be on time.

In the last year of their relationship, after a frazzled Peter told Anton that he would have to go to therapy if they were to stay

Anton

together, Anton openly signed up to hook-up websites. He told Peter that he had never been sexually satisfied by him, but that as Peter would never be able to find another partner, he would continue to live with him. Peter was in pieces; an emotional wreck, driven to despair by Anton's cruelty. To Anton, this was just more proof that Peter was mentally unstable, and he'd regularly tell him that he was 'crazy'. Anton calmly and logically explained that he did not see why it should be a problem him having other partners whilst living with Peter, as it was 'just sex'. He even began to taunt Peter, telling him that he had 250 men interested in him, and messaged them openly. But when Peter stayed out one night at a friend's house, just to clear his head and get out of the house, Anton was livid, demanding to know where he had been and what he had been doing. The hypocrisy of this did not seem to register with him, and Peter, increasingly worried about his behaviour, spoke to his doctor, genuinely wondering whether Anton might have early dementia or a brain tumour.

Another day, during another taunting about his sexual partners, a distraught Peter grabbed Anton by the shoulders in desperation, shaking him to get his attention, tears flooding down his face. Anton threw him off violently. Later he calmly told Peter that he had called the police about the 'assault' and that they had told Anton that Peter would have to leave the house immediately or be arrested. Even through his agony, Peter knew that this was another fabrication.

Several months later, after many failed attempts during which Peter would always end up taking Anton back, Peter finally plucked up the courage to throw Anton out of the house forever. Anton badmouthed Peter to everyone they knew, including his work colleagues, telling them that he was an abusive, violent, drug addict.

Thankfully, they had never married. Anton moved straight into another relationship, whilst Peter was left to mourn. He was not only grieving the loss of the relationship but coming to terms with the realisation that the relationship had never been about love; not as he understood it, anyway. The whole relationship had been a shallow lie.

Devaluing Narcissists are the narcissists who gain a sense of importance and superiority by putting others down, either subtly and behind their backs (if they are intelligent) or harshly and to their face if less so. They cannot bear others' successes, they see everyone as competition and are constantly comparing themselves to others.

They are particularly prone to vengeful behaviour in divorce and will stop at nothing to bring the other party down. They must win, at all costs, and compromise is not an option.

The Communal Narcissist

Jill

T he Communal Narcissist (or 'Altruistic' Narcissist) might, at first glance, appear to be a contradiction in terms. These are the narcissists who prop up their self-esteem and sense of specialness by giving to others. They obtain admiration, attention and a sense of specialness ('narcissistic supply') from good works and deeds, seeing themselves as the *most* generous, the *most* caring, the *most* kind.

They may start off in this vein with their significant others, but eventually their narcissism comes at the expense of those closest to them. They pride themselves on being 'nice', but quite often they give themselves away by becoming overly territorial in whatever arena they are practising their altruism. Whether they are intentionally deceiving others is unclear – it may be that they are trying to convince other people of their niceness in order to deceive themselves.

The Communal Narcissism Inventory asks participants to signify their agreement or disagreement with the 16 following statements about themselves. The more strongly they agree with the statements, the more likely they are to be communal narcissists.

I am the most helpful person I know.

I am going to bring peace and justice to the world.

I am the best friend someone can have.

I will be well known for the good deeds I will have done.

I am (going to be) the best parent on this planet.

I am the most caring person in my social surroundings.

In the future, I will be well known for solving the world's problems.

I greatly enrich others' lives.

I will bring freedom to the people.

I am an amazing listener.

I will be able to solve world poverty.

I have a very positive influence on others.

I am generally the most understanding person.

I'll make the world a much more beautiful place.

I am extraordinarily trustworthy.

I will be famous for increasing people's well-being.

Again, overlap between the different types of predominant narcissistic types can occur. For example, an Exhibitionist Narcissist can act as a Communal Narcissist in certain situations if it works to bring in narcissistic supply, say by giving a homeless person a large sum of cash when they have an audience to witness their generosity.

J ill, 50, is a devout Catholic, and will quietly bow her head and clasp her hands together piously as she takes Holy Communion, every Sunday, without fail.

She takes pride in having the barest of wardrobes – just a handful of long dresses hang inside, mostly picked up from charity shops, but you might notice that they do accentuate her ample bosom rather well.

Jill is heavily involved with the church, organising church fêtes and jumble sales, and she bakes a mean lemon drizzle cake; hers are always the first to sell out at the charity cake sale (on account of her secret recipe, which she will be taking with her to the grave).

Jill loves nothing more than to be right hand woman to Father Jameson, her priest, and she loves it when he tells her that she is 'a blessing'. "Ah, what would we do without our Jill?" he will say, and "Of course, a special mention goes to Jill McDonnell, without whom this fête would most certainly not have been possible – there'll be a special place in heaven for you, Jill, so there will …"

Jill works part time at the local convenience shop. Her name badge says 'Jolly Jill' on it, and she has a little sign propped up by her till with inspirational quotes on it, which she changes regularly. "No one has ever become poor by giving (Anne Frank)" is one of her favourites, and "There is no love without forgiveness".

"My empathy levels are off the chart," she will tell you as she scans and packs your groceries. "I just couldn't sit by and watch those poor children in Africa without helping".

"There's just something about my face that makes people want to tell me their woes …"; "I just love all animals … a poor bird broke its wing flying into my window last week and I cried for days … that's just the way I am …"; "A sensitive soul, that's me, just trying to make my little contribution to the world … well you have to, don't you?"

Recently, Father Jameson had an appointment at the hospital for his eyes. When Jill discovered, whilst cleaning the church with Margaret Massey, that Margaret had driven him to and from the hospital, and that she hadn't even been asked, she saw it as a personal slight.

Jill went home, kicked their old Border Collie out of the way, and ranted to her long suffering husband, Dave, livid. "That Margaret thinks she's better than me. She's just jealous because he chose *me* as churchwarden. I wonder how she found out about his eye appointment before me. It was so *humiliating* being the last to know. How *dare* they treat me like this. *Nobody* appreciates how much I do. Just because she plays the church organ. She's got ideas above her station…"

Dave was up a ladder, repainting the lounge to Jill's exacting standards, at the time. He knew better than to comment, but made sure he made the right number of sympathetic noises so as to avoid her wrath being directed at him, whilst their teenage daughter, Alice, rolled her eyes and slunk off to her room to drown out the raging with her headphones.

The Communal Narcissist

- ► gives to others publicly

- ► does good works and deeds

- ► prides themselves on being 'nice'

- ► sees themselves as the *most* generous, the *most* caring, the *most* kind

- ► territorial

- ► abusive behind closed doors

Dave has been worn down by Jill's impatience and judgemental attitudes towards others for years, but he plays his outward role of supportive husband in public on autopilot. He's used to playing second fiddle to 'handsome' Father Jameson too, with his 'fine singing voice' (who he's noticed Jill will always make sure she's got her lipstick on for). He's even had to host various lunches for the man, and tolerate Jill's alternate simpering and coquettish behaviour throughout. "Don't be ridiculous, Dave," she will scoff after such occasions. "The man's a *priest*, for goodness sake, a man of the *cloth*. Of course I don't have feelings for him, although you'd do better to take a leaf out of his book when it comes to grooming and personal hygiene …"

She's always been that way. Before Father Jameson, it was the 'saintly' manager of the animal rescue centre that she volunteered for that he'd have to be compared to, and hear about endlessly. "He's from Scotland too, but his accent is not at all coarse like yours …" she would tell him repeatedly. She was devastated when her volunteering services were terminated after she tried to take charge of a fundraising effort for the centre, annoying the staff who had it all under control, but she made out that she had left to spend more time at the church of her own accord.

Alice can't wait to go to university. "The softest thing about *my* mother" she tells her disbelieving friends who have only seen her outward persona, "are her teeth." Of course, only *she* knows that Jill slaps her dad repeatedly, until he cries and begs her to stop, and that she's been controlled herself for her whole life. She's not allowed to wear anything her mother considers to be vaguely 'tarty', and even though she's 18, she's not allowed to get her ears pierced, go to the pub with friends, or 'loiter' in town with them. Even her choice of university was dictated by her mother, who insisted that she knew best, even though she had left school without qualifications herself.

Alice has begged her dad to get a divorce as she can't bear the thought of him being at the mercy of her mother when she leaves for university, but Dave is resolute – Catholics do not get divorced, and he made his vows; "until death do us part." He tells Alice that underneath it all, her mother is a 'good woman', who 'loves her very much', and 'only has her best interests at heart'. He doesn't know that he is actually his narcissistic wife's 'enabler', and that his assertions are really narcissistic abuse by proxy.

Alice doesn't feel that her mother even knows the real her at all, but these assertions make her feel like a bad person for disliking her own flesh and blood, and she goes through cycles of trying to be a better daughter. She tells her friends that she intends to get a nose-ring and dye her hair pillar box red the day she moves out; but whether she'll actually pluck up the courage and risk the disgust of her mother remains to be seen.

Jill, not to be outdone, retaliated by putting Margaret on the church flowers rota for three weeks in a row, even though she knew she had terrible hay-fever, and made a point of visiting

Father Jameson with a get well soon card. She put on the voice she reserves for such occasions; soft and breathy. "Father, I wouldn't want to speak out of turn but may we talk *confidentially*? I wouldn't want to burden you with this, and poor Margaret would be devastated if she knew I'd told you but, just between us, she does like the odd sherry in the daytime, and it's a problem that I'm helping her with. But perhaps in the future I should drive you to your appointments? Just to be on the safe side, you know ...?"

Jill McDonnell was never to be upstaged – certainly not when it came to piety and helpfulness. Her very sense of self depended on it.

A deeper look at the narcissist's behaviours

2

First, let's talk about you

Are you surrounded by narcissists?

By now, some patterns may be emerging for you. If you have been in a relationship with a narcissist, you are probably also noticing some of these patterns in other people you know, and this can be very disconcerting. Your mother, your long-term friend, the neighbour you've just been getting to know. Your step-sibling, your real sibling. You may be thinking that you must be seeing patterns where none can really exist. You may be thinking that suddenly it seems that practically everybody you know is a narcissist. That you are in some awful horror movie where everything you once believed to be true is now thrown into question. You are, more than likely, even thinking that *you* are a narcissist.

Firstly, this is normal, so take a deep breath and be reassured that you are not losing your mind. All of this is a lot to take on board. But here is an important fact. Narcissists do in fact exist in clusters, and there are good reasons for this.

We will examine, in Chapter 3, the character traits of the people narcissists choose to become their victims, but if you have been targeted by one narcissist in your life because you have these character traits, chances are you have been targeted by many. It may not be just your imagination telling you that you are surrounded by narcissists. Whilst many people go their whole lives without becoming involved with a single narcissist, usually (although not always) those people who are unfortunate enough to become entangled with narcissists *seem to know a disproportionately large number of them.*

It is also very common that those who have been in a narcissistic marriage actually came from an upbringing where a parent was narcissistic (or neglectful, or toxic in some way). This results in that person growing up into somebody who cannot see toxic behaviour from others as being undesirable because, for them, it is their normal. Indeed, on a completely subconscious level, you may well actually be *actively attracted* to toxic personalities. Your brain may be pulling you towards the familiar, because that is where it feels comfortable.

Looking at your family of origin, if you were brought up by a narcissist, then so were your siblings. Which means that they have a higher than average risk of either becoming a narcissist themselves or, like you, attracting a narcissistic partner. So potentially here's another narcissist in your midst, be it your sibling or your in-law. And if your parent was narcissistic, was your grandparent also a narcissist? And how did that affect your aunts and uncles? Did they marry narcissists? Do they have narcissistic friends? Did they develop into narcissists themselves? If you look backwards and sideways along your family tree, you can see how the clusters arise, and you can see how narcissism is passed down the generations. Christmas dinner is generally an interesting affair in these extended families, as are family weddings.

If some of this is ringing true for you, then not only do you have a narcissistic partner to heal and grieve from, but an entire dysfunctional family system, the extent of which may only just be becoming clear. This is traumatising in itself. Be kind to yourself.

Staying single through the separation process

Here is a very important point regarding your future love relationships. If you have been attracted to a narcissist once, most likely it will happen again if you are not aware of the signs (and frankly, even if you are). Be vigilant, especially if you are being 'rescued' or feel an overwhelming 'chemistry' with someone new. In people who have been in a relationship with a narcissist, chemistry is actually *familiarity*. The new narcissist may superficially look nothing like the old one on the surface, but that does not mean that they are not narcissistic – narcissists come in many different flavours, and without warning symbols tattooed on their foreheads. If at all possible, try to navigate your divorce *as a single person*. The last thing you need during this process is what we call 'stereo narcissism' – two narcissists coming at you from each side. Patterns tend to repeat until healing has been completed – and, as a victim of narcissistic abuse, you have plenty to heal from, as we will discuss later.

Divorce lawyers commonly see the spouse of the narcissist in a new relationship where the new partner is controlling their partner – wanting to be involved in their divorce process, making suggestions, telling the victim what they should

> **"Try to navigate your divorce *as a single person*."**

be doing, all under the guise of caring for them, and wanting to help them through the process. If you find yourself with a new partner who you feel you have to have at meetings with your solicitor or run everything past, take note.

Tempting though it may be to search for love whilst newly separated and divorcing, *stay single for now.*

The narcissist's playbook

As we've already mentioned, narcissistic abuse is mostly *covert* emotional abuse, which isn't immediately obvious.

For the narcissist, the purpose of this abuse, and indeed of everything they do, is to secure *narcissistic supply*. The abusive behaviours work in two ways; the first is that narcissist gets supply directly from the sadistic satisfaction arising from drama and conflict; the second is that the abusive behaviours lead to their victims *becoming addicted* to the narcissist, losing their autonomy and becoming trapped in the relationship. They are therefore kept exactly where the narcissist wants them, as a reliable and steady source of supply, too invested and confused to break free. All victims relate to the vampire-like nature of the relationship, and some even describe a feeling of 'soul rape'. Whilst these terms may sound overly dramatic to the casual onlooker, sadly they really do give an accurate flavour of the experience of narcissistic abuse.

We've already explained the concept of trauma bonding, which is how abusive behaviours lead to victims becoming addicted to the narcissist. Remember the idea of 'intermittent reinforcement', where the narcissist keeps their victims hooked to them, by flooding the brains of their victims with certain brain chemicals during the initial honeymoon phase of the relationship? How they then withdraw their initial adoration and only give it back in unpredictable bursts, causing corresponding spikes in the brain chemicals of their victims? In Chapter 1, we explained how this, from a neurochemical perspective, is an addictive cycle, similar to the one employed by slot machines, and how it's the varying unpredictable nature of the 'wins' (in the case of narcissistic abuse, the adoration) that keeps the victim 'in the game'.

What follows now is a really deep dive into the trademark behaviours of those with NPD – here we expose the narcissist's abuse in detail. If you have been in a relationship with a narcissistic partner, be prepared for some 'lightbulb moments,' which may be uncomfortable. And please do not judge yourself harshly for not having seen it before. No one can know what they didn't even know there *was* to know.

It is also crucial to understand that narcissists abuse *everyone* they know to a greater or lesser extent, whether their targets know it or not. Their work colleagues, any underlings, the builder, the secretary, the nanny. The chap on the phone at the takeaway. Their brother, next door neighbour, best friend. The bank manager, their mother and their new partner. They will be abusing all the people in their fan club (they often have a fan club) and even their divorce lawyer. But if you have been a narcissist's primary source of supply, by being their main partner, you will have been abused the most.

The cycle of 'idealise' and 'devalue'

This cycle is the hallmark of those with narcissistic adaptations.

The idealisation (love-bombing) phase

The initial stage of a relationship with a narcissist is the 'idealisation' phase, also known as the 'love-bombing' phase, in romantic relationships.

Love-bombing is *always* described at the beginning of a romantic narcissistic relationship. The narcissist will spend excessive amounts of time either physically with the target of their affections or be in constant communication with them. They will appear completely besotted with their target who will be flattered by their attention and who will allow other things in their lives, such as friendships and hobbies, to drop away at this stage.

Narcissists appear to have an inbuilt radar for sniffing out the other's vulnerabilities, perhaps their attunement being as a result of their own dysfunctional upbringing. Although, by definition, they have little or no emotional empathy (they cannot *feel* another's pain or joy), they are able to employ 'cognitive empathy' (the intellectual *understanding* that certain situations may be painful for another) to their advantage.

In the case of Dennis, our Exhibitionist Narcissist, he was able to exploit Jane's grief at the death of her fiancé. He could not *feel* her anguish, but he was able to *understand* that people feel sad when a loved one dies. When he (an atheist) told her (a believer) that he had been sent from God to take away her pain, he knew he was answering her secret prayers. He would have understood that she was worried about becoming an 'old maid' too; he would have seen her as an ideal person to love-bomb.

Manipulation and exploitation are wired into narcissists' brain circuitry at an early age – not only have they learnt them from their parents, but they have used them all their lives as a defence against feeling their own pain and to get their needs met. Contrary to what some victims believe, those with narcissistic adaptions *do not* plot and scheme for hours about how they will manipulate others. It is completely natural and effortless. The ease with which such tactics are deployed in combination with the believability of the narcissist make it dangerously easy for *anyone* to be sucked in. You may be struck by how effectively your narcissist was able to exploit your own weaknesses, at the beginning of your relationship.

In romantic relationships, during the love-bombing phase, the narcissist will monopolise the target's time. Depending on what works best for that particular target, there may be gifts, meals, constant sex, helpfulness, displays of affection, and words of affirmation.

This is the *only* time in the relationship when the narcissist will listen deeply to the target's fears, stories from their past and secret hopes and dreams. The target will feel validated, heard and loved for exactly who they are.

Unfortunately, in exposing their vulnerabilities in this way to a narcissist, they have unwittingly handed the narcissist the key to their future exploitation and control.

Once the narcissist has uncovered the wounds of their target, and they know exactly what the target needs to feel healed and whole, they 'become' that person; the 'perfect' person for the target. It's common for victims to say: "I felt like I had known him my whole life" or, "It felt like he was heaven sent" and, "He was my soulmate". If the victim had lost a parent at an early age, the narcissist will play that role. If the victim had been neglected and unloved as a child, they will shower them with attention and love. If the victim had been cheated on in the past, they will speak of their high morals and faithfulness. If the victim was beaten as a child, they may speak of their perfect childhood, or may invent their own childhood dramas to show that they understand their target's pain. If the victim has a 'rescuer' mentality, they will re-write their own past so that they are the ones who need rescuing.

Targets will also invariably be taken in by the adoration which appears to be coming from the narcissist. Narcissists may stare deeply into the target's eyes, and make proclamations of perfect, true, never-ending love, far too early on in the relationship.

Essentially, the narcissist is holding up a mirror to the target. They are merely reflecting back the target's own adoration and love of the narcissist. The narcissist may *appear* to be in love, and most likely they *think* they are, but in fact, all that the narcissist is feeling is the positive effects of narcissistic supply. Their metaphorical suit of armour is temporarily gleaming and whole.

This is the point at which a reminder that "If it seems too good to be true, then it probably is" would be relevant. But by now, the target is hooked, and would not listen anyway.

Think back to the beginning of your relationship. Did you feel a strong sense of connection to the narcissist early on? Were you flattered to be considered special to them? Were you impressed by their status and achievements, or by their grand ambitions and plans for the future? Or did they play the role of hard done by victim, and did you feel an almost parental urge to help? Was this the great love story of your life?

The devalue stage

This stage follows love-bombing/idealisation. It occurs as the narcissist realises that their target is not the perfect human that they had idealised and put on a pedestal during the initial phase. It is usually not an abrupt change, but a gradual turning up of the heat, so slowly that you may not notice. The victim becomes the proverbial frog in boiling water, and does not jump out.

During this stage, the narcissist begins by employing subtle put downs to see how the target reacts. Remember that at this point that if *you* were the target, you would have been very favourably disposed towards the narcissist, so your defences will have been down. You will therefore have either completely missed the put downs or, if you did notice them, you would have made excuses for them. And, very cleverly, the narcissist will be devaluing you in those areas in which they have already identified you have vulnerabilities (your weight, your shyness, your social background etc.).

You may be asking how you managed to miss the put downs at the beginning of the devalue stage. Well, it wasn't actually your fault. The brain has systems whose jobs are to filter out incoming information that it does not consider to be relevant to the individual. If you noticed every single thing that was happening around you, if every single thing was to reach your conscious awareness, you would be pretty overwhelmed. Therefore, the brain filters out things that are not in line with your beliefs or your view of the world and those around you. These are known as 'deletions'. The brain also distorts reality, in line with our own personal prejudices due to former experiences, magnifying or diminishing our perceptions of things; so called 'distortions'. For example, if a person you like says something negative, "they can't have meant it". And finally, the brain's mental filters lead to 'generalisations' where we make automatic assumptions based on our past experiences, ignoring any exceptions that may be present, for example, "vicars are kind".

Your own brain filters will have been used against you by the narcissist during this stage with great effect, causing you to ignore or misread the devaluing behaviours.

The aim of devaluation is to gradually lower your self-esteem, so that you accept more and more bad behaviour from the narcissist, and eventually start jumping through hoops to try to get back the original feeling you had during the love-bombing phase. Some narcissists seem to be aware that they are doing this, but others are not, and they are unlikely to know *why* they behave in this way (unless they have particularly good insight).

The cycle of 'idealise' and 'devalue'

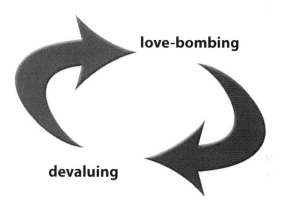

love-bombing

devaluing

Methods of devaluation

Verbal

These may be direct. If the target is a little self-conscious about their weight, the narcissist might say: "Perhaps you should wear something else – that doesn't do you any favours. I'm only telling you because I know you wouldn't want to be seen in something unflattering. *I* don't mind what you wear …"

They may thinly veil the devaluation with humour, delivering it with a jokey demeanour, and possibly following it up with: "I'm only joking – you are too sensitive!" For example: "Are you *sure* you should be drinking that full fat coke?!" Our Devaluing Narcissist, Anton, managed to put down his bride on their wedding day by telling the guests in his speech, with a big smile, that she had 'scrubbed up well' for the big day, rather than saying that she was beautiful. Her heart had sunk, but she told herself that she was being overly sensitive, and that this was just his quirky sense of humour.

There may be indirect insults, for example: "My friend thought that you looked pregnant – you aren't are you?" or "My dad was really offended at the way you didn't thank him enough for dinner" or "My mum is worried that you are making me materialistic." This way the narcissist is devaluing the target but not taking responsibility for it.

The narcissist often uses verbal devaluing to discourage the target from achieving anything that is important to them. If it doesn't impact the narcissist favourably or threatens to take the attention off them, they will not be supportive of their target's ambitions. For example: "Don't be too disappointed when it doesn't work out/you don't get the job/they change their minds."

The narcissist tends to start off feigning concern and having the target's best interests at heart, but if the target accepts these put downs, the narcissist will slowly ramp up the insults, testing how far they can go. Eventually, if the target tolerates this, frank name-calling and insults can become the norm. "You are boring"; "You are spiteful"; "You can't dance/sing/cook."

Being embarrassed by the other's behaviour at social events is another devaluing tactic, for example: "You shouldn't have drunk so much/talked so much/hogged that person's attention so much/told that story etc". These types of statements make the target feel like they are misreading social situations, and they start to mistrust themselves and to rely upon the narcissist to tell them what is appropriate or otherwise. The narcissist becomes their barometer of what is acceptable, their 'voice of reason.'

The target's taste in clothes, furnishing, houses, art, music or anything else can also be used to devalue them, as can their choice of career, parenting methods and so on. The way you stand, the way you speak, the way you blow your nose; the list is literally endless. Children will be demeaned and criticised, and spouses will be ridiculed for not earning enough, cooking well enough, keeping the house clean enough, being sexually adventurous enough. The narcissist's target will eventually believe that they are not enough in any way, as a result of these endless verbal put downs. This of course is true – they are not enough in the sense that they cannot top up the narcissist's narcissistic supply enough to keep them happy – because no one can.

Non-verbal

Examples of non-verbal devaluation can be wincing, pulling faces, looking disgusted, walking away, checking the phone at inappropriate times, watching TV during important conversations, yawning and looking bored when the other is speaking, looking at their watch, lateness, the silent treatment and emotional withdrawal and coldness. Physical abuse also falls into this category although not all narcissists employ this.

Our Devaluing Narcissist, Anton, did this all the time to Peter, who, if you remember, was an accomplished classical guitarist. During the love-bombing phase he would listen to Peter's playing with rapt attention, but in the devalue stage he would wince and walk out of the room if he played and even stick his fingers in his ears. This was to undermine Peter's confidence in his own abilities, and ultimately make him dependent on seeking Anton's approval for his own validation and self-worth.

Jill, our Communal Narcissist would employ physical abuse tactics towards her husband Dave, slapping him until he cried and begged her to stop.

Lateness is a common non-verbal devaluation tactic; it makes the target feel unimportant and undervalued, as if their time is not as important as the narcissist's. The target is simply expected to go along with the narcissist's lateness, which is often justified as a result of having important things to do; of being *more important* than the victim. What might start as a few minutes of tardiness could easily regularly become hours. This is surprisingly common, and the narcissist's sense of entitlement and lack of empathy also plays into this, and it boosts their sense of self-importance and control over others. How many times have you found yourself waiting for your partner?

Triangulation

This tactic is employed to get the victim to feel 'off balance' and to invoke feelings of jealousy and insecurity, which gives the narcissist a sense of power and sadistic enjoyment.

Triangulation is where the narcissist brings a third person into the equation. That person may be another unwitting victim of the narcissist, who is being groomed by the narcissist as another source of narcissistic supply. Narcissists generally have multiple sources of supply on the go at any one time, and many of these will be romantic interests waiting in the wings to take the place of the significant other. Others may just be hopeful fans, usually subordinates, who are flattered that the narcissist is shining their light on them. Young secretaries and junior work colleagues often fall into this category, and the narcissist will enjoy innocently dropping their names into conversation and texting them late into the night in front of their significant other who, desperate to not appear mad or crazy, will often downplay their unease about these relationships. Anton, our Devaluing Narcissist, would do this with young gay men he had met on the internet, and Jill, our Communal Narcissist, was triangulating Dave with the 'handsome' Father Jameson. Former romantic partners may be used for triangulation, and even members of the narcissist's own family ("It's not my place to insist that you are invited to my brother's wedding, even if we have been together for five years…", for example). The narcissistically disordered person will always deny all wrongdoing, or having any ulterior motives, if confronted. They may not even be aware of what they are doing or why, so deeply embedded into their subconscious are the programs on which they run.

Some narcissists cycle through so quickly that they blow hot one minute and cold the next. As a junior doctor, Supriya remembers working with a highly narcissistic registrar who would delight in praising her openly one day and giving her the benefit of his full charm offensive, and then completely ignore her the next, turning his attention to one of her colleagues instead. (His unsafe practices and tendency to play God with patients' lives got him sacked from that particular job, but he continued working in the medical profession elsewhere and no doubt rose to the highest ranks, due to his charismatic outward persona).

The cycle begins again

Once the narcissist has devalued you to the point where you are thinking about leaving, the cycle will begin again, and, quite abruptly, the narcissist will start to idealise you once more. Note that these cycles can be very short (days or even hours) or long (months or weeks), and the narcissist will typically vary the cycle length, which keeps you off balance.

In romantic relationships, this adoration will never be quite as pronounced as in the initial love-bombing phase, but somehow victims seem to accept this as normal. Do you remember experiencing huge relief at being back in favour, and making excuses for your partner's previous behaviour (they were stressed/tired/anxious/working too hard/stuck between a rock and a hard place etc.)? When the devalue stage then returned (as it invariably will have done), do you remember being thrown off balance once again, until the next idealisation phase?

As these cycles repeat, it is normal for the victim to begin to blame themselves for being unable to keep the narcissist happy, and to try harder and harder to do so. Walking on eggshells and tiptoeing around the narcissist's fragile ego eventually becomes the target's daily existence; the new norm. And in many cases, actually, it's not a 'new' norm at all, but a replaying of an *old* norm, most likely one enacted in childhood with a parent or primary caregiver. Can you relate to this in your marriage and maybe also your childhood?

Discard

Some describe the cycle not as a two part cycle but as a three part cycle, made up of idealisation, devaluation and then discard. Here the narcissist discards their victim, ending their relationship, before love-bombing them again, to draw them back into the cycle of abuse. However, more usually the narcissist does not actually discard their victim, but just makes them come close to thinking that they are going to do so. The victim then begs them to stay and tries to please them even more, until they are rewarded by renewed love-bombing.

But much more common than repeated discard by the narcissist is the situation where the victim ends or tries to end the relationship, only to be sucked back in. In fact, it is widely quoted that it takes, on average, seven attempts for a victim to leave their abuser, even one who is physically abusive. Of course, abusers do also leave their victims, but they more usually do this in one 'grand finale', rather than as part of a repeated cycle. For this reason, we do not include the 'discard' phase in our model of the cycle of idealisation and devaluation.

Hoovering

When a narcissist is on the verge of being left, or has been left by their significant other, their deep abandonment issues will be triggered. Hoovering is the term given to the narcissist's tactic to suck the target back into the relationship, so that the narcissist can continue to use them as a source of narcissistic supply. It is another form of idealisation but specific to imminent abandonment.

At this point the narcissist will turn back into the perfect partner. They will become seductive and charming. They will seem caring and helpful. They will put the bins out, load the dishwasher and stop texting their young attractive subordinates in front of their spouse. They will stop all devaluing behaviours and will apologise for the error of their ways, claiming stress or any other suitable excuse. Sadly, the trauma bonded spouse will be fooled by such behaviour, delighted that they still have a future with the narcissist. Of course, this is merely a temporary reprieve.

Given that it takes seven attempts to leave an abuser, if you are the spouse of a narcissist, you may well be hoovered back into the relationship even after you have instructed solicitors and moved out. To those around you, you may seem weak or indecisive, if they do not understand the highly addictive, neurochemical nature of trauma bonding (similar to a heroin addiction). It's normal to be indecisive when you are being hoovered by a narcissist. If it truly is your intention to leave, then one day you will be able to find the strength to walk away. But don't be surprised if it takes a few attempts. And don't then blame yourself. You are only human.

Rage

Narcissistic rage is another trademark sign indicating that one is dealing with a narcissist. This isn't anger. This is an intense fury that is unmistakable when one sees it. The way that a narcissist expresses their rage varies between narcissists. Some will physically attack. Others will throw and smash things. Dennis, our Exhibitionist Narcissist, would slash furniture with a knife. Some will clench their teeth and repeatedly hit a wall, or punch through a door. Some will scream and shout. Some will exhibit a chillingly quiet, psychopathic sort of fury like Anton, our Devaluing Narcissist, who would whisper threats whilst taking Peter's pulse as a lie detector test, and snarl at him through gritted teeth that he could read his mind.

Narcissistic rage is a consequence of 'narcissistic injury.' It happens when the narcissist's outer bubble is punctured; when the protective suit of armour is penetrated by some external event. It could be a perceived personal slight which brings on the injury, or any situation in which things do not go the narcissist's way. With little insight into what is happening, the rage quickly bursts forth, like a reflex response.

The number of attempts, on average, it takes to leave an abuser

People who have seen narcissistic rage often say the same things – it was terrifying to witness and it made them realise that it was one of only two *deeply, genuinely felt* emotions of the narcissist; the other being jealousy.

Narcissistic rage is generally accompanied by a type of communication known as the so called 'narcissistic word salad' (dealt with below).

Shallowness of emotions

It really does seem that many narcissists have a reduced emotional depth; that they feel most other emotions (apart from rage and jealousy) relatively shallowly, and that they have to sometimes 'play act' other *extremes* of emotions. Think of Dennis, and the way his eyes would well up in a display of emotion, short lasting and superficial. This is not to say that narcissists can't *feel* their emotions at all; they do. It seems to be the *extremes* of emotion (joy, despair etc.) that they struggle more with feeling.

Those relatively middle of the road emotions, (happiness, contentment, annoyance, mild irritation) are sincerely felt. But the difference here between narcissists and non-narcissists is the *depth* of the emotion. Narcissists can be happy one minute and angry the next, going right back to contentment in the next breath, depending on external circumstances. Their moods and emotions are *labile*. Think of a non-narcissistic person who is feeling happy in the moment. To them their happiness is deeply felt, like a very thick layer of ice on a frozen lake. It takes quite a bad event to penetrate that thick layer of ice, that feeling of happiness, and to change that feeling into a negative emotion. Now consider the narcissist, who is also feeling happy. Their happiness is shallowly felt; the layer of ice is thin. From the surface, it still looks like ice; it still looks like happiness. But even a minor external event or perceived slight can crack that thin ice and allow another emotion to surface.

Partners of narcissists frequently report occasions where the narcissist switches moods instantly, for example going from a foul mood to transforming into the life and soul of the party with a change in external circumstance such as a third party arriving. Their previous emotion is so shallowly held that it is easy to change. Think back to Anton, our Devaluing Narcissist, who would coldly blank his partner Peter during silent treatments, silently furious with him for his non-existent affairs, but would be able to laugh heartily at whatever sitcom was on the TV.

Going back to *extremes* of emotions, many partners of narcissists report that they never really properly cry. A narcissist who feels they should be desperately sobbing (for example, when a partner threatens to leave them) may make a sobbing sound with slightly watery eyes. A narcissist who recognises that they should be beaming with joy may turn the corners of their mouths upwards, raise their cheekbones, open their mouths and show all their teeth, possibly with a feverish look in their eyes, and tell people how joyful they are. With these *extremes* of emotions, one gets the feeling that one is watching someone deliberately trying to 'act like other people'. It just doesn't feel quite real, and it may seem overplayed or insincere. Does this resonate with you in relation to your partner?

We recall the story of an acquaintance being at a party hosted by a highly narcissistic middle-aged couple, who were commonly referred to as 'the beautiful people'. They were acting as if they were having the time of their lives, throwing their heads back and laughing at the smallest things, blowing on party whistles and letting off party poppers continuously. As our acquaintance explained, it felt completely false, as if they were trying too hard to look like they were having fun. Their slightly confused guests (our acquaintance included) mostly felt obliged to join in, dancing feverishly, as they did not want to appear ungrateful for their host's hospitality. But one person just sat and stared at the scene before him incredulously. Our acquaintance later heard that, to the couple, this had constituted an act of war. He and his wife were badmouthed and barred from future events from that day on, labelled as 'jealous' of their success and beauty and as 'boring'.

Jealousy

A healthy, non-narcissistic individual's sense of self-esteem comes mostly (around 70%) from their own intrinsic sense of innate self-worth, with around 20% coming from what other people think of them, and the remaining 10% coming from how they measure up when comparing themselves to other people. These proportions are very skewed in those with narcissistic adaptations, with a much, much higher proportion coming from what people think of them and how they compare themselves to others than from any innate sense of self-worth.

This means that narcissists are always comparing themselves to others; to what possessions others have, to the size and desirability of their houses, to their abilities and interests, to their relationships and social lives, and to their wealth and status.

Narcissists need to feel superior, whether overtly or covertly. They need to be winners.

They do not like it if their partner has a friend, sibling or anyone else in their lives who they perceive to have more than them, or be better than them in some sense. This jealousy manifests in a few ways.

Most commonly, the narcissist will accuse their partner of infidelity. They may also try to isolate them from the person they are jealous of, either by causing problems in the relationship with bad behaviour towards that person, or by manipulating or controlling their partner. They may directly ask their partner to stop seeing the person in question, giving their partner the silent treatment until they do so, or tell lies about the person they are jealous of, to put an end to the relationship.

Even nights out with long-term friends will be frowned upon or questioned. We recall the story of a woman who was raged at on and off for years about a ladies' only wedding hen night she attended, where the waiter (who she did not even speak to) was scantily dressed in 'Chippendale' style. She was made to feel guilty for being at such an event; her narcissist partner (who paradoxically, was a much better physical specimen than the waiter) simply couldn't deal with his own feelings of inadequacy. Perhaps there was some element of projection there, too, which will be discussed later.

Narcissists are constantly fearful about being replaced by someone else, someone better. They have deep abandonment issues. This will lead to snooping on phones and emails, and, often constant, intrusive phone calls, in order to check up on their partner's whereabouts.

They are also jealous of their partner being successful. Whilst they may initially seem proud of their achievements, this is only because they reflect well on themselves. The narcissist will initially bask in the glory of being capable of having such a successful partner to talk about to others. However, this will soon turn into a deep insecurity. If their partner is successful, he or she may leave them for better climes, after all. And no narcissist (other than the Closet Narcissist) is capable of having a partner who others perceive as being more successful than them. The narcissist will do everything in their power to undermine their partner's efforts to further their careers, by devaluing them, criticising them, attempting to destroy their confidence and sabotaging progress wherever possible. They certainly will not cheerlead them behind closed doors if they think they have a real possibility of success. Do you feel that you were fully supported in your aspirations and dreams by your partner? Or, in retrospect, did you find yourself pandering to theirs, at the expense of your own?

In divorce cases where this undermining of career advancement has gone on for years, it is important to acknowledge it. It may take many more years for you to recover your self-confidence and self-belief, and to be able to earn independently of the narcissist. Years of devaluing and mind games, such as gas-lighting, take their toll on a person. Healing and moving forwards is a long, drawn out affair and, in the ideal world, any divorce settlement should, if possible, take account of the extra time required to mentally recover in these cases. Unfortunately, because narcissistic personality disorder is not widely understood, especially by the legal profession, this may not happen. And labelling your spouse as a narcissist in court will tend to work against you, at the time of writing this book, and so should be avoided at all costs.

Being above the laws and rules

This is a very interesting pattern, which may appear less marked in Closet Narcissists, except behind closed doors.

It may be seen in many areas of the narcissist's life, from the laws of the land to the laws of physics and biology; from moral 'rules' to the rules of the road. It

> **"Labelling your spouse as a narcissist in court will tend to work against you and so should be avoided at all costs."**

often results in risk taking behaviours which others are carelessly subjected to, such as risky driving and drug taking.

Narcissists may insist upon having unprotected sex with multiple partners and not care about pregnancy or health risks (thus disregarding the laws of biology). Like our Exhibitionist Narcissist, Dennis, many drive recklessly, attempting to defy the laws of physics (driving through rivers, taking off on humpback bridges). They may accelerate around blind corners, ignore speed limits, and subject their passengers to hair-raising journeys.

They may flout the law (Dennis coerced his wife into accepting points on her licence by falsely accepting the blame for his speeding offences). They may even drive without a driver's licence.

When divorcing a narcissist, be aware that you will be subjected to woefully incomplete financial paperwork being presented to the court, as a result of the rules not applying to them. They will often flout court orders, or refuse to accept them until their own conditions have been added to them, giving them a sense of control. Your lawyer should be aware of this.

They may sell themselves as being highly moralistic, but in reality, morals are something for other people to adhere to. If it serves them and doesn't tarnish their reputation, they will lie, cheat, steal and ruthlessly exploit others, violating whatever code needs to be violated. Hypocrisy is a very marked feature here, but a high-functioning, intelligent narcissist can cover their tracks for years. Supriya is reminded of a very junior doctor she worked closely with who would turn up to work several hours late (expecting her co-workers to look after her patients on the wards) and then sneak off at lunchtime for a glass of wine on the grounds that it was the 'civilised' thing to do. She wasn't an alcoholic, just someone with a huge sense of entitlement and specialness as a result of her narcissism, who would moan incessantly if anyone left her to do any of their work in return. The rules just didn't apply to her.

Violating boundaries

This can occur on many levels, and is an effect of the narcissist's exploitative nature. 'No' often will not be accepted by a narcissist. In personal relationships narcissists will take up their victim's time and their money. They may violate physical boundaries and sexual boundaries. They may push verbal boundaries, enjoying making others feel uncomfortable with obtuse or flippant comments, 'banter' or rudeness disguised as jokes. They may have inappropriate social relationships with work colleagues and subordinates.

As a result of these blurred lines, secretaries will find themselves working late into the night for them for no extra pay. Subordinates will be flattered to be considered as 'friends' and so may find themselves driving them to the airport at 4am. Narcissists may refuse to tidy up after themselves, leaving others to do it. They may borrow things and not return them, or return them dirty or damaged. The Exhibitionist or Devaluing Narcissist is that person you know who will borrow your car and return it covered in mud and littered with snack wrappers, and then disarm you with a big smile. The Closet Narcissist might leave it with all the seats in the wrong position, the radio set to another channel, and the sat nav reset to avoid all major routes. And the Communal Narcissist, or any narcissist who wants to impress you in order to gain narcissistic supply from you, will return it fully valeted (by their long-suffering spouse, because they themselves were busy with other, much more important things) and with a fancy box of chocolates on the seat.

If you have been married to a narcissist, you may be the sort of person who naturally has very porous boundaries, and so find it difficult to stand up for yourself and what you find acceptable. This is very attractive indeed to a narcissist, and allows them to exploit you easily in order to get what they want. Alternatively, you may have had your boundaries (your barriers, demarcating where you end and another person begins) crossed so many times that you have allowed them to weaken. Have you been in a relationship with someone who just doesn't listen when you say no, ending with you giving in anyway?

Passive aggression

Those with narcissistic adaptions are masters of passive aggression. It serves them on various levels. It enables them to covertly devalue others, in order to control and minimise them. It fuels drama to provide narcissistic supply. And, all the while, its subtlety allows them to justify to themselves and others that what they are doing or saying is in line with their own image of 'niceness', and is not aggressive in any way.

Silent treatments are a classic example of passive aggression, as is persistent lateness, both commonly employed by the narcissist.

Procrastinating on jobs (such as cleaning or putting the bins out) that the narcissist feels they are above until others do them is also very common. In the work environment, narcissists will often not do the more mundane jobs that do not bring them an easy win of narcissistic supply, leaving others to fill in for them. Many narcissists will often do a household task so ineffectively that their spouse will stop asking them to help, or will deliberately make a mess in an act of passive aggression (think of Anton's daily habit of throwing wet towels on to Peter's side of the bed).

> **" Silent treatments are a classic example of passive aggression. "**

Sabotaging other's work is very common (Anton enjoyed sabotaging Peter's cooking for dinner parties by surreptitiously turning up the oven). Sabotaging relationships is also the norm; most narcissists tell believable lies about their targets as an act of passive aggression, so that others form an unfavourable picture of them and don't want to know them ("She hasn't cooked once in our whole relationship"; "He spends every night at the pub").

Name calling and insults re-framed as jokes are also a common passive aggressive tactic. If you have been in a relationship with a narcissist, you are highly likely to recognise some of these behaviours. Perhaps the way your spouse would load the dishwasher so the dishes wouldn't wash properly, or hang out scrunched up washing so that it wouldn't dry, wasn't so innocent after all.

Blameshifting

Those with narcissistic adaptations do not take the blame (except in the rare instances when doing so will give them narcissistic supply). They are never in the wrong, and simply cannot entertain the idea that this could even be a possibility. They will pass the blame on to others with lightning speed, almost as a wired-in reflex response which doesn't register consciously. We have some wonderful current examples of narcissistic politicians (a high risk group for narcissism) who do this beautifully.

They cannot take on blame, so they project it outwards on to others as a defence against feeling their own shame and the consequent deep depression that would result. As another example, during a rage a narcissist might repeatedly punch a wall, whilst blaming their terrified partner, "You are breaking my hand".

You will be used to taking the blame for everything from the smallest inconvenience to the biggest disaster if you have been the partner of a narcissist.

Lying

To a narcissist, the truth is not a finite entity. The truth is simply whatever they say it is at the time that they are saying it. This is so different to how most people are wired that it can be very hard to understand. Narcissists live a completely false version of reality every single day, as a defence against meeting and feeling their own shame and feelings of inadequacy. Lying to themselves and others about who they are is core to this personality disorder, so they are especially good at it, which is why lying about other things is extremely common – it's just a short hop, skip and a jump away from what they have to do anyway.

When a narcissist tells their version of the truth, they seem to believe it 100% – and that is because they often genuinely do, for the duration of the sentence, at least. They can take your hands in theirs and look deeply into your eyes, as they wriggle out of whatever it is that you have expressed concern about. It's extremely easy to be taken in. Affairs (physical or emotional) are rife in narcissists, but you will rarely get a confession.

In the context of family law, this has many ramifications. The narcissist will lie about every single thing if it serves them to. They will lie about their finances, hide money, accuse their spouse of being a drug abusing alcoholic prostitute who is unfit for parenting, claim that their new partner is being harassed by their spouse, call the police and claim that they have been assaulted by their spouse. They will lie on legal documentation (as they have no respect for the law) and to their own divorce lawyer. If you are divorcing a narcissist, you will need to be prepared for this, and for the woeful inadequacy of the legal system in protecting you from it, and its limited ability to penalise the narcissist for their lies.

Fluctuating morals, impaired conscience and inability to feel guilt

The above heading might sound somewhat demonising, so we'd like to reiterate at this point that we state this fact without judgement.

Those with NPD will often purport to have high moral standards, if this is in line with how they see themselves and their 'false self' but, in reality, moral rules apply to others, not to them. They seem to be able to intellectually understand their hypocrisy when acting in an 'immoral' way but again, psychologically bat off the feelings of shame that most people would feel so they don't have to face them. The same is true for guilt – they seem to know that they should be feeling guilt, but with guilt comes shame. They simply cannot take these feelings on board, so they don't, and they intellectualise their reasons instead, using what we call 'narcissistic pseudologic' – a nonsensical, contradictory type of logic delivered with utter conviction.

These impairments also go some way to explaining why the rules do not apply to them and, of course, why they lie.

Have you noticed how moralistic your partner can be, but how they don't live up to their own ideals? Have they told you that they are wracked with guilt for something they have done, but then done it again without a backward glance? Have they punished you harshly for something they themselves have also done, seemingly unaware of the hypocrisy? Or did they have you believing their high moral standards and trusting them so implicitly that you failed to see what was really going on?

Narcissistic pseudologic and word salad

Narcissistically disordered individuals can be very opinionated. Many seem to be able to 'change sides' with great ease, and seem to thrive on heated debates. It is almost the norm for narcissists to automatically take the opposite view to an opinion that is being expressed, and for many, compulsively playing 'devil's advocate' is an enjoyable game, precisely because of the frustration that it causes the other party.

Those with NPD need narcissistic supply. Arguing and debating gives them this by making them feel superior, special and clever. They need power struggles to keep things interesting. They need to 'win' in order to prove themselves and others that they are the best, in order to inflate their false self, so that they do not have to face their own feelings of shame and inadequacy.

Those narcissists that pride themselves on their intelligence (the cerebral subtype) may employ a grandiose, wordy, over complicated way of speaking, perhaps often also speaking very fast, in order to convey to the listener the great speed of their mind. They may speak as though they are highly logical, with high intensity. The listener often finds themselves believing the narcissist, as they seem utterly convincing and seem to know what they are talking about.

But, as we all know, the majority of effective communication is *non-verbal*, and this is where many narcissists have a big advantage. Their tone of voice, speed of delivery and body language convey great conviction, deep understanding and intelligence. But if you look at the *actual words* they are using you may be surprised to see a different picture. Nowhere is this more obvious than in written communication. Here it is easy to see the multiple contradictions, irrational conclusions, and loose associations between ideas that is the hallmark of the narcissist. This is what we call narcissistic pseudologic.

This pseudologic goes a step further when the narcissist experiences 'narcissistic injury' from being slighted, rejected or humiliated. Once the narcissist's defensive armour of superiority is punctured, narcissistic rage ensues, and their style of communication nosedives into full 'narcissistic word salad'.

Here the narcissist loses all sense of logic. They deny that things happened, blame the injured party using senseless reasons and re-written history, project on to the other party things that they themselves have done or have felt, make accusations, go round and round in circular discussions which descend into a downward spiral, say something one minute and deny having said it the next. They introduce new topics frequently or reintroduce old ones and try to logicalise events using nonsensical explanations. They make intimidating threats, and then profess undying love in the next sentence. The recipient of this ranting, raging, nonsensical, accusatory word salad is left reeling and breathless, utterly confused and questioning their own reality. They often feel the need to try to record conversations to prove to the narcissist that they have said certain things, and they find themselves trying to explain basic emotions, decency and empathy to the narcissist.

If you are in the throes of a divorce with a narcissist, you will receive emails and texts from the narcissist in full meltdown, where the contradictory word salad will be obvious. You will most likely find yourself recording every spoken conversation you have at the end of the relationship, and if you play them back, you may well be shocked by how nonsensical they are, and yet how convincing they seemed at the time.

> **"There is absolutely no point in trying to respond to either word salad or pseudologic in legal correspondence. "**

If you are already in the divorce process, then it is really important to know this. There is absolutely no point in trying to respond to either word salad or pseudologic in legal correspondence – you will be doing yourself no favours in engaging in costly and unproductive correspondence, and will be playing into the hands of the narcissist who will be trying to run up legal costs for you. More than likely you will wish to clear your name and respond to accusations and allegations. But you must understand that in doing this you will be inadvertently giving the narcissist what they need most - narcissistic supply as a result of the drama and conflict, as well as the ability to financially abuse you through your lawyer. Your lawyer's role in managing this effectively is crucial, which is precisely why you need a lawyer who understands this personality disorder. This piece of advice could save you literally tens of thousands of pounds.

Difficulty being alone

Narcissists need narcissistic supply to give them a sense of validation and self-worth. They need *people* to provide that, so they find it very difficult to be on their own where they are left with nobody to give them external adoration or attention. They may insist on their primary source of supply doing everything with them and not wanting them to have any time away from them; this is especially true of the older narcissists. They most likely will have multiple sources of supply on the go at any one time, and will often have a phone that buzzes and pings continuously as they are in constant communication with others.

The younger narcissists are often avid users of social media, where one is never really alone. They curate their posts to present an image to the world that will get the maximum numbers of likes, heart emojis and comments, all of which boosts their fragile senses of self. 'Me time', 'alone time' and 'screen free time' are not concepts that narcissists subscribe to. They descend into gloom and depression, or severe restlessness if forced into these situations, and may turn to drugs, alcohol or other addictive behaviours to distract them.

Some may gain narcissistic supply by propagating conspiracy theories online. These provide the narcissist with high drama, outrage and a reason to assert their own superiority whilst doing down others who they consider to be too stupid or blind to see the truth. Expressing extreme political opinions online is another way to get attention and so avoid feeling alone. Be slightly suspicious of the armchair Twitter warrior – their motives may not be as pure as you once thought.

It is characteristic of narcissists (especially the higher functioning, successful, intelligent ones, who are better able to hide their traits) to go straight from one romantic relationship into another with no gap or only a small gap. Because of their lack of emotional depth, they do not need to grieve or heal from former relationships, and they will use the breakdown of their relationship to garner sympathy from their next target who they may well have been grooming to step into their new role as primary supply for months or even years.

It is important to understand that, if you are separating from a narcissist, it is normal for them to move straight into another relationship in the separation period, or to jump straight into dating. But do not be fooled into thinking that this relationship is going to be any different or better than yours. Your narcissistic ex will be love-bombing and idealising their new love interest just as they did with you at the beginning of your relationship, and possibly rubbing your face in their new found 'love'. The truth is that they just need supply, and that they can't be alone. And please, *please* don't be tempted to warn their new partner that your ex is a narcissist. Just as you would never have believed it in the love-bombing phase, nor will they, and this can only backfire on you. Let their new supply take their journey – you have enough to be dealing with without trying to save them.

Think back to when you met your narcissistic partner – had they quickly replaced someone else with you, without a backwards glance? Were you so flattered that you didn't give it any thought? Have they ever really had times when they weren't either dating or in a relationship? Have you been stunned at how unscathed they seem when moving on from your relationship with them?

'Gas-lighting'

The term gas-lighting comes from the 1938 thriller 'Gas Light', in which a husband sends his wife 'mad' by repeatedly dimming the gas powered lights down to a flicker in their home, and then denying that they were flickering when she questions him.

To gas-light is "the act of undermining another person's reality by denying facts, the environment around them or their feelings".

It is a slow form of abuse which results in the victim questioning what is real, and wondering whether they are going 'mad'. Essentially, the abuser tells the victim that they are wrong on many levels and that they shouldn't trust themselves. It is a method of invalidation, whereby the victim slowly starts to feel unreal, and like a shadow of themselves. They then start to rely upon the abuser

> "To gas-light is "the act of undermining another person's reality by denying facts, the environment around them or their feelings".

as their 'voice of reason', no longer trusting their own perceptions of reality, and only trusting the narcissist's perceptions and point of view. There are a few presentations.

The narcissist will often tell a person that their *feelings* are invalid and wrong; that they shouldn't be feeling a certain way. They sometimes do it by deflection, or by twisting the other person's perspective. Think of the unhappy housewife who is feeling stressed by her mother's terminal illness. The narcissistic husband may invalidate her feelings by saying that she shouldn't be feeling stressed because her mother is old, and that he is the one that is entitled to feel stressed because his job is busy and he is doing long hours. Think of the wife who is upset that her husband has visited a lap dancing club and paid for a private lap dance. The narcissistic husband will tell her that she should be upset instead about the fact that society allows women's bodies to be exploited in venues which allow them to expose their breasts; that it is *society* she should be upset with, not *him* (this one also rather beautifully demonstrates narcissistic pseudologic).

Another common form of gas-lighting is simply to deny a person's *memory* of an event. "That didn't happen" and "I never said that" are common narcissistic refrains. Narcissists are renowned for rewriting history in this way, causing their target to question their memory and sanity.

Gas-lighting can also occur in the present, with everyday things in the environment. We recall a story of a narcissistic husband who would be drinking coffee, but would tell the wife that actually he was drinking tea, when he knew she had watched him make it.

Sometimes gas-lighting can be as extreme as the stuff normally reserved for fiction. We know of a narcissistic husband whose wife was thinking of leaving him, who would lean over her when he thought she was asleep and attempt to 'brainwash' her by repeatedly telling her that she did not want to leave him after all. The example of the (outwardly charming) Anton telling Peter that he could read his mind, and carrying out lie detector tests on him by taking his pulse and monitoring his breathing rate, is another true story.

Often the victim is repeatedly accused of having personality defects until they come to believe what they are being told, for example "You are crazy"; "There you go again, hysterical as ever"; "No one could ever love you because you are so unreasonable"; "You are paranoid/such a drama queen/boring/useless/a gold digger/ungrateful/selfish …"

Devaluing can also be used to gas-light victims about their own abilities. Consider the famous opera singer whose partner told her that she couldn't sing. Our Devaluing Narcissist Anton, who made Peter believe he couldn't cook by apologising about his food to others. The woman whose partner criticised her poor taste in interior design, although the house was featured in a design magazine. These victims had the reality of who they were, and what they were good at, deeply eroded to the point where they had lost confidence in their own sense of themselves.

The narcissist starts small at first and slowly turns up the volume on the gas-lighting, which can reach epic proportions. At this point, those outside the relationship may find the assertions outrageous and nonsensical (see the famous opera singer example above; a true story). However, to the long term, worn down victims, the narcissist's assertions seem true and believable.

If you have been in a relationship with a narcissist, you will have been invalidated in one of these ways. Look out also for those people who tell you that what you went through "isn't that bad" or that "all divorces are acrimonious", or that "it takes two to tango". They may not realise it, but they are also gas-lighting you. Do not accept this from people. If your divorce lawyer also does this to you, call them out on it. And if they do not understand what you are saying to them about this, find another lawyer – you need someone who is well versed enough in NPD to be able to give you the tactical support you need.

Projection

Projection is a psychological defence mechanism unconsciously used by many people, but by *all narcissists*. Anyone who finds it difficult to accept their failures, weaknesses and their own less flattering traits may unwittingly use projection as a way of feeling better about themselves.

In the case of narcissists, their sense of safety and self-worth depends upon maintaining a superior view of themselves. They are completely unable to accept the parts of themselves which are imperfect or flawed, as doing so would lead to an existential crisis, emotionally. They therefore assign those parts of themselves to other people, essentially giving away the feelings of deep shame that would come with acknowledging their flaws ('shamedumping').

So, when a narcissist accuses their partner of infidelity, it is actually the narcissist themselves who is cheating, or thinking of cheating. When a narcissist accuses a work colleague of stealing their work, they are the one who has considered doing that to someone or has done it. When a narcissist comments on a larger person's weight when they themselves are overweight, once again they are projecting their own disgust at themselves on to the other person. When they tell you that you are just like their mean-spirited father, they mean that *they* are just like their father. When they accuse you of being materialistic, they are inadvertently revealing this trait in themselves.

They project their thoughts, feelings, behaviour, insecurities about themselves, shame and fears on to their target. And the more intelligent ones may manage to do this by using a third party so that they absolve themselves of the act of projecting. "I've heard people say that you are arrogant…"

If a victim has also been gas-lit for years, it is quite common for them to actually take on and identify with whatever it is that the narcissist is projecting on to them. This is called 'projective identification'. They can start to believe the accusations. They apologise for transgressions they never made in the first place. They feel guilty for them. We knew of a woman who was so frequently accused of having affairs and making a fool out of her husband that she would feel great shame and apologise to him profusely even though she knew that she was innocent.

What did your narcissistic spouse accuse you of during your marriage? You can be absolutely sure that in fact they were the ones doing those deeds. Could you have been so busy defending yourself that you missed the truth of the matter?

Lack of empathy

All narcissists, without exception, lack empathy, which is of course *how* they are able to carry out their abusive and exploitative behaviours above without guilt or remorse. Lack of empathy is one of the 'Triple Es' of pathological narcissism, the others being entitlement and exploitation.

Those with narcissistic adaptations are unable to *actually feel* other people's pain or joy, or any other emotion. *They are therefore unable to really care about any other person*, other than in the context of what that other person can do for them, or how that other person can contribute to their own inflated sense of superiority (by making them look good, by giving them adulation, or food, or shelter or sympathy etc.) People are merely *tools* for those with NPD to use to obtain narcissistic supply, the oxygen that keeps their false selves alive, and so keeps them from facing their own deep insecurities, inadequacies and shame.

> "Lack of empathy is one of the 'Triple Es' of pathological narcissism, the others being entitlement and exploitation."

However, narcissists can *feign* empathy, and often do, particularly in the early stages of a relationship when they are seeking out to target another's vulnerabilities. This is because life experience and the careful study they have made of watching other people's behaviour has taught them under which circumstances they should *appear* to be sympathetic, and what they should do and say to convince others of their compassion. In other words, they have 'cognitive empathy' but not emotional empathy.

For example, if your mother died, a narcissist would be aware that this is a situation in which others would express sympathy, and would therefore have a stock phrase for dealing with this (for example, "I'm sorry for your loss"), and a behaviour to go along with it (perhaps a hug). However, they would not be able to really connect at all with how you were feeling, even if they had experienced bereavement themselves, and this might show itself fairly quickly. Perhaps straight after expressing their sympathy they would tell a funny anecdote, suggest that the bereaved person get on to a dating website or change the subject and talk about themselves. Some narcissists, in situations like these, miscalculate their responses in the opposite direction, and behave in an overly sympathetic manner, ringing people they barely know to offer their condolences and trying to be involved in helping with the funeral arrangements. The Closet Narcissists and the Communal Narcissists often fall into this latter category, and are completely unaware of how inappropriate this seems to others.

A big 'tell' of lack of empathy is that narcissists tend not to take care of their significant others when they are ill, and are very unsympathetic in these situations. They will not bring you soup and mop your brow. They will not massage your back for more than a second. They will still expect a meal on the table when you have the flu. Very often, if they can be persuaded to help, they will expect something in return (things are transactional to a narcissist), and they will usually point out how nice they are being.

Conversely, any opportunity to demonstrate how kind and compassionate they are to a new source of supply may be relished. We recall the story of the professional woman who rushed to her boss's hospital bed on Boxing Day after he broke his hip to sit by his bedside with his family for the day. She had left her own ill family including two young children (all of whom were incapacitated by the flu) in order to do so. She had been covertly grooming her boss as a source of supply for months at this stage, and he was beginning to fall in love with her, although she had been careful to ensure that she had *said* nothing that could be misinterpreted. All her advances had been non-verbal, and she had no intention of leaving her own husband and family. She just needed his adoration, and sadistically enjoyed devaluing her own husband by triangulating the pair. "But he's my *boss*," she told her husband when he questioned her actions. "It's the least

I could do – he's been so good to me…" Here she was feigning empathy for the boss, and having none for her sick family, all to obtain narcissistic supply.

Narcissists will often give away their lack of empathy by being cruelly inappropriate, with no idea that what they have said or done may be off the mark. Consider the narcissist who, on hearing that a family friend's teenage daughter was in hospital being tube fed for anorexia nervosa, felt it absolutely appropriate to suggest that letting the daughter die would be the best outcome all round. Or the narcissist who cheerfully suggested to the vet who came to the house to put down the family dog that he didn't believe she *really* felt sympathy for the family but that she must be putting it on, whilst the rest of the family sobbed. Or the narcissist on a boat who picked up his very young daughter unexpectedly and threw her into the sea. When she surfaced in floods of tears from the shock, he stormed off, for hours, furious that she could not take a joke, as her long suffering mother consoled her. Consider Dennis, our Exhibitionist Narcissist, and how he would drive so erratically that his wife Jane would suffer neck pain from being thrown around in the car. Narcissists are careless and thoughtless unless they stand to benefit in narcissistic supply terms, and those who are the closest to them are the ones who pay the highest price.

If a narcissist is having a good day, they will not thank you for bringing their mood down if you have not had such a good day. You may be struck by the poignancy of the story of the very little boy who was crying about his hurt finger. As soon as he heard his narcissistic mother coming home he said, "Quick everyone, act happy – mummy's home."

Sense of entitlement

This can take many forms. What lies at the core of this is the powerful, all pervasive need to *feel* special. They need to be *treated* as if they are special in order to prop up their fragile belief that they *are* special, and as all their validation comes from external sources, *how they are treated by others is the key* to this. This feeling does not, in narcissists, come from within.

It is often quoted that narcissists expect the best table at the restaurant due to their sense of entitlement, and that they will throw a tantrum if they do not get this. Another common example is that they may jump queues or complain loudly if they have to wait in line. Being rude to waiters and waitresses is another oft quoted red flag of NPD. Whilst this is true of many narcissists and should definitely be looked out for, in many cases their sense of entitlement to being treated as if they are special is much more subtle and they may manipulate situations much more cleverly to make sure that they are treated in the manner they desire, or so that they artificially create that feeling of specialness.

Lateness is one example of this. Arriving to an event late so others are left anxiously waiting for them to arrive, postponing the festivities until their grand entrance, is a great way to feel special. If part of a narcissist's sense of specialness comes from believing themselves to be the *nicest* person in the world, for example, they are not going to stamp their feet at having to wait in a queue as this would bust their own myth. They are going to arrive at the very last minute so that they don't have to wait at all, being publicly ushered in as the bride is walking down the aisle, as the curtain is lifting, as the judge is about to call you in, or as their child is about to blow their first note into their clarinet at the school recital. They are *entitled* to arrive late, as they are special.

Other narcissists, rather than treat service staff badly, treat them especially *well*, so that they are fawned over and receive special treatment as a result. Tipping the girl who sweeps up the hair at the hairdressers a fifty pound note can have *all* the staff at the hairdressers positively disposed towards you, and bending over backwards for you; sending someone out to get your special type of herbal tea, for example. Being extra charming to the waiters at the restaurant will mean that they will always find you the best table on subsequent visits, without you having to throw a tantrum. These intelligent narcissists will find the work around to ensure that they get this feeling anyway rather than risk putting themselves in a position where they aren't treated as if they are special. Remember the transitional nature of narcissistic interactions with others here.

As much as narcissists may feel entitled to be treated in certain ways and to have certain things, they also feel entitled to *not have to do* certain things. To not have to work, to not have to pay their way, to not have to tidy up after themselves, to not have to do domestic chores, to not have to get up in the night for the baby – each narcissist has their own unique list of things they feel entitled not to do. Many will work very hard in some areas (the ones which bring in the most narcissistic supply), and not at all in others. Of course, in order for these other important things to happen, they have to exploit others to get them done for them.

If you are divorcing a narcissist, they will arrive at court at the last minute or will be late (if they arrive at all), and may make a big show of having to leave early. They feel entitled to being treated as if they are special and they will make sure that this happens on their own terms. They won't stick to deadlines (giving a narcissist a deadline is futile), and they feel entitled to not fill in relevant forms or give a proper financial disclosure. They feel entitled to 100% of the equity in the family home, and to have spousal maintenance of more than your total salary, or (if they are the one with the money) to give you none of it, as only they are entitled to it. They feel entitled to drive you into the ground as you are no longer together. They feel entitled to do whatever they can to annihilate you. Be warned – this is tricky territory indeed, and this hardwired entitlement can leave you reeling in the divorce process.

Exploiting others

A natural follow on from entitlement, and another of the Triple Es. Again, depending the individual, this can have many presentations. Narcissists are able to exploit others for their own benefit because they do not care about other people's feelings, due to their intrinsic lack of empathy. Add to that their need to feel special through external means, and their sense of entitlement to have certain things and to not have to do certain things, and you have a recipe for interpersonal exploitation.

Work colleagues will pick up the slack for them and have the credit for their work stolen by them. Subordinates will be used in whatever way benefits them, and partners will find themselves doing whatever the narcissist feels entitled not to do, be that domestic chores, parenting or earning a crust. The list of exploitative behaviours is endless, and empathic givers who just keep giving are prime targets to be manipulated here. Are you one such empathic giver? Have you just kept on giving, as your spouse has taken and taken from you in various ways? If your partner is a narcissist, then, sadly, the answer to that question will be a resounding 'yes'.

The need to control

Narcissists need to control their victims. They do this in order to make their targets dependent on them in some way, so that they can keep them in place as reliable sources of narcissistic supply.

In the case of our Exhibitionist Narcissist, Dennis, he stripped his wife Jane of her autonomy by taking over all her roles such as cooking, choosing home furnishings and décor, making all financial decisions and doing all the driving. This had the effect of making her dependent on him; unable to live without him, especially as he had isolated her from her family. He de-personalised her, even deciding what hairstyle she would have. Many narcissists will appear to have strong feelings about what clothes suit their partner (which may initially be interpreted as caring for them), but which again is merely a control tactic and a manifestation of the fact that the narcissist only sees others as objects to be used for their own ends.

Narcissists typically control many areas of their targets' lives. An important point to make here is in regard to financial control. Whilst most narcissists tightly control their partner's spending, some (particularly affluent narcissists) use what looks (from the outside) like *generosity* to control their partner. They may give their partner full access to bank accounts etc, and encourage them to leave their jobs and stay at home, in reality making them completely financially dependent on them. Once the narcissist has them trapped, they turn up the volume on many or all of the horrendous abuse tactics described in this section. At first the target feels that they should be grateful to the narcissist for 'looking after' them financially but eventually they realise that they have been gifted a Trojan horse. The narcissist will expect them to do exactly what they tell them to do and to give up their own lives, hopes and dreams in return for their financial security. On the outside, these victims might look like spoilt, ungrateful brats; far from the birds in the gilded cages that they really are. Emotional support for them, when they try to leave, will be thin on the ground as a result. With narcissists there is never such a thing as a free lunch.

Narcissists will also control how their targets spend their day, often by giving them time consuming tasks to do (perhaps under the guise of "you would do this for me if you loved me, as I don't have time myself"). Constantly checking up on their partner's whereabouts through frequent messaging and calling is also a common control tactic, often under the guise of affection.

Furthermore, a narcissist will often control their partner's friendships by making them difficult to sustain. Here they might use a variety of ploys; directly alienating friends through bad behaviour or manipulating their partner into withdrawing from their friends through disapproval and sulking.

They may control what their partner does for a living, or even sabotage their chances of success. The children of narcissists suffer here too – their hobbies, university courses, careers and choice of friends may be dictated by the narcissist, as external appearances are desperately important. If a narcissist can control it, and it ultimately contributes to their own narcissistic supply, then they will. Children are merely an extension of themselves, and are not separate from them. Therefore, if the narcissist wants it, the child should want it too. And if the child wants it, but the narcissist does not, then the child should not want it either.

On the subject of control, some narcissists are also driven by a need to be perfect. These narcissists, as well as demanding perfectionism from others, demand it of *themselves* too, in various areas of their lives. These narcissists are prepared to work incredibly hard to be perfect.

We recall the example of a facial aesthetics doctor who was highly narcissistic, but was convinced that she was a kind and wonderful boss, wife, friend and mother. She needed to be those things, in her own mind. She wore flawless make-up every single day, even when not at work, and there was never even so much as a single hair out of place. She was immaculately dressed in designer wear at all times. She had built up a string of highly successful practices with multiple people working for her, of whom she demanded absolute perfection. She was a notoriously difficult boss, and even minor mistakes would make her employees feel like they had gone from 'hero to zero' overnight, and they would constantly be walking on eggshells. Her grand home was like something from the pages of a magazine, and staff would scuttle around continuously, scrubbing and polishing white floors and gleaming mirrors. When a married member of her live-in staff had an early miscarriage, she coldly fired her for having the audacity to get pregnant, which would have been highly inconvenient for the running of the household, and the distraught girl was given just a day to move out. Her children were also expected to be perfect in every way – high grades, the clothes they wore, the instruments they played, the level of sporting prowess achieved. She had been this way from childhood, brought up by a narcissistic father. Even as a medical student she had ironed her bedlinen and underwear.

This need to control often plays out in the narcissist having to have the last word on everything. If they cannot have everything their way, they have to have at least some of it their way. In the divorce process, you will find them putting their stamp on all manner of things. If you are thinking of divorcing them, they may unexpectedly start the process themselves, to gain a sense of control. They will insist on writing their own threatening letters to you which they will get their solicitor to copy and paste and sign so that it appears that you are being threatened by their legal team. They may insist upon trying mediation even though it will be unlikely to work in cases such as these. They will control court dates by being unavailable on certain dates and delay the process as much as possible by refusing to complete paperwork or provide financial disclosure. They will nit-pick over previously agreed matters, and constantly change the goalposts once an agreement is close. The list of ways in which this need to control plays out in divorce will be endless, and the process exhausting.

Toxic positivity

This is a really interesting behaviour that many Exhibitionist Narcissists, in particular, employ. It's especially confusing for the victim and for the people around the narcissist. Here, the narcissist lives their life telling everyone that it is perfect – that their job is great, their children are amazing and that their partner is wonderful. On the surface this may sound as if it is a good thing, focusing on the

> **"The need for control often plays out in the narcissist having to have the last word on everything."**

positives in this way, but actually, here it is a method of invalidation, denial and punishment.

The narcissist, who can only feel emotions on a very shallow level, believes that no one has the right to feel sad, deflated, upset, tired, stressed or annoyed. They may also deny these feelings in themselves, but they always do in others. As the partner of the narcissist, this makes you feel as if you are being ungrateful or churlish, just by having a normal, appropriate range of human emotions. You try to suppress these emotions, feeling that you don't have the right to them, especially when the narcissist seems so positive. If you do push it with the narcissist, asking for empathy or comfort, you may well find that the narcissist turns on you, calling you ungrateful, and then giving a diatribe about how difficult their life is but how they never complain. This leads to the partner feeling guilty about feeling the way they do – they have been gas-lighted in that their feelings have been invalidated, as if they shouldn't exist, and they come to believe that there is something wrong with having normal negative emotions. They often find themselves trying to 'act happy' around the narcissist, and they learn to push unwanted emotions away in order to keep the peace.

These narcissists are known by those outside the abuse for their smiley, happy, unstressed outlook on life. When you leave a narcissist like this, you are invariably seen as the ungrateful party by those who do not really know them.

Selfishness

Narcissists only do what *they* want to do, and they will drag others with them kicking and screaming. Because they have no empathy, they simply cannot fully understand other people's feelings, and so if they want to do something/go somewhere/have something/build something they will insist that others comply with their wishes, trampling all over their boundaries and needs.

Work colleagues will feel abused and unheard by them as a result of this, and partners and children may give up trying to object, developing 'co-dependency issues' where their own needs are so infrequently heard, and never met, that they stop having them altogether, instead focusing on meeting the many needs of the narcissist.

Narcissists are biologically wired to have no qualms about using others for their own ends, and genuinely feel completely entitled to exploit others to get what they want. They seem to have little or no insight into these behaviours.

The world revolves exclusively around them, a point made in the tongue-in-cheek joke we include here, for emphasis: *How many narcissists does it take to screw in a lightbulb? One. They just hold the bulb up in the air, and the whole world revolves around them.*

How they view others

Narcissists fluctuate between seeing people as either 'all good' or 'all bad'.

Here they are struggling with a healthy psychological phenomenon called 'whole object relations'.

They are unable to see people (or indeed themselves) as having both good and bad points at the same time – in other words, they cannot integrate both the liked and disliked parts of a person into a single stable picture. Instead they alternate between seeing the person (and themselves) as either being 'all good', when they are on the narcissist's pedestal, or 'all bad', when they have fallen off the pedestal and are exhibiting an annoying human flaw.

Related to this is the fact that narcissists also have problems with what is known as 'object constancy'. This means that they are unable to have positive feelings towards someone when they feel disappointed, angry, hurt or frustrated by them. It's as if any positive feeling there was instantly evaporates, leaving the victim walking on eggshells, scared to be anything less than perfect. In a healthy relationship, if your husband forgets your anniversary because he is swamped at work, you might be hurt, but you still love and care for him. Not so with the narcissist, who will vilify that husband for his cruel act.

Those who have struggled at the hands of a narcissist will recognise this instantly. They can feel as though the narcissist loves them one day, and then feel utterly despised the next because they have exhibited some minor human imperfection or have offended the narcissist in some way. Children (who inevitably misbehave) can feel these fluctuations acutely and, as the development of whole object relations and object constancy occurs in childhood, poor modelling of it by their narcissistic parent can cause them to suffer from such problems themselves, as adults.

Do you relate to this concept of being on a pedestal one day (when you are playing ball with the narcissist) and reviled the next (when you try to express yourself or stand up for yourself)?

The narcissist's experience of 'love'

Narcissists do not experience love deeply, if at all.

This is a very tricky one for the spouse of a narcissist, and one of the hardest things of all to come to terms with as a victim, especially one who has given the narcissist years of their life and had a family with them. I'm afraid there is no other way to put this. If you are married to a narcissist, you will at some point have to come to terms with the fact that they could not love you – not in the deep way that you are able to love, anyway.

If you ever question a narcissist about their concept of love, you might get some interesting answers. Many (if not most) will idealise it, fantasising about a Disney-style, perfect, love at first sight, never-ending, til death do us part type of love. A minority may reject the concept entirely, if pushed. And others may bring a slightly more bizarre notion to the table. We remember a Devaluing Narcissist once telling us about a husband and wife team he had known who had both contracted the same type of bowel cancer, the wife just a few months after the husband. His eyes welled up momentarily as he explained that this was an unmistakable sign of true love (see also 'narcissistic pseudologic' above). To him this was the ultimate beautiful romantic gesture from the wife; dying from the same cancer.

Narcissists do not experience love in the same way as healthy adults. To them, love is completely conditional. It's dependent on whether the recipient of their charms is giving them enough narcissistic supply, by doing what they want, being a flawless human being, and by adoring them, regardless of the abusive behaviours they are being subjected to. Of course, no one person will ever be enough to keep the narcissist topped up adequately with narcissistic supply, and the narcissist's partner has an impossible task in trying to meet the terms above. Love is transactional, and this also applies for the children of a narcissist.

It often causes the victim of narcissistic abuse much confusion when they first realise this, and they alternate between memories of the narcissist in the early days of love-bombing, staring deeply into their eyes and vowing their undying love, to those when the mask of the narcissist finally drops. They start to see the devaluing, and the gas-lighting, and all the other behaviours described above, but they cannot reconcile this with how the narcissist behaved towards them at the beginning (and in all the subsequent times when the narcissist 'hoovered' them back in, just as they were about to leave

> **"Narcissists do not experience love in the same way as healthy adults."**

the relationship). "It looked so much like love" you might find yourself saying, "but how can it have been?"

At this point, the victim is experiencing a difficult psychological phenomenon; so called 'cognitive dissonance' which we touched on in Chapter 1. Here they are struggling to hold two opposing beliefs about their relationship or marriage in their brains at the same time. This is still likely to be going on during the separation period, and you may find yourself fluctuating wildly in your beliefs on any one day to begin with. "He loves me, he loves me not." It's extremely difficult, but it will subside eventually, although it can take months to settle.

At this point, we want to mention the grief process. Divorce or loss of an important relationship will trigger a grief process in healthy people. The five-stage Kubler-Ross model consists of denial, anger, bargaining, depression and finally, acceptance. But the spouse divorcing a narcissist has a particularly traumatic process to go through (even greater we would say than in a 'normal' divorce, and perhaps even in many cases of bereavement). This is precisely because the spouse is grieving the loss of a relationship that was not at all what they had believed it to be. *They are grieving the loss of something that was never real*, which makes it especially difficult. Many simply cannot process their grief, as they believe they are not entitled to it. When these people try to revisit happy memories, through their new lens of awareness, they see the darker side of that same image; the bad behaviours that they had filtered out and ignored at the time. Everything they had previously thought of as a 'good time' may be negated, essentially wiping out years or even decades of their past.

Others will prefer to believe that the good times were genuine and that their partner just took leave of their senses. They may choose to romanticise the relationship, and may not move on, remaining wedded to the image of their partner as they were in the idealisation and love-bombing phases. So many people find themselves in this position, and tend to live their lives as victims, often blaming the new partner of their narcissistic ex for 'stealing' them away from them, and never moving forwards with their own lives. Many secretly hope that their former partner will return, even after years, or that they gave all their love away to the narcissist and will therefore never love again. It's terribly sad to see, but if this is you, it is your choice, and it should be respected.

If you tell people that you have been living a lie, you may receive well meaning comments such as "But surely you can't regret all? There must have been love there for you to get married in the first place?" These comments are not helpful or true. You've had your feelings, thoughts and beliefs invalidated for years already – you do not need more of the same. You may need to consider who you choose to surround yourself with in this period of separation, divorce and healing.

Living in the 'drama triangle' – the narcissist's home

Karpman's drama triangle was first described in the 1960s as a description of conflict in social interactions. There are three roles within the triangle – victim, rescuer and perpetrator. In high conflict relationships people tend to move around the triangle taking up the different roles at different times, perpetuating the drama, so that it continues on and on. If one person switches role, the other person has to also switch role to take up one of the vacant positions in the triangle, often completely unwittingly. People tend to get stuck in the drama triangle, unable to break out, and nowhere is this more apparent than in a relationship with a narcissist who manipulates the triangle to their own end with great skill, sucking people in to fill the vacancies.

For example, narcissists will often enter a person's life when they are vulnerable, and they will play the role of rescuer; the knight in shining armour. They will help their target sort their affairs and take care of them. Notice the way our Exhibitionist Narcissist Dennis swept Jane off her feet after the death of her fiancé, claiming that he had been sent by God to take away her grief. Here Dennis was the rescuer and Jane, the helpless victim of her awful circumstances.

Once the rescue has been effected, the narcissist will at some point take on the role of perpetrator, gas-lighting and devaluing their target. The target, rather than being the victim of circumstance, now becomes the narcissist's victim, and is utterly confused. But as soon as they try to address the issue, the narcissist will pull a quick role shift out of the bag and play the role of victim themselves, for example telling their target that "they do not understand how difficult life is for them at the moment, how stressed they are, and how they are making it all even worse". The target has been made the perpetrator now – everything is their fault. The empathic target, without even consciously registering it, feels their heartstrings being pulled, and they move into the role of the rescuer themselves, placating the poor narcissist and trying to solve their problems.

Often there will be other people in the triangle that you may not even know. For example, the narcissist may be telling his young new secretary that you, his wife, does not love him. Here you (in his mind) are the perpetrator. The secretary puts herself in the rescuer role, flattered to be important enough to be confided in and hoping for more, and the narcissist happily plays the victim. When you find him texting his secretary late into the night, you become angry, reinforcing your position as perpetrator. The narcissist continues to play the injured party (victim), you feel guilty about your anger and you try to rescue the narcissist from his own pain, at the same time blaming the secretary (now the perpetrator) for obviously trying to steal your husband.

The Drama Triangle

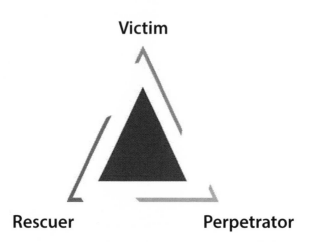

Victim

Rescuer   **Perpetrator**

There are an infinite number of permutations of the exact ways in which the narcissist can play in the drama triangle, and divorce provides the perfect backdrop for multiple triangles to be in motion at any one time. Your solicitor will be sucked in, as will your barrister. Even the narcissist's legal team will be drawn in.

You cannot step out of the drama triangle if you do not realise that you are in it in the first place, but simply noticing what positions you are taking up in it is all that is required to make major shifts in the game. And make no mistake – for the narcissist, sadly, it is just that; a game.

The dropping of the mask

As we have already mentioned, narcissists wear a mask (or sometimes many different masks depending on who they need to be in a given situation to secure the most narcissistic supply). We've previously referred to this as their 'armour' to illustrate the protective nature of it, but it is more commonly referred to as a mask.

The mask is the outward projection of the narcissist's false self. But when the narcissist does not get what he or she wants from their target, the mask will drop to reveal their true nature. Some narcissists can keep their mask on for years, fooling their long-term partner, for example, although they may drop it at work or in other situations. Others are less stable and drop their masks more frequently, whenever they experience narcissistic injury. Some are able to only partially drop their masks in response to mild narcissistic injury, showing relatively controlled rage, but others will drop the mask entirely.

During the divorce process, especially if it is the narcissist who has been left (triggering deep abandonment issues and severe narcissistic injury), the mask will drop, most likely completely.

At this point you, as the narcissist's target, the recipient of their abuse, will finally get a true glimpse of the person that you have slept soundly next to in the marital bed and it is likely to be a moment that you will never forget.

The Narcissist's Playbook

The cycle of 'idealise' and 'devalue'

Hoovering   RAGE

Shallowness of emotions   Jealousy

Being above the laws and rules

Violating boundaries

Passive aggression

Blameshifting

Lying

Fluctuating morals, impaired conscience and inability to feel guilt

Narcissistic pseudologic and word salad   Difficulty being alone

Gas-lighting   **Projection**

Lack of empathy   Sense of entitlement

Exploiting others

The need to control

Selfishness

Why me? 3

So now you have gained a deeper understanding of narcissists, and hopefully have worked out whether your partner fits the criteria for narcissistic personality disorder or not. But just as important *is understanding yourself*, and understanding how your background and character traits might have made you a ripe target for a narcissist. There are two pieces to this puzzle, and victim and narcissist generally fit perfectly together.

Who do narcissists target?

The question so many people ask, when the penny finally drops and they understand that they have fallen for a narcissist, is *why me*? What made the narcissistic pick me? And will it happen to me again?

Well, anyone can be targeted by a narcissist, but the people who tend to fall the hardest and for the longest tend to have some or all of a number of specific traits; if you have them, then recognising them and working on yourself to change them will make you more 'narcissist-proof' in the future.

Rescuers. Those that need to rescue others are often taken in by the narcissist's pity plays, time and time again. Rescuers usually need to rescue others to feel needed and to matter and, although they may think their rescuing tendencies are generous in nature, in fact, even with non-narcissists, they are disempowering to the recipient. A narcissist will exploit this trait time and time again, pulling the target into the drama triangle and keeping them there.

Those who are blindly compassionate and empathic. Despite being hurt by the narcissist, or seeing others hurt, these people (who tend to believe that all people are intrinsically good) continue to forgive poor behaviours endlessly. They believe that 'love conquers all', and they give more and more of themselves to the narcissist. The problem is that, in terms of empathy, this is one-way traffic. A severely narcissistically disordered person will not be cured by love or kindness, no matter how much they receive. And in repeated forgiving, they are actually giving the narcissist *permission* to re-offend, ad infinitum. (Forgiveness is not something that should be given to another person so that they can continue to abuse. For those who have been narcissistically abused, it is something that may be given, without telling the narcissist, some months or years down the line, when they are safe from the narcissist. And here, it is not for the narcissist, but as an act of love for *themselves*, to save themselves from the toxicity of their own bitterness).

Those who were brought up in narcissistic households. You can only know what you know, and these people have been wired to accept poor narcissistic behaviours from an early age, to dance to the tune of their narcissistic parent, and to develop workaround strategies as second nature. These people are very attracted to narcissists, and feel a strong 'chemistry' towards them. They probably don't realise that what they are actually feeling is *familiarity*, especially as the narcissists they are drawn to may be superficially very different to the type of narcissist they grew up with. Our brains subconsciously draw us to what feels familiar and safe to us; to what we know, in order to re-create the patterns of our upbringing. *You find the person whose teeth fit your wounds*, as the expression goes. These people may be surrounded by narcissists, unwittingly collecting them and bringing them into their lives as friends, clients, colleagues and partners.

> **"You find the person whose teeth fit your wounds. "**

It's very common indeed for those divorcing a narcissist to realise that they were brought up in a narcissistic family system. Your narcissistic parent may be a different type to your narcissistic spouse (for example, you may have had an Exhibitionist Narcissist father, but then been drawn to a Communal Narcissist spouse), making the connections relatively hard to see initially.

Echoists. The term 'echoist' was coined in 2005 by Dean Davis, an American psychoanalyst. In Ovid's myth of Echo and Narcissus, Echo had a curse put on her so that she wasn't able to speak her thoughts, and could only repeat the thoughts of Narcissus (who she was in love with, but who could never love her back). He famously fell in love with his own reflection and drowned as he dove into the pool to try to be with himself.

Echoists are essentially the polar opposites of narcissists, on the opposite end of the spectrum which we will be looking at later in this chapter. They have poor interpersonal boundaries, and do not like asking for or accepting help or gifts. They feel uncomfortable having needs at all, and prefer to focus on fulfilling other's needs and wishes. Unlike Closet Narcissists, they do not feel special at all – quite the reverse; they have an aversion to feeling special. They feel under-entitled and undeserving, and are emotionally fragile. They find it difficult to accept compliments and can suffer from anxiety and depression. Like narcissists, they suffer from low self-esteem, but they do not create a false self of superiority to mask this. They overlap with the category above in that they are also the sons and daughters of narcissists. (What determines whether a child of a narcissist becomes a narcissist, an echoist or indeed a healthy individual with good self-esteem, is not yet fully understood. Even within the same family, three children subjected to the same parenting may grow up to be one of each of the types above).

Echo and Narcissus (1903), a Pre-Raphaelite interpretation by John William Waterhouse (courtesy of Wikipedia)

Co-dependents. Those people who have previously been in co-dependent relationships are particularly prone to repeating this pattern and falling for a narcissist. Co-dependency is "a specific relationship addiction characterised by preoccupation and extreme dependence – emotional, social and sometimes physical – on another person…" Co-dependents feel extreme amounts of dependence on loved ones in their lives and they feel responsible for the feelings and actions of those loved ones. A co-dependent can only feel ok if their partner feels ok, and they feel responsible for making their partner feel this way. They therefore subjugate their own healthy needs to this need for their partner to be ok, and they often don't even know what their own needs are, so preoccupied are they with their partner.

Who is likely to be a co-dependent?

Co-dependents are essentially caretakers of another, and they are themselves addicted to needing to take care of the other person.

Often, the person they are taking care of also has an addiction of some sort. Partners of alcoholics and substance addicts are co-dependent. Partners of narcissists are also likely to be co-dependents. Interestingly here, some see *narcissism itself* as an *addiction to needing to feel superior*, in which the cravings to feel superior are like the incessant cravings for a drug. Just as drug addicts need more and more of the drug to satisfy their cravings, narcissists require more and more narcissistic supply in order to feel superior.

So, if you are someone who has previously been in a relationship with an alcoholic or drug addict, you are at risk of becoming the partner of a narcissist, and vice versa. People who have had to take care of a close family member with a chronic illness may also become co-dependent, as can children who were forced into a caretaking role with their own parent. It also seems that any type of deeply traumatic upbringing can result in co-dependency issues. Those who have developed co-dependent personalities often find themselves repeating relationship patterns in their new relationships with different alcoholics, substance addicts and narcissists. If you've been with a narcissist in the past, until you break your co-dependency issues, you may well find yourself with another in the future.

> " **If you are someone who has previously been in a relationship with an alcoholic or drug addict, you are at risk of becoming the partner of a narcissist.** "

It's as if the co-dependent person is almost defined by the other person's addiction or needs. They are those who have a hard time saying no, who have poor boundaries, and who deny their own needs, thoughts and feelings. They confuse love and pity, and have a need to control others and to take care of others. These types often fear abandonment and have a need to always be in a relationship. They typically are so busy taking care of another that they forget to take care of themselves, and so lose their own sense of identity. Indeed, many long-term partners of narcissists report feeling as if they didn't really know who they were anymore. The good news is that co-dependency can be overcome with awareness and some work. (See the Further Reading section at the back of this book).

At this point we will reiterate that, especially if you recognise yourself as falling into any (or even all) of the categories above, you are at risk of being targeted by another narcissist again. This is especially risky *now*, when you are at your most vulnerable, most needing support and craving the love you may have only just realised you never received from your narcissistic spouse. Be wary of getting into another relationship during your separation and divorce. All too often people make this mistake, and do not recognise the new love-bombing (which will invariably be different in some way to their former partner's previous love-bombing) for what it is. If your new partner wants to rescue you, or get involved with every aspect of your divorce in order to 'help' you, hear the warning bells. And be warned – narcissism is usually mostly noticeable in retrospect, in the cold light of day.

Am I a narcissist? The spectrum of narcissism

By now, you may be wondering whether *you* are a narcissist. After all, every now and then, perhaps *you* secretly feel that you are a bit special.

Well, as it happens *most* people do not see themselves as being merely average. Studies have consistently shown that *most people think of themselves as being exceptional*. This is known as the 'better than average effect'.

People who see themselves as being better than average are happier, more sociable and often healthier than those who do not. They are confident, more able to endure hardship, creative, good leaders and have high self-esteem. They also see their partners as being more special than they really are.

Conversely, the opposite is true for those who do not feel special; they have higher rates of depression and anxiety, and do not admire their partners as much. Not feeling special is officially bad for your health.

It is interesting that the biggest predictor for success of a romantic relationship is one or both people in the relationship thinking that their partner is better than they actually are by objective standards. People in successful romantic relationships think that their partner is more beautiful, more intelligent and more talented than they actually are, and as a result, they feel special by association.

So it would seem that feeling special per se isn't actually a bad thing after all. It is a question of degree. *It's a question of to what extent a person **clings to the need to feel special at the expense of others**.*

So, narcissism exists on a spectrum. Those at the lowest end of the spectrum who do not feel special are the echoists, after Echo, the voiceless, presence-less character in the myth of Echo and Narcissus. They have little sense of self and of their own needs. They are 'negative narcissists' as it were, with *not enough* healthy self-belief and self-advocacy skills.

Those at the opposite end of the spectrum are the narcissists, after Narcissus, who are blind to the needs and feelings of others, concerned only with meeting their own needs to feel special.

And those in the middle of the spectrum balance their own inherent healthy sense of specialness with the capacity to care for and meet the needs of others. *This is the ideal place to be on the spectrum; in a place where your own sense of self-worth keeps you boundaried, healthy and happy, with a healthy amount of self-advocacy.* (Some people call these traits 'healthy narcissism'. We believe that this is a confusing oxymoron, and that the term 'narcissism' should only ever be used in its correct, pathological sense).

In Dr Craig Malkin's book, *'Rethinking Narcissism'* he describes a spectrum from 1 to 10. The echoists lie at the left hand side of the spectrum, with those who are the least able to be seen, heard and self-advocate occupying position 1. Those who are better at self-advocacy and expressing needs are at 2, 3 and 4. These people could still do better for themselves, however. Positions 5 and 6 are where the optimally healthy people lie, and the narcissists lie at 7 through to 10, with the most pathologically narcissistic at 10.

The spectrum of narcissism

0 Echoist   Pathological Narcissist **10**

Interestingly, narcissism is not fixed. People can move up or down the scale a few notches depending on their life circumstances. Some moves may be permanent, others not.

For example, consider the heart surgeon, who started his adult life off as a 7. He may have been selfish and arrogant, but not always at the expense of those around him. He may have only occasionally devalued others, and may not have been overly entitled, perhaps not expecting too much in the way of special treatment. As he progresses up the career ladder, getting ever closer to the top, he gets more and more narcissistic supply. More and more young nurses may see him as a better prospect, and will fawn over him, vying for his attention. He will thrive on this, and feel more special as a result. He may have his pick of them, and may conduct affairs with them, discarding them as more attractive ones come in. He has just hit an 8 on the spectrum.

His empathy for those he has discarded may decrease. He may start to feel entitled to have these affairs as his wife is no longer worshipping him as much as these ladies at work. Concurrently, as his surgical ability increases, he will cure more patients of their conditions, and they will be grateful to him and impressed by his ability. His narcissism may increase further. He may start devaluing his other surgical colleagues, commenting on their lack of skills relative to his. He may start to look as though he believes his own hype although, underneath this, his intrinsic self-esteem is low. He deflects from this feeling by acquiring more and more narcissistic supply. He earns more money and buys fancy cars and holidays, impressing his junior colleagues who suck up to him, hoping that one day he will recommend them for a job. He is now at a 9.

By the time he reaches the upper echelons of his surgical career, he is regularly saving lives and people around him are hero-worshipping him. His wife has not been on her pedestal for a long time, and he now feels far too important to participate in mundane domestic tasks. He runs her ragged. He starts to gaslight her, demean her and criticise her. He projects his own affairs on to her. At work, he is considered a God, and he starts to expect to be treated like this as the bare minimum. Those around him cater to his every whim, laugh at his jokes, and want to be associated with him. He grandiosely sweeps in to work to see his patients, late. He does not bother to learn the names of his junior colleagues. He keeps his staff working after hours and performs operations which are so risky that no one else will do them. Some of his staff are starting to feel abused by his demands on them. He needs to believe he is the best of the best. His secretaries are exhausted, chasing him for paperwork which he feels he is too important to do in a timely fashion. He is at a 10.

He chases even more power, wealth, status and possessions to feel special. He needs a younger, prettier wife who is more of a trophy; the cue for his wife's divorce lawyer to enter stage left. And at this point, to the narcissist, to para-phrase Shakespeare, all the world is indeed a stage, and all its men and women merely players. Sadly, at this stage, *all* empathy has left the building.

At this point, it is probably far too late to bring the narcissist back down the scale to his original 7. It may, however, have been possible for a specialist psychother-apist to have made some progress earlier, perhaps when he was at an 8.

Note that *all* of us have times in our lives when we slide, usually temporarily, up the scale a few notches. If we have been bereaved, for example, we will feel entitled to be treated with special care. We may be selfish and introspective, fo-cusing on how we are feeling above all else, putting our own needs first.

Adolescents also typically slide up the scale, becoming selfish and unempathic, relying on a sense of artificially feeling special to get them through. Once adults, they slide back down again, able to consider others once again.

The elderly also experience a surge in narcissism, often as ill health takes hold, making them feel vulnerable, sad and self-centred as they struggle to hold on to their sense of self-worth.

It is also possible for those at the lower end of the spectrum to move up, towards the healthy zones of 5 and 6, with awareness and perhaps therapy.

Turning to those who have been in long-term narcissistic relationships, often when they look back at their own behaviours, they find that they have actually 'taken on' some of their partner's narcissism. This is a very common and tempo-rary phenomenon. This happens when the non-narcissist places the narcissist on a pedestal, and then is subjected to invalidation and devaluation. Once their confidence in who they are is eroded, they find themselves emulating the ac-tions of the narcissist, holding up some of those behaviours as their new ideal. If you recognise yourself here, self-forgiveness will be important. After all, you were the narcissist's biggest fan, and probably also their 'flying monkey'. A flying monkey (named after those in the wizard of Oz who did the evil bidding of the Wicked Witch) is a person who enables the narcissist's bad behaviour, and ac-tually unwittingly carries out such behaviour on their behalf, enmeshed in their belief that the narcissist is perfect and always right. Be assured that awareness and recognition of these behaviours in yourself is enough to put it to an end.

If you wish to know where *you* currently are on the spectrum of narcissism, please refer to Dr Craig Malkin's book, *'Rethinking Narcissism'* in the Further Reading section of this book, where there is an excellent questionnaire. And be-fore you do, be aware that pathological narcissists generally would not have the insight to wonder if they were narcissistic, and would be very unlikely to care even if they found out they were.

Am I a Closet Narcissist?

You may also be concerned that you may be a Closet (also known as 'Covert') Narcissist, particularly if you were drawn to the charm and charisma of an Exhibitionist Narcissist, and have noticed that they made you feel special by association. To reassure you, *everyone* feels special by association when they are involved with an Exhibitionist Narcissist, as that is how they pull you in in the first place. The 23-item scale below was presented at the 2013 Association for Research in Personality conference by Jonathan Cheek, Holly Hendin and Paul Wink, and is a questionnaire which will help you determine whether you fall into the Closet Narcissist category.

Maladaptive Covert Narcissism Scale (MCNS)

Please answer the following questions by deciding to what extent each item is characteristic of your feelings and behaviour. Fill in the blank next to each item by choosing a number from this scale.

1 = Very uncharacteristic or untrue, strongly disagree

2 = Uncharacteristic

3 = Neutral

4 = Characteristic

5 = Very characteristic or true, strongly agree

Question	Score
1. I can become entirely absorbed in thinking about my personal affairs, my health, my cares or my relations to others.	
2. My feelings are easily hurt by ridicule or the slighting remarks of others.	
3. When I enter a room I often become self-conscious and feel that the eyes of others are upon me.	
4. I dislike sharing the credit of an achievement with others.	
5. I feel that I have enough on my hands without worrying about other people's troubles.	
6. I feel that I am temperamentally different from most people.	
7. I often interpret the remarks of others in a personal way.	
8. I easily become wrapped up in my own interests and forget the existence of others.	
9. I dislike being with a group unless I know that I am appreciated by at least one of those present.	

Question	Score
10. I am secretly "put out" or annoyed when other people come to me with their troubles, asking me for their time and sympathy.	
11. I am jealous of good-looking people.	
12. I tend to feel humiliated when criticised.	
13. I wonder why other people aren't more appreciative of my good qualities.	
14. I tend to see other people as being either great or terrible.	
15. I sometimes have fantasies about being violent without knowing why.	
16. I am especially sensitive to success and failure.	
17. I have problems that nobody else seems to understand.	
18. I try to avoid rejection at all costs.	
19. My secret thoughts, feelings, and actions would horrify some of my friends.	
20. I tend to become involved in relationships in which I alternately adore and despise the other person.	
21. Even when I am in a group of friends, I often feel very alone and uneasy.	
22. I resent others who have what I lack.	
23. Defeat or disappointment usually shame or anger me, but I try not to show it.	

Now add together all the numbers to come up with a total score.

Results

Below 40: you scored very *low* in covert (closet) narcissism.

82 and above: you scored *high* in covert (closet) narcissism.

The average score on this scale is in the mid-upper 60s. So, if your score hovered around that range, you're about average in closet narcissism.

The narcissist and their children

4

First, let's talk about you

You may by now be building up an understanding of the behaviours of your spouse and recognising some of their actions for what they were – an attempt in some way to gain narcissistic supply at the expense of those around them. If you are not dealing with a narcissist, this may also be becoming apparent by now. Note that these realisations, these 'lightbulb moments', don't come in a neatly linear series just whilst you are sat actively researching NPD. They can come out of the blue, when you least expect them – when you are in the supermarket queue, or drifting off to sleep, or as you stare blankly out of the train window. They can sideswipe you, or run you over like a huge steamroller. They can wake you up in the night, and take your breath away. In the trauma of narcissistic abuse, flashbacks can start to appear as your brain, constantly working away in the background, starts to put two and two together. These flashbacks might be vivid and intrusive.

Anger might now be a prominent emotion – the second stage of grief. You might find yourself vacillating between anger and denial. You almost certainly will be angry at your narcissistic spouse, but you may well also be angry at yourself for letting this happen. For being so foolish. For being so gullible and for wasting so much time. For giving up on your own hopes and dreams, perhaps. You may be angry at all the narcissist's enablers – their family, their fan club, their work colleagues – and perhaps even your own family and friends. You may have started to realise that you were also an enabler of your narcissist, sticking up for them, looking away, perpetuating their perhaps subtle abuse. You may even be at the stage of realising that you were as much a fan club member as the others

– and, actually, perhaps the narcissist's number one fan, cringeworthy though that might now seem.

With narcissistic abuse, it helps to take ownership of the part you had to play in all of it, difficult though that might be. To understand that although the perfect storm drew you in, you stayed. You denied and minimised the narcissist's abuse, and allowed it. That is not to say that things could have been any different – you were most likely a lamb to the slaughter. But to accept your percentage of the blame, even if that is a mere one percent, is actually oddly empowering. It marks the beginning of you moving from hapless victim to a person who is in control of their own destiny. You might not be ready for this yet, but bear it in mind for the future. To accept the part you had to play *and to be able to forgive yourself for it* is a big step towards healing, when you are ready.

We've already looked at what personality traits in *you* might have subconsciously led you to becoming fodder for a narcissist but, to become really informed, we now have to turn our attention to the other really important people in your life (if you have them) – the children, the innocents, who had arguably even less say than you did in having narcissism enter their lives.

How the narcissist behaves towards their children

If you have children with your narcissistic spouse, it's crucial to be aware of the effect that a narcissistic parent can have on a child. As we have already established, narcissists abuse everybody that they come into contact with to some degree, whether that person ever realises it or not. (Someone who has very limited contact with a narcissist, and who gives the narcissist good narcissistic supply on the occasions they do come in contact with them might hardly be abused at all, and certainly not to a level that is noticeable to them. Perhaps they are simply badmouthed behind their back or come to realise that the narcissist has never bothered to remember their name – relatively minor, but hurtful behaviour at worst).

However, the child of a narcissist is also not exempt from narcissistic abuse, but in their case, they are likely to spend a significant amount of time with their narcissistic parent, and be subjected to plenty of abusive behaviour, albeit often subtle. But of course, *they know no different* – the way the narcissist behaves towards them is their normal, setting them up for difficulties as adults. In this chapter we explain how narcissistic parents behave towards their children, both in general, and during and after separation and divorce from the other parent. If you are considering leaving your narcissistic spouse, you will need to be prepared for these quite disturbing 'divorce behaviours' towards your children, as well as for the limitations of their parenting skills. We also take a look at the effect narcissistic parenting can have on the emotional and mental development of the child, and how this may affect them in adulthood, and at what you, as the non-narcissistic parent, can do to limit the damage.

It's important to understand that those with narcissistic personality disorder view others *not as people*, with hopes, dreams, desires, wants and needs of their own, but more as *objects* to be used for their own benefit. The lack of empathy which is fundamental to this disorder is the reason for this; a narcissist has a very limited ability to step into another's shoes, and view the world from their perspective. Although it may not superficially appear to be so, they cannot deeply feel another's pain or joy, or anything in between, although they may be able to cognitively understand it, and so use it to their own advantage. Team this with a tendency to exploit others and a sense of entitlement and you have a recipe for unsatisfactory relationships, including those with their children, even in two parent households.

The children of a narcissist are, like all people, simply a means of securing narcissistic supply, directly (from their adoration of the narcissist) or indirectly (by making the narcissist look good to others).

Putting it bluntly, in staying with a narcissist 'for the sake of the children,' you may, in fact, be enabling their abuse, particularly if you would be the person with whom the children would primarily live if you left the relationship. In these cases, in leaving, if you can summon up the momentous strength required, you are at least attempting to save them from becoming damaged by the narcissist, or even from becoming narcissists themselves. You are, at least, trying to break the generational chains of narcissism – a hugely significant task.

The situation is much more complicated if the narcissist is the person with whom the children would mostly live. Here you have a terrible conundrum – balancing your own welfare in leaving the relationship with the welfare of your children who will largely be staying. It's a decision which only you can make, but if you have to make it, then we can at least try to arm you with as much information as possible. And be aware that, as things stand, in the UK family court system, it is not possible to give NPD in your spouse as a reason for the children to live primarily with you – the courts simply

> **"In staying with a narcissist 'for the sake of the children,' you may, in fact, be enabling their abuse. "**

do not yet recognise this entity, and any assertion of this nature will most likely backfire on you. (This is not to say that you cannot highlight the unacceptable *behaviours* of your spouse, if necessary – but, sadly, you cannot give it a name).

Bear in mind that narcissists rarely look like the Childcatcher from Chitty Chitty Bang Bang or the Wicked Witch of the East. They can appear to the outside world (and sometimes to their own children) to be caring parents. They may even, on the surface, seem that way to *you*, the other parent. Remember that the narcissist in your life may have even built their false persona to appear to be the 'perfect' parent, in order to obtain narcissistic supply from others. It's more complicated than it may seem on the surface. Are they the fun parent, the crazy parent? The parent that never tells them off or sets any boundaries? The parent that shows them off and idealises them? Are they the parent that makes over the top proclamations of love for their children? Regardless of how things may appear, if the other parent of your children is a narcissist, underneath whatever veneer is presented to the world, damaging behaviours *will* be playing out as a result of their miswired brain.

Narcissists view children as extensions of themselves

With their own children, the way a narcissist behaves is even more complicated than usual. Not only are the children used as mere objects, or accessories to the narcissist, but the narcissist also has trouble separating their own sense of self from the child; they view their children, not as individuals, but as *extensions of themselves*.

> " **Narcissists view children as *extensions of themselves*. "**

This makes boundary violations with children particularly common, as the narcissist does not see themselves as separate. What the narcissistic parent wants, the child should also want and if they assert their boundaries, they will cause narcissistic injury and rage and find themselves at the mercy of their narcissistic parent's wrath.

These boundary violations can take various forms. They may constantly demand to know exactly where their children are, what they are doing and whom they are seeing. They may walk into rooms without knocking, read diaries and look through their devices. They may feel threatened by the idea of the developing child separating from themselves, and may try to stop them from becoming independent by not letting them leave home or making them financially dependent on them in adulthood, perhaps even insisting that they work for their own firm where they can be kept under the thumb.

In divorce and separation, issues also frequently arise in relation to the new partner or partners of the narcissist. As we have established, narcissists find it difficult to be on their own, and therefore, without the insight required to heal from the loss of a significant relationship, tend to quickly jump into a new relationship. This has nothing to do with you, as the old partner, and everything to do with them, and is a pattern that is likely to repeat should there be further relationship break-ups.

Very often, they do not consider the feelings of their children when introducing them to their new partner, again as a result of their lack of empathy and inability to see the children as separate from themselves. (What is fine with them should be fine by their children too). The children can be forced into spending time with the new partner when they feel uncomfortable about it, or find themselves thrown in at the deep end, being introduced without warning. They may even be subjected to exhibitionist public displays of affection, perhaps when they are still getting used to the fact that their parents are no longer together.

If the children try to avoid such situations, perhaps by refusing to visit the narcissistic parent if their partner is present, they will be turned upon, or the former spouse will receive accusations of alienating the narcissist from their child. Narcissists do not accept blame for their actions. They are unable to see themselves as anything other than special or perfect; if they did, they'd risk puncturing the false image they need to have of themselves, to avoid feeling their underlying feelings of shame and worthlessness.

This view that children are extensions of themselves can also lead to other issues. Remember Susan, our Closet Narcissist? She was unable to tolerate the suggestion that her son, Sebastian, had dyslexia, and refused to get him tested for this, in spite of the school suggesting it. Sebastian struggled throughout his school years as a result, and long term his confidence in his own ability became severely eroded. This is very common indeed. Narcissists need to believe that they are perfect and special. It is often the case that this need for perfection is extended to their children. In the case above, Susan refused to take on the belief that their child could have learning difficulties, even at her child's expense.

A narcissist may block a child's diagnosis and treatment, and should a diagnosis be obtained, they might even refuse to accept it as true and may refuse to administer prescribed medication as a result, even for potentially serious illnesses such as asthma. Where a child needs counselling or psychotherapy, a narcissist may also step in and prevent this, deeply uncomfortable with the child revealing anything they cannot control to a third party.

Narcissists are often risk-takers and, again as a result of seeing their children as their own extensions, they may not consider that the risks they are taking are inappropriate with children in tow. Bad driving at high speeds, taking the children on the back of motorbikes without the other parent's consent and leaving young children unattended near swimming pools are just some of the many safety issues that can occur during narcissistic parenting.

Conditional love

A narcissist will generally purport to adore and love their children but, as with their other relationships (and tragically for the children), love is merely conditional and transactional. As with all matters of the heart with a narcissist, they themselves truly believe that what they are feeling is love, but once again it is merely a reflection of the amount of adoration or supply they are receiving from the child. It is a *sort* of love, in a way, but a shallowly felt, easy to break kind. And, of course, a narcissist does not know any different. And nor do their young children.

This brings us on to the topics of 'whole object relations' and 'object constancy'; psychological attributes which develop in healthy individuals, as described in Chapter 2. Narcissists have not developed these and so have a tendency to see others (and themselves) as being either 'all good' or 'all bad'. They therefore swing between the two extremes in their view of others, behaving accordingly.

They are also unable to maintain positive feelings to someone who has hurt or disappointed them, making their feelings towards others highly unstable. Narcissists are unable to accept or like people as they truly are – imperfect beings with a blend of good and bad traits. A narcissist therefore idealises their children in their own minds, and when they fall off their pedestals due to their imperfections, they vilify them. Needless to say, this is a cycle that is confusing and damaging to children.

Consider the toddler, who is beaming sweetly at their parent and tottering around dressed as a bear. The narcissistic parent, most likely, will feel positively disposed to this child, and may pick them up and toss them playfully into the air, especially if they have an audience. The child might chuckle and squeal in delight. All is well. The narcissistic parent is happy and feels their version of love for the child. The child is responding just as the narcissist wants them to, affirming their own abilities as a parent. But just a few moments later, the child is suddenly hungry and becomes grouchy. Within moments this good-natured child has started to cry and is on the way to a full blown tantrum. The narcissistic parent, unable to coax the child back into their former state of happiness, becomes angry. This is not what he or she wanted. Suddenly the child is a monster, and their feelings of love vanish. It's not just irritation, but with love still running underneath. It's a disappearance of the feelings of love. The child is now 'all bad', and the narcissistic parent has stormed off, hurriedly withdrawn, or is shouting at the child, having lost their all-important control of the situation.

Narcissists have a sense of entitlement

A narcissist's sense of entitlement can also play out in the parenting arena. Often narcissists do not want to engage in menial jobs that do not give them the gratification of narcissistic supply. As any parent knows, parenting, especially of younger children, involves a never ending loop of thankless tasks, from nappy changing, to meal preparation, to refusal of the child to eat the carefully prepared meal, to tantrum throwing in public etc. Unless the narcissist is receiving supply from these tasks (perhaps by developing the outward persona of 'perfect parent' when in public), they may simply refuse to do them. This is well and good when another parent can step in, but in separation and divorce, the parenting deficiencies of the narcissistic parent can quickly become an issue, and you may find yourself shocked at the apparent ineptitude of your narcissistic ex.

Narcissistic parents, for example, can forget to feed their children altogether until they themselves feel hungry. Children, even young ones, may end up cooking un-nutritious meals for themselves when staying with a narcissistic parent. If a child is ill, the narcissistic parent's intrinsic lack of empathy can mean that symptoms are ignored, or no sympathy or care is forthcoming. We have heard of narcissistic parents who have failed to seek medical attention for suspected broken bones for their children whilst in their care. They can forget to ensure their children are bathed, and may fail to even think about providing their child with a toothbrush or toothpaste when they are staying with them, teeth going un-brushed for days as a result.

Emails from the school may be deemed as unimportant and not looked at. They are unlikely to ensure that homework is completed, and may not even consider doing their children's laundry or ensuring that they have clothes, or even made up beds at their house. Parents' evenings and sports days are often not attended (unless there is an opportunity to gain admiration and supply in attending, or if they are helicopter parenting, gaining supply from controlling their children's lives and achievements). Routine appointments, such as for opticians and dentists, will usually fall upon the non-narcissistic spouse, regardless of who the children primarily live with.

And, to be brutally honest, the narcissist's sense of entitlement over you as their ex-spouse does not end with a decree absolute. They will simply expect you to continue to follow orders, pick up the pieces or take up the slack when their own parenting falls short. We recall the tale of a narcissist who was financially abusing his ex-spouse by refusing to pay child maintenance. When his father died after a long illness, he refused to contribute to suitable clothes for the children to wear to the funeral, but criticised his ex-wife heavily for not having bought the children new outfits for the occasion. Due to limited funds, she had borrowed clothes from friends instead, which he found unacceptable. He simply could not see that this was now his responsibility, not hers.

Lateness is another typical behaviour that will be seen with narcissistic parents, as a result of their sense of entitlement. They can be hours late picking up their children for visits, with no prior warning, but if made to wait on *their* arrival, can fly off the handle. They will often change arrangements and visitation days without notice, or cancel altogether. Lateness can also be used against the non-narcissistic parent in other ways: for example, if their ex-spouse has somewhere important to be (if they have a flight to catch or a function to attend) and the narcissist gets wind of this, the narcissist will very often attempt to sabotage the other's plans, using lateness in picking up the children or sudden cancellation as their excuse. This can be wearying and stressful for the other parent who will eventually learn to make contingency plans for situations such as these. Also, getting children to school or to out of school activities in a timely fashion seems difficult for many narcissistic parents as these

> **" Lateness is another typical behaviour that will be seen with narcissistic parents, as a result of their sense of entitlement. "**

are not areas of high priority for them and it is common for children to miss out here.

How the narcissist uses their children as weapons

One of the most shocking behaviours in divorce is the way that narcissists will punish their children in order to get back at their spouse. This is the one behaviour that will have even the narcissist's diehard enablers raising their eyebrows. Narcissists do not feel remorse or guilt – they cannot, because those feelings threaten the existence of their false selves which they have worked so hard to establish and maintain. Moral standards, in reality, apply only to others. They show no mercy when dealing with their ex-spouse, and using the children is a perfect way to punish that spouse; one of the best tools in the narcissist's war chest, in fact.

Children are *objects* to be used in whatever way is in the narcissist's interests. They are pawns in the narcissist's game of needing to win, of needing to crush their 'opposition' (the former spouse).

Financial abuse is such an area, ripe for exploitation, and in divorce a narcissist will not hold back, even at the expense of their own flesh and blood.

A narcissist may deliberately reduce their earnings in order to reduce their child maintenance payments. An affluent narcissist whose children are in private education will commonly stop paying school fees so that the children may be forced to leave their schools, in order to burden the other parent with the guilt.

When they have the children with them, they may refuse to take them out for food or to events or to buy them birthday presents, claiming that the other spouse has all the money and they cannot afford it. They may refuse to continue to contribute to much loved hobbies, activities or school trips in order to guilt trip the other, less affluent parent into paying. They will often have inappropriate discussions with the children about the finances relating to a divorce.

If the narcissist is not the main earner, they can also try to exploit the children for financial gain, and may take the other parent back to court repeatedly to this end. It is not uncommon for this behaviour to go on for years until the child has reached their 18th birthday. Consider the case of a narcissistic mother, 15 years post-divorce, who took her high earning husband back to court in order to claim child maintenance. This narcissist lied to the court that the child, who was 17, was in full time education, even though he had left school and had a full time paid apprenticeship. After two years of fighting, the court finally asked the narcissistic parent for evidence of the full time education. The case collapsed at this point, but significant anguish and pain had been caused to both the father and the child. The child, although he knew what was happening, did not dare stand up to the wrath of his mother and, despite pleas from his father to write to the court explaining the truth of the matter, felt unable to do so. Narcissists are masters of guilt tripping and have an enormous hold over their children who have been worn down through abuse which has lasted their entire lifetimes. It is interesting to note that, even though this narcissist had already been given a jail sentence for child benefit fraud some years previously, she was still able to wreak havoc in the legal system, using it to perpetuate the abuse of her ex-husband.

Less extreme narcissists will do all manner of things to control their ex-spouse's finances through separation, divorce and beyond, pettiness featuring highly here. One narcissist we heard of took both TVs from the family home in an attempt to force their spouse to buy another, purely to run down funds. And another, who did not live with the children, insisted upon taking the Christmas tree and all the Christmas decorations from the family home just a few days before the big day. We have even heard of narcissists removing their children from their film and music streaming accounts, even though they had spare accounts available, just in order to get their spouse to buy accounts for the children. Threatening to remove beloved pets from the home in which the children live is another real life example of just how far a narcissist will go to seek revenge, even at the emotional expense of the children they believe they love.

Children may even be enlisted to remove things from the other parent's house, either on the grounds that they are merely 'borrowing' them, or that they are the narcissist's to take. Of course for children whose parents have relatively recently split, this is confusing as they were used to things being shared and also don't understand why their parents shouldn't be friendly towards one another. If the non-narcissistic parent tries to resist having items taken from their home, the narcissist will inevitably turn it on them, suggesting to the children that they are being unreasonable and mean spirited. In fact, by trying to maintain a friendly relationship with the narcissist you, as the ex-spouse, are actually opening yourself up to more abuse and boundary violations yourself, as you will eventually come to realise if you try this route.

Some narcissists may seek to highlight the difference between their life and the non-narcissistic spouse's circumstances to their children. We recall the story of the very wealthy narcissist who failed to pay interim maintenance pending suit to his spouse with whom the children lived so that even buying food became an issue. When the children visited him, he would alternate between telling them that he had no money and could only afford to feed them beans on toast, to offering them fillet steaks and high end mouthwatering treats. He would confuse them further by taking them away to 5-star luxury resorts, to show the ex-wife what she was missing out on as a result of her desire to divorce, all the while purporting to the children to be poor.

Narcissists will also use their children to destabilise their spouse. They may use the children to give them information about the spouse, such as regarding a new partner or a new job. We know of a narcissist who used her son to obtain the spare key to her ex-husbands flat, which she then had copied. She would regularly visit the flat, go through the paperwork on his desk, look at pictures on his mantelpiece and rifle through drawers, looking for his new partner's underwear. You can see why many former partners of narcissists end up changing the locks, setting up a webcam, and resorting to locking important paperwork in a safe through the divorce process.

Badmouthing

Narcissists will always carry out a smear campaign, telling frank lies about their spouse to others so that they are seen as the long-suffering injured party. They will also enlist others (their 'flying monkeys') to badmouth their former spouse.

Narcissistic injury leads to narcissistic rage as we have already ascertained. Narcissists need to hurt their spouse, to punish them, regardless of who instigated the split. What better way than by attempting to alienate the children from the other parent?

Unfortunately, it is absolutely typical for the narcissist to badmouth their ex-spouse to their children and blame them for their new, less salubrious, living situation. They often lie to them in order to confuse them and turn them away from their other parent. Projection is often employed here, by telling

> **"Narcissists will always carry out a smear campaign."**

the children that their other parent is guilty of things that *they themselves* have actually done. Narcissists may tell the children that the other parent has mental health issues, has had affairs, is lazy, is a drug addict; whatever works to undermine them in the eyes of their children. The children may know in their hearts that these accusations are not true, but begin to believe them anyway. Of course, they do not know that this is gas-lighting, a hallmark of narcissistic abuse.

Badmouthing the other parent to both sets of grandparents and to the children's aunts and uncles is another common tactic. Of course, this has knock on effects for the children, affecting their relationships with cousins and other important extended family members. This is very wearing indeed, especially when the narcissist is convincing enough to succeed in turning your own family away from you, perhaps even having cosy visits with your family with your own children in tow. This really does happen. It can eat away at your resilience and actually start to affect your own ability to parent optimally. You may well find yourself conflicted, not wishing to stop your children from having a relationship with other members of your family, but deeply hurt that you yourself have been ousted by them due to the narcissist's lies.

Issues regarding where the children live

It is extremely common for narcissists to demand that the children live with them, regardless of what would be in the best interests of the children. A narcissist experiencing narcissistic injury needs others to see them as special, perfect, a nice person, the 'good' parent. They need topping up with narcissistic supply urgently. They need others to see them as 'all good' so that *they* can see *themselves* in this way. They need to discredit and devalue the other parent to others, so that they are viewed by others as *they* see them; as 'all bad'. This pushes the narcissist's sense of superiority up further, and validates them even more.

The narcissist may insist that their spouse attends mediation regarding child arrangements issues, particularly over the issue of which parent the child might primarily live with. This is commonly employed as a scare tactic and as a method to reduce the spouse's funds further. As explained later, on page 178, mediation is usually not an effective method for tackling issues involving a narcissist, and the process is highly likely to break down. The narcissist merely uses the mediation process as a way to create drama, fear and conflict, whilst attempting to feel superior by running rings around all parties involved with constantly shifting goalposts and attempts to undermine the impartiality of the mediator.

If the narcissist is particularly aggrieved, the matter may reach court where they will relish the adversarial environment, where they can prove their superiority and cleverness. The worry here is that the narcissist may well have the advantage. They seem initially plausible and charming. If very high up on the spectrum (tending towards psychopathy) they are often able to behave in a fearless manner, coming across as the calm, rational parent.

They can play the quiet victim with aplomb, and as lying is second nature to a narcissist, they are able to make realistic sounding arguments explaining why the other parent is unfit for parental duties. The frightened parent on the other side, whose fight, flight or freeze response has been activated and whose stress hormones are flooding their system, diverting blood away from the logical and thinking areas of their brain, may not come across as quite so rational. This may well come at the cost of their children if they and their legal team are unprepared.

Another common ploy, designed to punish the non-narcissistic parent, is to threaten to move to another part of the country, or indeed to another country altogether, taking the children with them. This may also be used as leverage in order to procure a better financial settlement, where the narcissist will attempt to blackmail the other parent into agreeing to give a greater proportion of the assets to them so that they do not move to a part of the country which they claim is more affordable. Again, the children are weaponised here.

The golden child, the scapegoat and the invisible child

When there is more than one child, other patterns of behaviour often manifest.

The narcissist enjoys drama and will usually favour one child over another. This is whichever child is the most effective at securing the most narcissistic supply for the parent. The child may be the one who is most adoring of the parent, the one who subjugates their needs most, or the one whose achievements bring the narcissist attention and praise. It may even be the child who most closely physically resembles the narcissist. Whichever child is living up to the expectations and demands of the narcissist the most is the 'golden child,' and is treated differently to the others. They will be spoiled with gifts and praise but, like all children of narcissists, will eventually come to know that being loved by that parent is conditional on them being who the narcissist wants them to be, rather than who they actually are. They are likely to carry this pattern into their adult lives, either becoming narcissistic themselves or attracting a narcissistic partner.

Where there is a 'golden child' there is often also a 'scapegoat.' The child who stands up for themselves, with healthy, non-porous boundaries may find themselves in this position, or perhaps the child who may be unfortunate enough to physically resemble the non-narcissistic parent, the now reviled former spouse of the narcissist. They will be subjected to all the normal narcissistic abuse tactics. Devaluation, projection of the narcissist's own actions on to them, gas-lighting, passive aggression, name calling, triangulation with others. They will watch the other child receiving no-expense spared gifts, whilst they are left out. They will be forced to always eat what the other child wants, watch the movies they want, and they will be subjected to silent treatments when they are visiting their narcissistic parent. If they decide not to visit, they will receive a tirade of abuse by text and multiple phone calls. They will be drawn into arguments involving the other parent. They will experience the narcissist's pseudo-logic and word salad. In some cases, the narcissist will enlist the whole family in scapegoating this child.

We recall a parent describing this dynamic to us. The narcissistic parent would be sending loving texts full of pet names to one child, whilst *simultaneously* demeaning and criticising the other child in short sharp sentences, also by text. The two children, who were teenagers sitting on the sofa next to each other, would incredulously compare the messages they were receiving, in real time, shocked at how their mother could be so cutting to one of them at the same time as being so warm to the other. Manipulation came absolutely naturally to her.

The golden child/scapegoat dynamic may not be a stable one, however. It may take months or even years, but at some point the roles may well be switched. This could be as a result of external circumstances, or if the golden child learns to assert their own autonomy. At this point, the golden child moves out of the idealisation phase into the devalue phase (becoming the scapegoat), and the former scapegoat may then enter the idealisation phase, grateful at last to be the 'golden child.'

Another child in the dynamic may be forced into the role of the 'invisible child'; this is the child who simply is not seen. They jump through hoops to try to get noticed, and are usually the affable, compliant child who was always ignored and overlooked.

The invisible child learns that they do not matter. They grow up without the concept of having rights, wants or needs, and this plays out in their adult relationships where they either develop their own narcissistic defences in order to feel special, or they become echoists with a revulsion to feeling special, thus becoming magnets for narcissists and other psychologically unhealthy types.

Narcissistic mothers

Interestingly, although narcissistic fathers are more common (there is a gender bias of around a 3:1 male to female ratio in narcissism), it seems to be the narcissistic *mothers* who cause a disproportionate amount of damage to their children as they are more likely, due to societal norms, to be the primary caregivers in the early life of the children and also, post-divorce, to be the parent with whom the children spend more time.

Narcissistic mothers have an even more complicated dynamic with their daughters in that not only do they see their daughters as extensions of themselves, they also see them as threats, and may be envious of their youth, looks, achievements and even boyfriends. They may, in public, flaunt their daughter but, in private, criticise and demean them for not being good enough. They see them as frank competition and may even flirt with their boyfriends to assert their own superiority, put down their daughter and gain narcissistic supply. Far from preparing their daughters for the world of adulthood and independence, they place the focus on themselves.

Harmful behaviours of narcissistic mothers are not just limited to daughters, however. With sons, a narcissistic mother may compete with, and be jealous of, his girlfriends or wife. Criticism and devaluation will take place as she fails to live up to her mother-in-law's exacting standards. A narcissistic mother needs to be her son's number one, and if he is used to tiptoeing around his mother's needs above all else, he may fail to set appropriate boundaries with her and end up losing his significant other altogether.

A narcissistic mother may also use her son as a confidant or companion, enlisting him to support her emotionally, to glorify her and to attend to her physical comfort; his needs, on the other hand, will be seen as irrelevant, and he may well be told to 'man up' if he expresses them or his own emotions. Narcissistic sons are often forced to become enmeshed and over-involved with their mothers, and they may be parentified, finding themselves taking over the role of their father.

Adult sons may be relied upon to make decisions and manage the narcissistic mother's finances, with guilt and a sense of misplaced duty running the show.

The long-term effects of narcissistic parenting

Symptoms of narcissism inevitably affect the narcissist's ability to parent as behind the scenes they subject their children to the same abuse as everyone else. With unchecked abuse, the children of narcissists may go on to:

- become narcissists themselves

- become narcissist 'magnets', due to becoming co-dependents or echoists

- develop insecure attachment styles with others, leading to difficulties in adult relationships

Narcissists will shame and devalue their children about anything they can; the way they look, their weight, their lack of achievements, their friends. This is not always done with overt cruelty; subtle put downs or disguising criticism as 'jokes' is common too. Narcissists will use their children for narcissistic supply, expecting adoration. They will be highly controlling, expecting them to do exactly what they want them to do so that they reflect well on themselves, in all areas of their lives. They may demand perfection but never be satisfied by the child (unless they happen to be the 'golden child').

> " **Symptoms of narcissism inevitably affect the narcissist's ability to parent as behind the scenes they subject their children to the same abuse as everyone else.** "

They triangulate their children with each other (why can't you be more like your brother?), their peers, cousins, or anyone else they can. They use the children's friends as sources of supply in whatever way they can, sometimes even in highly inappropriate sexual ways. A narcissistic mother we knew of once sent topless selfies to her 13 year old son's friends as a way of securing adoration and attention, with no empathy or regard for her son. By the time he was an adult, sadly, he was highly narcissistic himself.

They can be highly manipulative, and interpersonally exploitative. They can be quick to anger and may be prone to physical violence, passive aggression and giving silent treatments. They will invalidate (and may even ridicule) their child's emotions, thoughts, wants and needs. They will prioritise their own needs and expect their children to do the same so that life becomes about tiptoeing around their egos to keep them happy, at the same time avoiding incurring narcissistic rage. They are devoid of true empathy, and unable to care when the child needs their support most.

You could be forgiven for thinking that such behaviour would simply result in turning the children away from the narcissistic parent, but it is not quite that simple. Don't forget that Exhibitionist Narcissists can be charming and great fun; when they are receiving enough narcissistic supply, they can be the 'coolest' parent, the magnanimous parent; they can shine brilliantly, and the child will love being the apple of their eye, feeling special by association and worshipping their greatness. They can be amazing and awful, in equal measure. This is confusing enough for adults who know about NPD, so what chance does a child have in making sense of it? It's easy to see how they come to accept things as they are, taking the rough with the smooth.

The emotional consequences on the child

Children want to be loved by their parents. They believe that their caregivers know best. When the narcissist is behaving badly, the children may make excuses for them, blaming themselves for it and internalising these feelings.

They can believe that if they tried harder, or did better, that they could make things better. They learn to ignore their gut instincts about what behaviours are right and wrong, and suppress and invalidate their own negative feelings. They may feel extreme guilt if they dislike the narcissistic parent and so try to overcompensate for it.

They may come to feel that they are 'not enough'. They may learn the psychological phenomenon of 'learned helplessness', where they just accept that they cannot make anything any better, and they should just accept things as they are. This can be a lifelong affliction, affecting all future relationships, careers etc. Children may learn to subjugate their needs, prioritising the needs of their narcissistic parent instead, simply to keep the peace.

Becoming a narcissist magnet

This subjugation of needs is *co-dependency in the making*, and may lead to similarly unhealthy future relationships with narcissists, alcoholics or substance addicts. The child of a narcissist accepts their parent's behaviour as *normal*. It is little wonder that, as an adult, they then accept such behaviours from others in their adult lives. In romantic relationships, they may feel intensely drawn to narcissists due to the subconscious pull of the *familiar*, mistaking it for 'chemistry'. This can perpetuate a lifetime of abuse. The adult children of narcissists should be very wary indeed of 'instant chemistry' when dating – for them, what most people hail as an essential component in a new relationship is actually a recipe for disaster. Their new partner, to whom they are so powerfully drawn, may be the polar opposite of their narcissistic parent on the surface, but *underneath* the similarities may be striking as they will likely discover with the passing of time.

> **"The child of a narcissist accepts their parent's behaviour as *normal*."**

Becoming a narcissist

Narcissistic parenting can also, of course, lead to the development of narcissism in the child and they can go on to become the abuser themselves. These children adapt to their deficient upbringing by developing their *own* false self, in order to feel special. These children are bound by (and find themselves perpetuating) the generational chains of NPD.

Alternatively, it may be that a child 'gets away with it', and neither of the two scenarios above unfold. What determines whether a child raised by narcissists becomes a narcissist is determined by a complex interplay of factors.

Some children have a stronger, more resilient inborn temperament than others. Others may be from households where perhaps gender differences and expectations played a role in how they were treated, with a daughter being treated differently to a son, thereby reinforcing narcissistic behaviours more in one gender than another. And some may have had other, more healthy relationships modelled to them, by grandparents, friends or teachers, which negated some of the adverse effects of the narcissist's parenting.

Forming insecure attachment styles

A child's development, ability to regulate their emotions and ability to form secure healthy attachments to others is largely determined by their mother. If she validates their pain and meets their needs effectively, and is empathic and securely attached to them, then they will be positively impacted by this.

So, even if a child does not become narcissistic nor attract other narcissistic relationships into their lives, they may still be emotionally damaged to some extent by a narcissistic parent, especially a mother, who simply cannot give them what they need emotionally.

So called 'attachment styles' with significant others will likely be affected, with the child of a narcissist either having a 'dismissive avoidant', 'fearful avoidant' or 'anxious preoccupied' attachment style, leading to difficulties forming close, stable, secure bonds with a partner. Briefly, in spite of craving closeness, they may avoid or drive others away through fear of abandonment, a feeling of not needing anyone, or by an anxious neediness. (The good news with these is that, with awareness, they can be overcome, and secure attachments formed).

What can the non-narcissistic parent do to limit the damage to the children by the narcissist?

Now that you know what you are dealing with, the first thing is simply to *stop enabling* the narcissist's bad behaviour. Whilst living with the narcissist, you may have found yourself agreeing with the narcissist's behaviour at times, minimising it or even denying it – this is actually classic gas-lighting, and so many victims of narcissistic abuse end up unwittingly doing this to their own children in order to keep the peace with the narcissist, or because they have been led to believe that the narcissist knows best. You may feel great shame in admitting this to yourself if it has been a feature of your home life, but there is nothing wrong with feeling that shame – and then forgiving yourself and vowing to change in the light of your new found understanding about your partner.

Modelling good behaviour is key in making up for the parenting deficiencies of the narcissistic parent. If you can do this effectively then your children will eventually come to see the contrast between the two of you as parents, and make up their own minds about who they wish to trust and eventually emulate. The non-narcissistic parent has to be consistent, establish clear boundaries and rules and be emotionally available for the children. They should listen to them, hear their fears and be interested in who they are as people. Supporting their wants and needs, celebrating their successes, and commiserating and encouraging when they fail will also be essential. The non-narcissistic parent will need to be on time for the child, and will need to make it clear that they are *unconditionally loved*; that they are *more than enough, exactly as they are*. Of course, none of this is rocket science, just good parenting, and that is all that is needed.

A really important part of this is modelling and encouraging the development of *empathy* in the child. Talking about empathy and discussing how people in real life or characters in books or movies must be feeling are all helpful. If a child can develop true emotional empathy, developing narcissism is unlikely. Bear in mind that in adolescence, empathy takes a natural nosedive for a number of years as the brain's neural networks are heavily pruned back. You will, most likely, fret that your teenage child is becoming a narcissist. But think back – if they were empathic before the dreaded teens, then they will be empathic again. Fear not.

Trying to explain the behaviours of the other parent to the child is a tricky issue and one that can lead to claims from the narcissist of parental alienation, so it is best avoided. Expressing empathy for your child when they tell you about things they have experienced at the hands of the narcissist, and explaining that those behaviours are not desirable or how most people relate to others, is the best that one can do here. Encouraging the child to set boundaries and stand up for themselves with the narcissist and others is also important. Also, passing on communication tips when the narcissist is sending threatening, ranting, guilt-tripping, accusatory messages to the child will help them enormously; explaining to them how to disengage for a while when "daddy goes off on one" in order to let things cool down. Of course, stepping in immediately if the child is in physical danger is essential.

In no longer being in a relationship with a narcissist, one finally has the ability to step away from being the narcissist's enabler. Whilst many unhappy non-narcissistic couples *stay together* for the 'sake of the children', it is not surprising that many former spouses of a narcissist report having found the strength to leave them for very same reason.

Parenting with a narcissistic parent after divorce or separation

Even though you are coming to understand the complexities of NPD, you might still be hoping that healthy, co-operative, empathic co-parenting with your former partner may be possible once the dust of your separation has settled. You may believe, even though it is extremely unlikely that the narcissist ever co-parented with you *during your relationship*, that they will become motivated to learn the skills required and, in time, overcome their negative feelings towards you, 'for the sake of the children'.

You may well have expectations of being able to invite the narcissistic parent in for a cup of tea when they come to collect the children to take them to an after school activity, perhaps. You may expect to be able to discuss how your child is doing at school and to sit down together to discuss choice of secondary schools and GCSE or A level subject options. Attending parents' evenings and sports days together may be an expectation, or sharing university open day visits. Fairly splitting extra child costs, and flexibility on helping each other out regarding childcare if work or other commitments arise may be hoped for. Perhaps even being at the child's birthday party together or jointly contributing to a present. You almost certainly may hope to see eye-to-eye on safety issues for your child, such as wearing helmets and protective pads during certain sports. And surely some compromise regarding Christmas arrangements, Mother's and Father's day and holiday time will be a given?

Sadly, this is highly unlikely to ever be the case and if you are in the throes of divorce, not only should *you* understand this but *so should your lawyer*. If your lawyer is uninformed they may well be *projecting the expected qualities of a good, cooperative, loving, giving parent on to a narcissist*, and this is deeply unhelpful, and actually is unintentional gas-lighting, denying the reality of the situation.

Realism would serve all concerned much better instead and both you and your lawyer need to understand that the narcissist is wired to be selfish and unempathic. This will not change even if they are able, on the surface, to play act the role of 'perfect mum', or 'fun dad'.

Unfortunately, at the very least, they will continue to wish to manipulate and control and upset you, using the children as previously discussed, for as long as you have to be in each other's lives.

There is no such thing as co-parenting with a narcissist – unfortunately, narcissists only 'counter-parent' – reflexly and deliberately going against your wishes

> **"If your lawyer is uninformed they may well be projecting the expected qualities of a good, cooperative, loving, giving parent on to a narcissist, and this is deeply unhelpful. "**

and values when it comes to the children. We will discuss how to manage this in detail later, in Chapter 11, in the section on 'parallel parenting'.

Deciding to leave

5

First, let's talk about you

So, here we are, at crunch point. Perhaps by now you are pretty sure that your partner has NPD. (Or as sure as you can be, given that you could be suffering from all the emotional and mental difficulties described at the very beginning of Chapter 1, including fluctuating cognitive dissonance, addiction to the relationship through trauma bonding, grief, hope that things will change and anxiety).

More than likely, at least for some of the time, you are telling yourself that this whole 'NPD thing' cannot possibly be true, and that you have made it all up, or unconsciously and incorrectly made your partner's behaviour fit with what you have learnt about it. That's normal – the truth doesn't just hit you like a freight train – it creeps up on you, taps you on the shoulder and then runs away again, until the next time.

You may have tried to leave before and always ended up back with the narcissist, lured in by hoovering, with renewed love-bombing and promises of change. After all, it takes seven attempts to finally leave an abusive relationship, according to America's National Domestic Violence Hotline. Could this be your seventh time?

You may have previously refused to abandon ship, simply on the grounds that you have invested so much time/money/love/hope on it, and so you feel you might as well stay – the so called 'sunk cost fallacy'.

You probably still deeply love the image of the narcissist that you originally fell for, the person that you thought they were, and want desperately for that person to have been real. Euphoric recall (a tendency to remember past experiences in a positive light, whilst overlooking the negative experiences associated with those events) may be hijacking you here.

Perhaps you are struggling with the concept of NPD, perhaps viewing it as an 'illness' rather than as a personality disorder, having promised your partner a lifelong commitment 'in sickness and in health'? Guilt may be keeping you stuck. Perhaps no one ever told you that, as a human being, *you have the right to change your mind, even without explanation.* If you are a co-dependent, used to putting your needs behind other people's, this may literally have never occurred to you.

Perhaps, you, as so many do at this stage, are thinking that you should try to get your partner some sort of brain scan before you make a decision in case they have a brain tumour or some form of early dementia – that you should leave no stone unturned before you commit yourself to the hard finality of NPD.

You may be having difficulty sleeping, the chronic tiredness blunting your capacity to think rationally, making everything more difficult, putting you on edge and making you wonder if you can trust your own thoughts.

But could it be that slowly, out the fog, a picture has formed which, apart from during your vacillations to and fro (which are *normal*), is getting clearer and clearer? You see, *once you've really seen NPD for what it is, you can't ever really unsee it.*

It may be that now you have a decision to make – whether to stay or whether to go.

Choosing to stay

It could be that you feel you have to stay – for financial, religious, family, community, timing, immigration, or health reasons, to name just a few. But if you do (and we are not judging here – this is an individual choice), *you have to be aware of the limitations of the relationship you will be staying in, and you have to radically and fully accept that these limitations will not change.*

- The narcissist cannot love you, not in the way that you understand love, and will never be capable of it.

- The narcissist will never truly understand (or care) about how you are feeling, regardless of their acting ability.

- The narcissist will not 'get better' – they may slide up and down the scale of narcissism a few notches depending on life circumstances as described in Chapter 3, but they will always be a narcissist, at the right hand side of the scale. (Only 5% of them will try to work on their empathy in specialist psychotherapy over the ten year period usually required to make a difference).

- The narcissist will always put themselves first, regardless of who they hurt in the process.

- *You* cannot cure the narcissist. No matter how much you love them, no matter how much you pledge to give up for them, no matter how much you pray. Magical thinking will not help you here. This is not your disorder to cure – it is *theirs*, and actually, trying to cure the narcissist isn't your responsibility anyway (even if you could cure it).

> **"*You* cannot cure the narcissist. "**

If you choose to stay, then perhaps we have come to the end of our journey together in this book, at least for now, and we wish you strength and good fortune. It may just not be the right time for you now, and it may never be – and that is ok as long as your eyes are open and you can protect yourself and your children from narcissistic abuse. You will need to learn to assert your needs and erect strong, immovable boundaries, and teach your children to do the same, leading by example. Consider therapy and co-dependency support groups such as CoDa. Build up strong friendships and do not allow the narcissist to isolate you from friends and family – you will need them to keep you grounded, validate you, empathise with you, look after you, commiserate with you, encourage you and celebrate your successes. You will need them to make up for all the shortfalls of your narcissistic partner, and to keep you emotionally safe and happy. They will need to be your barometers of what is 'normal' and trustworthy. Choose them wisely, and do not tolerate bad behaviour. You may not be able to leave your narcissistic husband or wife, but you absolutely do not have to tolerate toxic friendships.

How the narcissist will react when you tell them that you are leaving

Like non-narcissists, narcissists do not like rejection.

But if you are planning to leave a relationship with a narcissist, be prepared for the fallout. Because narcissists will do quite a bit more than simply throwing their toys out of the pram upon being left. And if you were ever in any doubt about whether your beau or belle was a true narcissist, you will most certainly know once you've walked away, in the most unequivocal terms.

You see, rejecting a person with narcissistic personality disorder triggers a variety of highly predictable responses, borne out of what is termed 'narcissistic injury.' As we have discussed previously, although certain types of narcissists (especially the exhibitionist type) may *appear* to have high self-regard and self-esteem, in actual fact all narcissists actually suffer from highly unstable self-esteem.

This is why they need to appear perfect, or to appear to have the perfect life. This is why they have to believe themselves (overtly or covertly) to be superior to others. This is why they often have to believe that others are envious of them, and that those who are not simply do not understand their brilliance and uniqueness.

Being rejected does not fit in this need to appear and feel special and superior. Once you walk away their already fragile, artificially propped up self-esteem takes an enormous beating, and they spectacularly fall off their own self-made pedestals. And what happens next, which can last for months or even years, is a desperate attempt to claw back their sense of self-worth. When a narcissist is rejected, and their supply is withdrawn, they are suddenly forced to actually *feel* their own pitifully lacking low self-esteem and their shame, and this is unbearable for them – the avoidance of it being the whole reason why they constructed their protective false persona in the first place. It is this intense emotion that the narcissist feels as 'narcissistic injury.' It's even worse if they suffer the humiliation of being left publicly.

But before your empathy kicks in, just be aware that the callous, cold, manipulative, controlling, vindictive behaviour that results from narcissistic injury can be so shocking that you may find it hard to believe that any human being could be capable of it.

Very often people who have been in long-term relationships with narcissists find this the hardest to believe – incredulous that after years of loyal servitude, they could be treated which such ice-cold heartlessness. Of course, due to arrested emotional development, the narcissist has never developed the ability to feel *genuine* empathy. This explains why they simply cannot care about the pain that they are inflicting on you as a result of their response to their narcissistic injury. Your pain is irrelevant, unreal, and if it is real, deserved. And most importantly, *they can't feel it*, and therefore can't feel guilt or remorse about it.

In addition, narcissists have a problem with 'whole object relations', as we've mentioned previously. What this means is that they are unable to see people (and themselves) as having a mixture of good and bad attributes. They are only able to see you as being 'all good' or 'all bad' at any one time, depending how they perceive you are acting towards them. Obviously, if you have left them, you will have severely slighted them and this will make them see you as 'all bad', meaning that any punishment they inflict upon you as a result of their narcissistic injury will be entirely justified.

Even more sadly, the narcissist is not capable of loving in the unconditional, accepting, reciprocal way that typifies healthy love, no matter how convincing their love seemed at times. As we've already explained, the narcissist did not adore or love *you*, he or she adored or loved *the way you made them feel, and what you did for them*. And that is another reason why the narcissist's reaction to you leaving can seem so inhumane and cruel.

In short, if you leave a narcissist, *expect no mercy*. They will wish to annihilate you, and this is no exaggeration.

Which type of narcissist they predominantly are dictates which (and how many) of the following strategies they will employ in response to their being left by their significant other.

So, here's what you can expect in the immediate aftermath, as they try to stop you from leaving.

> **"If you leave a narcissist,** *expect no mercy.* **"**

Guilt tripping

The narcissist is a natural master manipulator and will often threaten suicide or even carry out an act of deliberate self-harm to make you feel guilty for thinking about leaving. They are keen to make you think that their blood will be on your hands if you go through with abandoning them. They will often tell you that they have been suffering with undiagnosed depression or stress and that that is the true reason why they have been difficult to live with. If you are married, they may pull the 'in sickness and in health vow card' in conjunction with this last ploy. They may go through the motions of having therapy to appease you, or suggest couples therapy. If you have children they will use this to their advantage, most likely telling you that leaving will ruin the children's lives. (It is ironic that many people leave their narcissist partners to *improve* their children's lives, as we've already discussed). Guilt tripping is classic of the Closet (or Covert) Narcissist, although all types can use it.

Threats and intimidation

A common strategy to make you rethink your position is to threaten to make you suffer financially, or in some other way, if you go through with walking away. Custody threats regarding any children or pets, threats to smear your name, threats to destroy your possessions (for example to burn down your house) are all common, and delivered with such conviction that you will find them believable and scary. Unfortunately, these threats may not be empty, and you should consider legal advice regarding them. You may be expecting such threats but they come as a big surprise to many.

Playing on your insecurities

If you've had a relationship with a narcissist you will be familiar with the idealise, devalue cycle that all narcissists employ to keep you off balance, hooked into the relationship and unsure of what is coming next. If you look back, this is the pattern that will have been present throughout the bulk of your relationship.

When you threaten to leave a narcissist they often tend to ramp up these cycles to quite alarming levels, so you may find yourself in the 'devalue' stage once more. Here the narcissist may play on your insecurities, by telling you that you will be alone forever if you leave them and that you are unlovable, unattractive, boring, unintelligent, fat or whatever else they have learned you may be insecure about. Do not be drawn into staying by this – after all, if you are as undesirable as they say, why are they so keen to hang on to you?

Hoovering

You are already familiar with this term, and, looking back you may have experienced this a few times in the course of the relationship already. But when threatened with divorce, a narcissist is likely to pull out all the stops to suck you back in, most likely on the grounds that they love you so much that they cannot live without you.

You will doubtless have tried to explain to the narcissist what it is about the relationship that you cannot live with anymore, and they will be able to change some of these things in the short term to demonstrate their love for you, so great is their fear of abandonment. These tactics are often hard for the victim to resist, and if you not aware that this is happening, you may well be drawn back into the relationship, pulled by the magnetism of the empty promise of true love, and the demonstrable improvements that the narcissist has been able to make.

The inevitable demise of the relationship will not be far away, however, when the devalue phase is upon you once more.

Insisting on marriage guidance counselling

Many couples during the breakdown of a marriage will try marriage guidance counselling as an attempt to find strategies to either try to save the marriage, or to break up in an amicable way. But when attending such counselling with a narcissist you have a dynamic at play which the counsellor is unlikely to be able to see, certainly from just a few sessions, if ever. In fact, the counsellor is most likely untrained in personality disorders especially here in the UK, where even medical professionals and psychologists do not receive training for the reasons described in the introduction of this book. The counsellor is likely to go on what they see and what they are told and they are unlikely, like most people, to understand the manipulation that both they and you are being subjected to in sessions, at the hands of the narcissist.

Your problem is that marriage guidance counselling is a wonderful place for a narcissist to gain narcissistic supply, both from the people they tell about the counselling and from the counsellor themselves, and *that* is the true reason for them attending. It's not about saving the marriage or trying to change – although if you are the one threatening to leave, they may want you to stay because of their fear of abandonment, and the consequent narcissistic injury, which they would do anything to avoid. Don't mistake this for love, however – it isn't.

Narcissists love this game, this chance to pit you and your counsellor against one another, to triangulate you both. They relish playing the victim, telling tales of how you are so unforgiving, or of how difficult you are as a partner, hurt exuding convincingly from every pore. Narcissists are excellent at subtly throwing statements into the ring to make you feel uncomfortable, which have just the right amount of truth to them so that you will be left justifying your actions, or wondering whether you are entirely to blame. They will push your buttons with absolute ease, and then sit back and watch you get angry or upset with an innocent air, or with raised eyebrows and a resigned shrug of the shoulders.

> **"Marriage guidance counselling is a wonderful place for a narcissist to gain narcissistic supply."**

They will pull the counsellor into the drama triangle (described in Chapter 2), effortlessly moving them and you from victim to rescuer to perpetrator, like pieces on a board game. The counsellor will quickly be manipulated by the narcissist, flattered by them, and the narcissist will initially appear keen to do whatever they suggest, pretending to place them on a pedestal.

This game of manipulation, as they devalue you and idealise the counsellor, feeds the narcissist in every way – with attention and perhaps even adoration from a new audience member (the counsellor), and drama and conflict (with you). You may find yourself harshly and unfairly judged by the counsellor, and have your reality denied or minimised by them as the narcissist expertly turns them into tools of their own abuse, getting them to unwittingly gas-light you on their behalf.

Eventually of course, if the charade continues for long enough, the therapist or counsellor themselves will be devalued and thrown under the bus by the narcissist, true to their hardwiring. It is unlikely, unless you happen to chance upon a marriage guidance counsellor or therapist who fully understands NPD, that there will be any benefit to this circus for anyone in the triangle – least of all you. Narcissists don't try to learn or evolve from the process of marriage therapy or counselling – they merely try to *win* at it.

This is not to say that you shouldn't give it a try if you feel you ought to, but just to warn you that you may come out doubting yourself and your truth even more than before you went in. But equally, knowing what you now know, it may give you a chance to sit back and watch the dynamics of narcissism at play if you can remain dispassionate enough to do so – and this might even help to solidify what you already know and fortify your resolve to walk away from the relationship.

Phase 2

Once the narcissist has accepted that your mind is made up, phase 2 begins. Here you should expect the following behaviours as standard.

The mask will drop

If it hasn't already, it will now, and you will get a terrifying glimpse of what lies beneath the façade of your narcissistic partner.

Here is an account from a woman who had been married to a narcissist for 20 years, who had finally plucked up the courage to leave:

> *"He turned around and looked straight at me. His eyes, normally a washed out blue, were black; suddenly beady, boring into me with a hatred I didn't think any human could have for anyone else. I know that doesn't sound possible, them being black, but they were, or at least, I thought they were. His upper lip was curled upwards in a vengeful snarl, like a creature from the bowels of hell. A vile creature, full of rage and mockery and loathing. The closest thing I'd ever seen to the devil; I hadn't even believed in <u>him</u>*

before. I remember trying not to recoil in horror as he hissed (yes hissed) at me that he was going to take the children, and that I would be left with nothing. And that the police would be coming to take me away. There was a chilling emptiness there. A bottomless void of darkness from which venom emanated. This snarling, spitting, hissing, ridiculing creature was the <u>real</u> man I had married. 'Smiling Death', someone had once called him, and now I knew why. Finally, I understood how all those other times of fury and rage had barely scratched the surface of what really lay beneath. It lasted barely a minute. And in the next moment, he was promising to change, declaring undying love, saying we could make it work. Eyes blue once again, pleading."

You will be quickly replaced

Most narcissists will already have a number of adoring fans waiting in the wings who they have been triangulating you with during your relationship. This stems from their insatiable need for admiration and attention as a source of narcissistic supply. It is simply impossible for one person to be enough to provide all that the narcissist needs supply-wise, so the more people they have orbiting around them, ready to jump into their arms, the better.

A narcissist is unable to be relationship-less for any length of time, as without a relationship their narcissistic supply needs are simply not being met. They cannot run the risk of having to feel the reality of their empty self-esteem, and so you will be replaced instantly. Expect your narcissist to be on a dating website within hours, dating within days and in another relationship within weeks, no matter how long or serious you thought your relationship with them was, even whilst they play the role of inconsolable deserted lover.

They may hide their new relationship from you, but subtlety is definitely not a given. You may well find out about their new relationship practically from the outset, and the pain that results from this gives the narcissist a wonderful sense of power and superiority.

Instigating divorce proceedings before you do

This is very common indeed – a narcissist needs to be a winner, and winners do not get jilted. Do not be surprised if a divorce petition lands on your front mat before you've even had a chance to choose a solicitor.

You will be stolen from

We will go into this in much more detail in Chapter 8, but we include this for completeness here also. Do not assume that they will not carry out at least some of the actions that follow – they are now operating from a place of unparalleled narcissistic injury, the likes of which you may not have seen from them before. Do not tell the narcissist that you are leaving them without being prepared for the following, and without various contingencies in place:

- Money may be removed from joint bank accounts, usually in huge amounts, and spent or hidden.

- Mortgages may be extended and cash released and spent.

- You will be quickly cut off from access to the finances, especially if you are the lower earner. If you share online banking passwords, expect these to be changed without your knowledge.

- Joint credit cards for which you are liable may be maxed out.

- New cars or other expensive items may be bought, reducing the amount left in the financial pot for division.

- Expensive items may go missing, or be given away.

- Treasured belongings and photographs, or anything else of sentimental value to you (even things that the narcissist has never liked) might be removed.

Intimidating mind games

Narcissists need to feel that they are in control, and destabilising you mentally is a good source of narcissistic supply. The more they are able to intimidate you the better, and it is important to try to appear unfazed by such behaviours, difficult though that may be. Responding in ways that could make you seem unstable is one of the narcissist's desired outcomes. Be prepared for a variety of tactics, including:

- Refusing to move out of the marital home.

- Stalking you.

- Leaving abusive messages for you, sending abusive texts and emails and ringing you repeatedly.

- Threatening to bug you, or actually bugging the house or car.

- Threatening to take the children or pets.

Invading your home and privacy

Narcissists are expert boundary violators as you will already have experienced, and this can get taken up a notch during narcissistic injury.

Moving out but coming and going as they please, taking with them whatever possessions they want and leaving you on edge in your own home is common.

Looking through or removing your paperwork (bank statements and tax information) is another frequently reported issue, or looking through important items such as home computers, and even removing these.

The smear campaign

This is another expected narcissistic move which most types of narcissists seem to pull without hesitation.

Expect to be labelled a prostitute, drug addict or alcoholic, or all three. Expect the word on the street to be that you were the one having an affair and that was the reason for the split. Expect to be described as a violent controlling abuser.

Expect to be called an inadequate or abusive parent and to potentially have a fight about who the children live with on your hands.

Expect your family and friends to be contacted and lied to about you, with characteristic convincingness. The narcissist will play the victim here, and crocodile tears will fall. The narcissist will also badmouth you to work colleagues and acquaintances. Expect to lose friends and respect in the community and possibly even at work.

> **" Expect to be labelled a prostitute, drug addict or alcoholic. "**

Expect the narcissist to recruit their 'flying monkeys' to help with the smear campaign. Flying monkeys are the narcissist's fan club who would do anything to curry favour with him or her, including spreading malicious gossip. They are usually eager love hopefuls waiting in the wings or impressed subordinates (narcissists are often unable to sustain meaningful friendships with people at the same intellectual level as them as they generally do not provide them with enough unconditional admiration or attention).

If you share children with the narcissist be prepared for them to attempt to alienate the children from you with a mix of charm, victimhood and lies about you. This type of badmouthing is a particularly challenging thing to deal with, particularly if the children are not old enough to understand the narcissist's true personality. For other expected behaviours regarding the children, see Chapter 4.

In summary, leaving a narcissist may be one of the most traumatic experiences of your life, but it will be one of the most worthwhile. Know that if you can prepare for the worst, as we will detail later, you will survive it, although it is rare to emerge unscathed (at least in the short term). It can rock the very foundations of your world but it is more than possible to grow and reconfigure from the experience (so called 'post traumatic growth'). As you are the sort of person who is learning about NPD by reading this book, you are exactly the sort of person who will do just this – heal, grow and evolve into a better life, one that is lived on *your* terms, for you.

Practical early steps to take

6

First, let's talk about you

Perhaps you did not get to make the decision as to whether to stay or leave – perhaps the narcissist in your life did that for you, unceremoniously dumping you in a brutal discard. Perhaps you have been left reeling in a state of shock as the narcissist basks openly in the glory of fresh narcissistic supply, a new doe-eyed partner cluelessly in tow. Maybe you want them back. Maybe you don't.

But regardless, you are in pain – and you are entitled to that pain. Remember how we discussed how the pain of rejection lights up the same areas in the brain as when you are in physical pain, such as the pain of having a limb sawn off? But you have the added complication of having been trauma bonded to your narcissist – that neurochemical addiction we talked about earlier. Not only have you had your leg ripped off but you are withdrawing from heroin at the same time. That's why it hurts so much – and that's a level of pain that not everyone has experienced and can understand. 'Tough love' will not work here – so avoid anyone who tells you to 'just move on' or to 'let it go' or to 'get over it'. You've had more than your fair share of having your feelings criticised, invalidated or shamed already, so be choosy as to who you lean on.

So, punch and batter your pillow. Scream as loudly as you can, whenever you feel like it. Howl at the moon. Dissolve on your closest friends – and forget about dignity with them. Try not to self-medicate with alcohol. Eat what you want, if you can eat at all. Do whatever it is that gives you comfort (as long as it is legal and safe). Treat yourself as you would an injured child. Talk to yourself only as you would speak to your best friend. When your inner critic (the 'narcissist in your head') pipes up with criticisms and name-calling, telling you that you deserve it, or accusing you of being pathetic, unworthy or unlovable, notice it and silence it, every single time. That is one narcissist you *can* be in control of. Remember to love yourself, exactly as you want to be loved – perhaps not as easy as it sounds at the moment.

In order to get over the pain, you have to allow yourself to feel it. Turn towards it and welcome it in without pushing it away or trying to change it. The Buddhists (whose teachings have been shown to be inextricably linked to neuroscience) have taught us that that is the only way the brain can process unwanted emotions – to actually feel them and accept them as they are. Once the processing is done, the brain then relegates those emotions, that pain, to the deep storage areas of the brain, and you are free of having to feel them. So don't fight it. Your (non-narcissistic) Granny was right about the merits of having a good cry.

It's hard to believe right now but one day you might conceive of the idea that perhaps, in leaving you, the narcissist did you a favour, especially now that you know what you are dealing with.

But, if you are early in the process, irrespective of whether your narcissist has decided to divorce you or whether you have made the momentous decision to leave them, there are some practical things to consider, as soon as you can.

Who stays in the family home?

When you have accepted that your marriage has broken down, co-existing under the same roof can be extremely difficult. Financial matters can take months (and sometimes even years) to conclude and the desire to physically separate can be high.

Having to share a home with someone you have fallen out of love with – and in fact may not even like – can be extremely stressful and difficult. The urge to move out can be enormous. There are, however, things which you need to be aware of and consider very carefully before you do.

- Once you have vacated the family home it can be extremely difficult to move back subsequently.

- It may take many months or even years for financial matters to be resolved.

- If you move into rented accommodation you may be spending money you can ill afford for a period of time which is longer than intended.

- You should never move out without the children if you see yourself as their primary carer.

If the property is not in your name you should register a Matrimonial Home Act Caution to protect your financial interest. This will remain in place until released by you or it is extinguished when the marriage comes to an end following pronouncement of decree absolute.

> **" You should never move out without the children if you see yourself as their primary carer. "**

You might want to try to persuade your spouse to move out. Bear in mind that any lawyer will advise their client to stay put – largely for the reasons set out above.

Trying to remove your spouse from the house

If your spouse refuses to leave the family home, you may wish to consider whether their behaviour is sufficiently bad to warrant making an application to the court to have them removed, under the Family Law Act 1996. A costs order can be made in favour of the person who wins, so that the other party pays their legal bill. So, if you lose your application to have your spouse removed from the home, you could end up paying their fees.

But it's important to understand that such applications should only be made if you are advised by your lawyer that the likelihood of success is high – and be aware that, in most cases, it is not. Bear in mind that removing a person from their home is the most draconian step a judge can take in relation to a person's liberty, and it is not something which they will do lightly. It is far more likely that they will make the couple accept 'undertakings' (which are promises to the court) to behave reasonably towards each other whilst co-occupying the house during the divorce process. It's not hard to see how ineffective this is likely to be with a narcissistic individual.

So, losing a court application of this nature can have devastating effects. Not only are you likely to have to pay the legal costs incurred by your narcissistic spouse, but they will feel that their bad behaviour towards you has been vindicated – and worse, you will have to continue living under the same roof as them.

If you feel unsafe in your home as a result of the behaviour of your spouse or partner, or you feel that your children are unsafe, the best step to take is to call the police. If they deem the situation to be serious enough, they will deal with it by bringing a criminal prosecution (which will cost you nothing) and this will usually result in the offending partner moving out.

Bear in mind that if the police are called but they decide to take no action and bring no criminal proceedings, they may suggest that you make an application under the Family Law Act, as described above. But be wary of this – even if they do suggest this it doesn't mean your application would succeed, especially as they are not taking action themselves.

Co-existing in the same household whilst separated

Once a decision to separate has been taken the home environment may well be turned into, at best, a 'no man's land' or, at worst, a battleground. That is bad enough when only two adults are involved but if you have children, the need to maintain a bearable home environment for them is a must. If one of you cannot move out for financial (or other) reasons until the house is sold, here are some things to consider when living 'separately but apart'.

Dividing up time with the children

It's a very good idea to start making arrangements for the children as though physical separation has actually taken place, with parents taking responsibility for the children on designated days and alternating weekends and time in the school holidays. This may help deal with any contact issues which might arise ahead of actual separation and demonstrate what is actually workable or achievable. For example, if the narcissist is insisting that they want a 50% child arrangement but cannot demonstrate that this is plausible in this part of your separation, this can be used as evidence by you for a more realistic permanent arrangement. In addition, as children thrive on structure and routine, it will help them get used to what the future holds, but with both parents still on hand.

Practical living arrangements

Divorces can be very drawn out, and regulating the occupation of the home for what could be a long time (1-2 years or more) is vital, and ground rules will be essential. Personal space for both of the couple must be respected – narcissists are natural boundary violaters, so this will not come easily to them. If you can, take control of the implementation of arrangements within the home yourself. Be positive and proactive rather than reactive. This will surprise and wrong foot the narcissist, who is probably used to being in control, and will send a clear message that you are now in the driving seat.

There is a legal requirement, if you are to get divorced, to be able to confirm that you have not lived together for more than six months since the date of the petition for divorce – you have to confirm this when you apply for your Decree Nisi. So try to structure living arrangements rather like housemates sharing a house.

As the spouse of a narcissist, this legal requirement can be an effective way of getting the narcissist to comply with the boundaries that you will have to lay down. Specifically, this means:

- Having separate rooms. Sorting out where everyone will sleep needs to be done as a priority. As far as you can, don't make changes for the children but remember that a parent who is working probably can't continue for long with an arrangement that involves a put-up bed in a reception room. If children have to share a room because parents can no longer do so, so be it.

- Making and eating meals separately. The narcissist will expect, if you are the main cook, that you continue cooking for them if you do not make it clear that you will not. This is not pettiness – it is starting as you mean to go on, and is part of being legally separated.

- Not doing each other's washing or shopping.

- Sharing housework. An agreement regarding sharing household chores will need to be reached at the start of the separation. Many narcissists often feel too important to do housework, but do not be tempted to clean their room for them.

Also, both of the couple should be allowed to conduct their own lives without question from the other except when they are responsible for the children. This is another good reason for sharing the responsibility of the children while under the same roof. Be prepared for hypocrisy, however – you may well be constantly quizzed on your whereabouts by the narcissist, who of course will be expecting total freedom and privacy themselves.

You will need to keep your divorce related paperwork under lock and key when sharing your home with your narcissistic ex, and changing passwords on your computer and phone will also be essential – make sure you prioritise these. A lock on your bedroom door would also be a good idea.

Keeping cool

Try to stay calm and unemotional in front of your narcissistic 'housemate'. They will try to push your buttons and provoke you into an argument, for the drama and conflict. They may not want the relationship to be over and may continue to try their hoovering tactics on you – or they may want to maintain a sexual relationship with you while continuing a relationship (or multiple relationships) with others.

The narcissist may openly rub your nose in their dating endeavours to cause you pain or see you squirm. They may make phone calls to love interests with you in the room, or even try to show you dating profiles – they can exhibit unparalleled callousness in these situations.

The 'grey rock' technique is essential when co-existing under the same roof (see page 216). Do everything you can not to rise to their bait – it is common for narcissists to try to trap you into saying things in conversation which they will use against you in court. If you have to speak at all, try to converse with them as if every conversation they try to have with you is being recorded – because, frankly, it probably is.

> **"The 'grey rock' technique is essential when co-existing under the same roof. "**

The emotional road ahead will be rocky and you will need all your strength and determination to stay on track. Keep your eye on the prize – your freedom.

A word about Christmas when you are living under the same roof

One of the most difficult times of year is Christmas, particularly if you have no option but to live in the same house as your ex. Again, try to be child focused, but understand that giving the children false hope by emulating a Christmas of times past, spent with both you and your ex at the same time, is not in anyone's interests. Time with the children will need to be shared in some way, but separately, if you are to get them used to what is happening. Be prepared to put your guilt aside here.

If you sense that the narcissist wants a row about the children over Christmas as they so often do, it may be worth letting them have the children this year on the understanding that you will have them the next (by which time hopefully things will be more settled and the whole occasion will be much more enjoyable).

Of course, you will have to brace yourself for how you will feel spending Christmas away from your children, especially the first time – but at least it is a day which can be replicated on another. The feelings of loneliness, regret and disappointment do subside, and there will be a day when you can truly enjoy the season once again – only this time on your terms, unencumbered by the yuletide demands of a narcissistic spouse.

In summary, be under no illusion that sharing a house with a narcissistic spouse or partner from whom you wish to separate will be fraught with difficulties. Be careful not to try to remove them from the house if their behaviour is sufficiently subtle not to constitute grounds to do so. Try to regulate the occupation of the home as much as you can, especially for the sake of children. Don't be goaded into behaving in a way that could give the other person grounds to have you removed. Try to find a method of resolution which will bring your divorce, the finances and the child arrangements to a conclusion relatively quickly (see page 178 for details on the different available types of dispute resolution).

Important early steps to take when separating from a narcissist

The Do's

1. Protect yourself financially

Urgently contact all financial institutions with whom a joint account is held, and joint credit card providers, and tell them of your separation to ensure that funds cannot be withdrawn except on joint signature.

Take copies of all relevant joint paperwork in case it might be removed from the house – bank statements, mortgage statements, savings account statements, paperwork related to shares. Be sure that you only remove documents to which you have access. It's important to be aware that documents taken from your spouse's personal desk, filing cabinet, computer, bedside table etc. without their knowledge or permission will *not* be disclosable or admissible to the court (*Immerman v Immerman* 2009).

Change your Will in contemplation of divorce so that the narcissist is no longer a beneficiary.

Change all passwords for online banking etc. which might be known to, or discoverable by, the narcissist.

2. Limit communication with the narcissist

If at all possible, completely cut off communication so that there is no contact at all. If you have to have some contact (perhaps you have children together or have to continue living in the same house) be ready to cut it down to the bare minimum in the early stages of separation. We will discuss this in much greater detail, and the reasons for it, in Chapter 9, but in brief, the narcissist's rage always leads to accusatory rants which may be entirely nonsensical or, worse, be based on half-truths. You will find yourself drawn into horrendous arguments as you seek to defend yourself and inadvertently become a source of narcissistic supply, making things even worse. You may find yourself saying things in anger which might be taken out of context and used as evidence against you in divorce proceedings. It's vital to cut out as much communication as possible, and limit the potential damage.

Block the narcissist's phone numbers if you can, and if you can't, for child related reasons for example, reduce the number of methods of contact via phones to just one, perhaps text. Messaging platforms such as WhatsApp enable the narcissist to see when you are online in a conversation which can be intrusive. The narcissist will expect instant replies from you if they can see that you have seen their messages, or are online. It is wise to turn off your 'read receipts' if you can't block them.

Ideally, ensure that all communication with the narcissist takes place in writing, preferably by email. Be very careful to retain all emails from the narcissist – you will need them later, maybe even years down the line.

Work out how to download WhatsApp conversations into an archived file so that a recorded version is available should the narcissist become abusive.

Screenshot and file text messages, so that you have a record of them.

Note that if you have asked for no contact (and you can prove this), but contact from the narcissist persists, two or more such incidents amount to harassment and should be reported to the police.

3. Protect your privacy

Consider changing locks where appropriate (although your lawyer will not be able to advise you to change the locks on a jointly owned property).

Find out about the latest methods of bugging (actual physical bugging or through phones and computers) and install the latest phone updates to lower the chances of this happening.

Set up a completely new email account for divorce-related correspondence which is kept private from the narcissist.

Change passwords to email accounts that the narcissist might know.

Buy a safe, or similar, to keep paperwork and documents under lock and key, especially divorce-related correspondence. If you are having to share the house with the narcissist, consider putting a lock on your bedroom door and keeping paperwork there, or at a friend's house if there are no other safe alternatives.

4. Protect yourself emotionally

Therapy or counselling

If you can find a therapist or counsellor who understands narcissistic abuse, this could be a valuable tool. However, by wary of those who do not specifically understand it, particularly in these early stages – they could end up invalidating your experiences if they are not completely au fait with the behaviours that you are being subjected to. Your GP should be able to refer you for free counselling on the NHS for a limited number of sessions, but there may well be a wait and the type of therapy offered in your region may not be the correct type for you.

If you can afford to pay for private counselling or psychotherapy then finding an accredited member of the BACP, BABCP, UKCP or the NCS could be a good choice. Be aware, however, that working on the PTSD symptoms of abuse, such as flashbacks, might not be helpful at this stage as it might intensify your symptoms for a while at the beginning or make you emotionally less stable to start with. You need to be firing on as many cylinders as you can be during the process of divorcing a narcissist, so delaying treatments of this nature might be appropriate – be guided by your therapist.

There is also a growing number of narcissistic abuse/divorce coaches here in the UK who may be even better suited to supporting you through your divorce and beyond, and who may work nationally on Zoom, Skype or similar.

Your solicitor may have links to a family coach and this may be another suitable option for you if they are well versed in NPD.

It's important to understand that, even if you have formed a trusting bond with your solicitor, letting off steam to them about the latest developments with your narcissistic ex may not be the best use of their time, and will be more expensive on an hourly rate than one of the other options above.

If you are sure that you wish to divorce, make sure that you are emotionally ready – you may wish to use the resources above to help you to become stronger, before you proceed with your divorce.

Re-set your amygdala

At this time in your life you will be in a highly reactive state, easily triggered by the narcissist's bad behaviour. You may find yourself flying off the handle, short tempered and angry, or frozen with indecision. Feeling this way is as a result of activation of the part of your brain called the amygdala – the part responsible for your fear and survival reflexes of fight, flight or freeze. Your brain is on high alert for threats at this time and often overreacts to situations, and once activated it results in the production of the stress hormones cortisol and adrenalin. These quickly flood the system and, crucially, *divert blood flow away from your brain towards your muscles so you can escape the threat.* (This part of the brain is from an evolutionary perspective an old structure – it still perceives threat as if you are a caveman being attacked by a bear and responds accordingly). But the important point here is that blood is being diverted away from the logical, thinking part of your brain – making logic and thinking difficult. None of this is great when you have a narcissist manipulating you during the divorce process and a solicitor asking you to make important decisions about your finances, future and children.

So, your amygdala needs a system re-set – the threshold at which it fires needs to be lowered. Now bear with us on this next bit, especially if you are a sceptic. It has been shown again and again that meditation and mindfulness are practices which reduce this activation threshold, as well as having a whole host of other benefits. We strongly recommend that you develop a daily practice of meditation and mindfulness. Consider attending a course in Mindfulness Based Cognitive Therapy (MBCT) or Mindfulness Based Stress Reduction (MBSR) – these courses are recommended by NICE (the National Institute for Clinical Excellence) and they run for a couple of hours every week over eight weeks, with some daily meditation based homework. They have been shown on brain scans to increase the density of grey matter in the pre-frontal cortex area of the brain after just eight weeks. There are also a number of meditation apps available that you may wish to start off with instead, such as Headspace and Calm. The sooner you start, the sooner you'll feel the difference, and you are likely to be amazed at the difference this will make to you and your ability to cope.

Line up a couple of supportive friends who are good listeners

Sometimes you will just want to pick up the phone and need to rant or cry at somebody at odd times of the day, at no charge. Work out who the best people you know are for this and use them. Try not to feel too bad – although it is undeniably a stress on them, take comfort in the fact that one day you may need to do the same for them. You are probably not used to asking for help (especially if you are a co-dependent), but here is a good opportunity to learn that people actually like to be able to help, and that asking for help forges closer relationships full of authenticity. Being able to be vulnerable in front of those who love you, because it is hard to do, is actually a strength. You may have forgotten this whilst in a narcissistic relationship, as any vulnerable moments may have been ridiculed, criticised, shamed or used against you.

Online narcissistic abuse forums

Consider googling some of these – there are closed Facebook groups, for example, which may be helpful in assisting you to understand that you are not alone, but be sure to come off them as soon as you can. Some people stay on them for years and start to identify purely as a victim – this bitterness is not empowering and can actually prevent the incredible post-traumatic growth that is possible after leaving a narcissistic relationship. There comes a point, usually sometime post-divorce, where continuing to obsess about the narcissist actually wires in such thoughts as habits. For now, just be aware of this if you do join an online forum.

Social media

Block your former partner from all your social media such as Facebook, Twitter and Instagram – the phenomena of 'orbiting' and 'breadcrumbing' are common narcissistic practices, and they may 'follow' you now even if they haven't before. Be aware that the narcissist may view and 'like' your posts, whilst treating you badly in real life. They get narcissistic supply from these tactics, by orbiting your life without actually engaging with you, or by throwing you breadcrumbs of hope, to keep you hooked to them. It's destabilising and confusing – blocking them will remove their opportunity to do this.

It is also healthy for you to do this as you won't then be tempted to look them up – you won't have access to their profiles if you have blocked them. Reducing contact to as close to no contact as you can is an important part of your detox from your trauma bonding to the narcissist, and is a step towards your eventual healing. Looking at 'loved up' photographs of them with their new partner or surrounded by sycophants is simply self-torture. Don't do it.

If you need someone to keep an eye on them to make sure that they are not spending the marital financial pot (which should be being preserved to divide between you), then ask a friend to do this for you – and ask them only to tell you what you need to know, and what might be useful. Posing next to their new car, on a lavish holiday, or with their new baby (a new dependent, important to know) might be relevant examples here.

Don't be surprised if the narcissist subscribes to one of your online channels (e.g. YouTube) or follows you on media that you might not have thought of

(Pinterest, or LinkedIn, for example). Again, block them, and any members of their fan club you can think of – they frequently will send them to stalk you if they can't do it themselves.

Prioritise sleep

This is not always easy, but it is more important than you might realise.

A lack of sleep makes you more prone to mental health issues such as depression, anxiety and suicidal thoughts. You are already at high risk of these things due to the adverse life events you are experiencing when divorcing a narcissist, so you can see how adding in lack of sleep could tip you over the edge, into a full scale breakdown.

Brain scans of poor sleepers show an amplification in the reactivity of the amygdala, the area of the brain mentioned previously, which leads to one being on a shorter fuse than usual with increased anger and rage. Again, at this time in your life, you need to be as calm and non-reactive as you can be in the face of whatever is being thrown at you by your narcissistic ex-partner. Science tells us that a good night's sleep can actually help with this, by down-regulating the reactivity of the fight or flight system.

Sleep is also important for decision making (crucial in high conflict divorces), creativity and forming new memories. But not only do we sleep to remember, we also sleep to *forget*, with dreaming, which takes place in deep sleep, being a factor in helping us to deal with emotionally charged experiences, making them easier to tolerate – a valuable resource at this time in your life. Sleep has too many physical effects to describe here (such as producing chemicals that break down toxins, reducing the risk of cancer, heart attacks, strokes, Alzheimer's disease and diabetes). Sleep scientists are only just starting to get these messages heard by the world.

In order to cycle through the different phases of sleep, you need to be actually asleep for at least seven to eight hours a day, preferably in an unbroken stint. Only then can the essential processes, that are actually the purpose of sleep, be effectively carried out. Even losing an hour of sleep a night has adverse effects. (There are decades of data proving that, when the clocks go forwards every year, admissions to hospital for heart attacks rocket over the subsequent days. The reverse is true when they go back due to the associated extra hour in bed).

Be aware that prescription sleeping tablets don't actually give you true sleep. Prescription sleeping tablets (odd though it may seem) don't give you the crucial restorative phases of sleep that you need, although they do knock you out. The same is true for alcohol – the sleep you get if you've been drinking is short on the type of sleep you actually need. The only type of sleeping tablet that leads you into true sleep is melatonin which is the naturally occurring chemical that the body already produces, rising at night and telling your brain and body that you are ready for sleep, lulling you into it. Melatonin tablets will get you to sleep, and the type of sleep you will have is proper sleep, but it may not keep you there. Although melatonin is available on prescription in the UK, it is rarely prescribed. In the USA and many other countries it is available over the counter.

You will need to be firing on all cylinders and getting a good night's sleep is a must have – after all, you are about to engage in what will probably be the fight of your life. Don't underestimate the power of this one simple, free and natural resource – it could make all the difference to you.

So, reduce alcohol and caffeine, have a hot bath or shower so that you can cool down afterwards once in bed (the cooling off being a signal for the brain for sleep), and try to develop a sleep routine which your brain will eventually associate with shutting down for the night. When you bath a baby, you lower the lights and read a soothing bedtime story to them. Here you are actually establishing a bedtime ritual to signal to their brain that it is time to increase their own natural melatonin so that sleep can begin. Consider nurturing yourself as if you are that baby.

5. Tell the children of your decision to separate

So many adults believe that even quite young children do not pick up on what is going on in the home; that they don't listen to conversations (or more usually rows) between their parents after they have gone to bed. In fact, children often draw the wrong conclusions and become confused and frightened, not wanting to ask questions for fear of the answers. However difficult family life might be, most children would prefer their parents to remain together (regardless of the age of the children). If separation is definite, telling the children at as early a stage as possible is important to provide them with reassurance and stability. If at all possible, this should be communicated by both parents together.

However, a parent with NPD is more likely to want to communicate this:

a)   alone

b)   first

If you think this might happen in your case, as the non-narcissistic parent you need to try to head this off, perhaps by raising the issue when all the family are together without giving the narcissistic parent advance warning. Whatever happens, they won't want to look like the bad guy, but they may be less likely to

157

openly blame you for the split if the conversation is not one they have had time to prepare for.

Stick to the facts, stay calm and don't criticise the other parent, remembering that the children love you both. Even if the conversation doesn't go as well as you might have hoped it will be better than the narcissist telling the children their own version of events without you even being present.

The narcissist is likely to want a hysterical response, and for the children to be inconsolable – if they are not, they are likely to feel disappointed. Don't be surprised if this happens in your situation – it's just another play for narcissistic supply.

6. Take your wedding ring off

This is another good way to signal to both the narcissist and the children that the relationship is really over. The narcissist is likely to delay doing this themselves in order to gain sympathy from you and others, although they probably will be removing it as soon as you are out of sight for liaisons etc. Be aware of this, and don't fall for any pity plays relating to it. As you are learning, the narcissist will exploit anything they can to get supply.

Important early steps: The Do's

▶ **Protect yourself financially**

▶ **Limit communication with the narcissist**

▶ **Protect your privacy**

▶ **Protect yourself emotionally**

▶ **Tell the children of your decision to separate**

▶ **Take your wedding ring off**

The Don'ts

1. Don't tell the narcissist that you think they are a narcissist

You might think that this is a perfectly reasonable and possibly even a helpful thing to tell your narcissistic ex-partner. You may think enlightening them will help them to understand why you are leaving, or why they behave in the way that they do. You may find yourself wanting to sling the word at them in an episode of anger or frustration.

Don't do it. Narcissists are masters of projection, and more than likely they will label *you* as the narcissist, to your face and to anyone who will listen, including the court. Not only will this have you wondering whether you are one all over again (it's still too early for you to be immune to the narcissist's gas-lighting), but it may be harmful to your reputation and may lose you friends, family and work. Bite your lip. Think: "Narcissist? What's one of those?" when tempted to spill the beans to your former spouse.

Narcissists will also commonly search for an alternative diagnosis for *you* if you tell them that you believe they are a narcissist. They may label you as 'borderline' or 'bipolar' or 'unstable', for example. Borderline personality disorder (cousin to NPD, and actually often coexisting with it) is typified by, amongst other things, sudden intense anger, mood swings, impulsivity and tension which builds up and explodes in rage and which is then followed by regret. You may well currently relate to these symptoms yourself, but do consider that *anyone* who has suffered narcissistic abuse and is undergoing a breakdown in a narcissistic relationship will suffer from these symptoms, *as they are appropriate to the situation*. This does not make you borderline and if the narcissist tries to convince you that you are, be aware that this is just another attempt at gas-lighting.

2. Don't tell the narcissist's new partner that they are a narcissist

You are, most likely, a nice person. Empathic. Kind. Possibly a rescuer. These qualities drew the narcissist to you in the first place, after all. You cannot bear the thought of someone else being pulled into the narcissist's web. It is a completely natural instinct to want to warn them – to tell them to run, to help them to save themselves.

Don't be tempted to do this. Remember how you felt in the early days of your relationship with the narcissist? When you were being love-bombed and believed that you had met your soul mate? Those pesky feel good brain chemicals that were sky high *literally made your love blind*. Even in 'normal' love with a non-narcissist, the 'love chemicals' in the early stages (a potent combination of dopamine, serotonin and oxytocin) remove your ability to be objective about your partner. It takes months for those chemicals to subside and for you to be able to see your belle or beau more clearly. This is no accident – nature designed us like this so that we would procreate to propagate the species in these early stages of 'love'. In narcissistic abuse, the chemicals drop for a while but then rise again, due to the repeated cycles of idealisation and devaluing. If an ex-partner of your narcissist had told you about their true nature, there is no way that you would have listened – and you would have labelled them as 'crazy' or 'bitter' instead.

The narcissist's new supply is on their own journey, and it is not your job to rescue them. It's high time you focused on yourself for a change. Any attempts you make to do what feels like the 'right thing' will backfire on you and accusations of harassment may be forthcoming. Just don't go there – you owe it to yourself.

3. Don't expect marriage guidance counselling to work

As we have discussed previously, if your partner is a true narcissist, no amount of marriage guidance counselling will cure them and, although you should take your own share of responsibility for what you genuinely can in your marriage, the fundamental problem here is your partner's miswired brain. By all means give it a shot if you feel you ought to exhaust every possibility, but look out for the narcissist's 'crazymaking behaviour' and expect to be blamed by them (and possibly your counsellor) for the demise of your relationship. Narcissists are charming, plausible and attractive and your counsellor may well be drawn in by them, just as you were. The narcissist will be an expert at making inflammatory suggestions about you, under the guise of the poor victim, and then sitting back smugly to watch you try to justify yourself.

4. Don't put anything on social media other than a brief announcement of your divorce

It can be tempting to offload on social media with blow by blow accounts of the narcissist's outrageous behaviour, and your suspicions of their personality disorder, but actually, this will not be helpful. Even if you have blocked them (which you definitely should) the narcissist will send members of their fan club to stalk you online and report back. There will be no chance of you having the upper hand in negotiations in divorce proceedings if the narcissist knows what you are thinking, and they will get immense narcissistic supply from seeing your meltdowns and outrage at their behaviour. This is not what you want – you need to starve them of narcissistic supply from you so that they bother you less. You need to disappear from their lives and pretend not to exist as far as possible.

In addition, you will be upset, your mood will be labile, and you will be highly reactive and prone to tears and despair for at least a few months. Advertising this on social media could have serious repercussions, particularly in relation to any children, as the narcissist will use whatever they can to discredit you and make you look unstable. Be careful. Narcissists often go after the children as an attempt to hurt you by insisting that you are an unfit parent.

Chronicling the narcissist's behaviour online will also drive people away from you – unfortunately not enough people are aware of these personality types. Many perfectly nice people may just not believe you and think you are unreasonable and a drama queen.

If you possibly can, come off social media altogether for a few months. Your dignity will thank you for it.

5. Don't tell anyone other than your very closest allies that your former partner is a narcissist

It is absolutely true that awareness of NPD needs to increase in the wider community and that all of society will be better off for understanding it, but no one, other than your best friends, will believe you if you try to enlighten them as to the character of your narcissist ex during your divorce.

They will just think you are being bitter or that it is just an 'acrimonious divorce'. They may tell you that it takes two to tango and that you are equally to blame. Many people will even tell you that *they* don't believe in drama, the implication being that this drama is something you have brought upon yourself as a result of who you are as a person. The majority of people are utterly ignorant about NPD and they may well end up gas-lighting you themselves by making the statements above. Accept their ignorance, and don't bother trying to explain anything to them until you have come out the other side of your divorce, when you are back to being yourself. Be prepared for the harsh reality of losing friends during this time – but, if you can, take comfort in the fact that they were only the ones you needed to lose.

6. Don't expect to be able to get the narcissist formally diagnosed

As we've already ascertained, the UK lags behind the US in recognising NPD, and it is extremely unlikely that you will be able to get the narcissist diagnosed. They are masters or mistresses of charm and deception anyway, and may slip through the diagnostic net because of this. Perhaps one day the courts and medical profession will understand the importance of recognising this personality adaptation, but at the moment, we are nowhere near this. The only lawyer or legal professional you should be uttering the 'narcissist' word to is your own. Don't even think of bringing it up to a judge – whilst it's fine to show the patterns of behaviours that occur, which they will recognise as being undesirable and abusive, they are highly unlikely to accept the term narcissist as shorthand for those behaviours, and, ridiculous though this is, it may go against you if you do use the term.

Important early steps: The Don'ts

► Don't tell the narcissist that you think they are a narcissist

► Don't tell the narcissist's new partner that they are a narcissist

► Don't expect marriage guidance counselling to work

► Don't offload your emotions on to social media

► Don't tell anyone other than your inner circle that your former partner is a narcissist

► Don't expect to be able to get the narcissist formally diagnosed

Early legal considerations **7**

T here are three separate areas where you may require legal assistance – the divorce itself, the finances, and the children. In the court process the finances are dealt with in the 'financial remedy proceedings' and matters related to the children are dealt with in the so-called 'Children Act proceedings'.

Costs for the divorce are likely to be charged on a fixed fee basis. Most lawyers will charge in the region of £1,500 to £2,000 including court fees at the time of going to print. Bear in mind that this cost only covers the divorce itself – financial matters or issues relating to your children will be separately charged and tend to be the expensive parts, especially where a narcissist is involved.

Most lawyers charge on the basis of an hourly rate which will be higher or lower depending upon the seniority of the lawyer in question. Hourly rates can be deceptive as it is hard to tell how much work will be undertaken in an hour and how quick or efficient a particular lawyer is. Bear in mind that, even if you are on a budget where legal fees are concerned, the instruction of the right person (as opposed to the least expensive) could be crucially important for you.

Finding a lawyer

So, you have reached the point where you are looking for a divorce solicitor, whose effectiveness will determine your financial future and perhaps also your children's.

Choosing the right professional representation is an extremely important, yet difficult, decision. Getting this selection right at the outset can save you a great deal of time and money in the future. Your spouse is likely to behave in a very predictable way for those lawyers who recognise NPD, who will be able to advise you and act on your behalf accordingly. But be warned – those who do not understand, particularly through lack of experience, will run the risk of simply becoming a pawn in the game of the narcissist, who will delight in extending their manipulation skills to your lawyer – an excellent form of narcissistic supply. At the time of writing, we estimate that only 20% of UK family lawyers fully understand NPD, for the reasons outlined earlier.

You will be relying heavily upon your solicitor to get you through the ordeal ahead of you with:

- a financial outcome which allows you to move forward with your life

- workable child arrangements

- the return of your independence

The objective of the narcissist will be to punish you for having the audacity to leave them or to uncover their true self. In either circumstance narcissistic rage will have been triggered and revenge is what will be sought, almost at any price, even to the narcissist's own detriment.

Your solicitor needs to understand exactly what they are dealing with and the fact that they will be sucked into the narcissist's games unless they are very resilient and aware. It is also highly likely that the narcissist will be representing themselves (without a lawyer) at least for some of the time, and so your lawyer will be in direct contact with them. The wrong solicitor may well, therefore, be at risk of being charmed by them.

Although cost may be an issue, your lawyer's hourly rate should not determine who you select to represent you. Nor should you necessarily be looking at who has historically represented those in the public eye. You are looking for someone who:

- is a specialist family solicitor.

- has a sufficient level or air of seniority to hold the awe of your spouse – you do not want your case to be passed to the junior solicitor on the grounds of lower cost. Whilst there may be work which can be carried out by a more junior lawyer, you need someone with robust experience to deal directly with the narcissist.

- understands all methods of possible dispute resolution currently available, and specifically which methods should be avoided with a narcissist, as well as which ones have a good chance of success (see page 178 for out of court dispute resolution methods).

- will recognise the behaviour traits to which you have been subjected, and if they don't already fully understand NPD, will be prepared to listen carefully and learn about what they will be up against.

- can manage the process and advise you specifically on how to deal with your particular situation (some lawyers prefer to just ask for your instructions without advising you – this will not be appropriate in your case).

- is also a trained mediator, as their wider skill set may mean that they are more able to recognise traits of NPD and as a consequence be more able to provide the level of care and support which you will require.

- has adequate time to devote to your case, and who, once again, will not simply be overseeing a junior solicitor.

Reading through online biographies can be time consuming and unhelpful. The court will rarely provide a recommendation and at best will give you a list. Citizen's Advice will usually hand out the names of firms who volunteer for them on a rotation basis. This is not what you want either.

The best possible route to the right solicitor for you is a personal recommendation. Do you have a friend who has been in a similar situation, perhaps in a particularly acrimonious divorce? Who did they instruct? How successful was the outcome? Do you know anyone from the world of family law? A school friend, a barrister's clerk, a PA – anyone who might give you a steer in the right direction? It's the personal recommendation that you need – you need to know exactly how someone works and their level of understanding of what lies ahead for you.

Make sure that you delete any online searches – especially on a shared computer or one to which your spouse might have access.

Although access to funds for legal fees might be an issue, don't be attracted to a 'free' initial consultation. They are a marketing ploy to attract work. The person you want to instruct won't need to do this.

Don't be afraid to ring solicitors up – as many as you have to. The right solicitor will be able to give you five or ten minutes on the phone before you set up an initial consultation. Tell them that you suspect your spouse may have NPD and ask them specifically whether they understand this condition and the divorce behaviours that those with NPD exhibit. Those solicitors that do will tell you. They won't say that they 'don't believe in labels', or that you are simply in an 'acrimonious' or 'high conflict' situation. Remember that only one in five do understand at present, and do not be put off by this. Keep going until you find the right solicitor for you, and don't be tempted to go with someone just because they seem 'nice' if they don't have a specific understanding of your situation.

A narcissist may want to try to restrict where you can go to obtain legal advice, and may play on the strict rules that lawyers have to abide by. A lawyer may not act for a client if they have previously had dealings with their spouse. It used to be commonplace for one person to contact a number of good lawyers in the locality for an initial chat, simply to prevent their spouse from instructing that individual or firm.

The rules are that the lawyer is prohibited from acting if they have direct knowledge of the circumstances of the other person, to the extent that it would be unfair or inappropriate to then represent the other side of the couple. However, most lawyers have processes in place to prevent any underhand potential exclusion of representation happening. They will not be keen to consider an individual as a 'client' without setting up a proper chargeable appointment. If that appointment turns into a 'one off' and the client goes elsewhere, it is unlikely the same lawyer would be prepared to take on the other party as a client, but it would be a matter for the lawyer's discretion.

The first consultation

You need your first meeting with your lawyer to be an in-depth discussion during which you can fully explain the predicament in which you find yourself and structure a way forward that will enable you to get your life back under your own control. Your first meeting with your lawyer will be vitally important. You will need to evaluate, either at or shortly after that meeting, how comfortable you are with your choice. Don't be afraid to tell your story. Don't be afraid to ask questions. You should leave the meeting feeling that you and your lawyer have a common understanding and objective.

Ahead of your first meeting provide a written account of what your life has been like with your spouse and what is important for you to change in the future. Explain what you are frightened of.

Provide some background to your own relationship with your parents. Was your relationship with either of them difficult and if so why? How did you cope with that?

What sort of person do you see yourself as being and how do others see you? Is their view of you the same or different to that of your partner/spouse?

If you have a supportive close friend or relative (not an adult child) in whom you have been able to confide, take them along with you to your first meeting with your lawyer. The step which you are taking is a very big and brave one. It will help to have someone familiar there with you until you have formed a working bond with your legal advisor.

Your lawyer needs to know:

- What motivates your partner/spouse.

- What irritates them.

- What sort of relationship they have with each of your children and whether that has historically changed – if so when and for what apparent reason.

- Which of the financial assets in your case will be of significance to them.

The more background information you can supply, the better placed your lawyer will be to represent you.

Spend time talking to your lawyer at the outset of the case. This may feel initially expensive but it will definitely be worth it in the long term and will undoubtedly save fees further down the line.

Your lawyer must understand that the objectives of the narcissist will be:

- To undermine your confidence in your own lawyer.

- To take charge of the process in every way possible.

- To prevent resolution and cause as much delay and chaos as they can – even to their own detriment or expense. Even if it is the narcissist who has ended the relationship, they need to keep you in play as a source of narcissistic supply for as long as possible – the "can't live with you, can't live without you" phenomenon.

If your lawyer does not understand, you will both find yourselves:

- Bombarded with correspondence which serves only to increase costs, as you are unnecessarily drawn into a 'war' in correspondence which simply follows the agenda set by the narcissist. In Chapter 9 there is a letter to Maggie from her narcissistic husband which we have decoded. A narcissist is highly likely to insist on writing their own correspondence which is just sent out on their own lawyer's notepaper (unless their lawyer is strong enough to prevent this from happening). Your lawyer needs to be able to translate what is being said exactly as Maggie does, and respond only to the relevant points in a clear and calm way. Being sucked into a line by line response will only increase costs and acrimony/anxiety and serve no useful purpose.

- Constantly reacting to an erratic approach taken by the other side instead of being proactively in control.

Barrister or solicitor?

Barristers are trained advocates. Their role is to present your case to the judge in the best possible way, using their skill and expertise at a court hearing, and to give advice about your case to you and your solicitor – a sort of second opinion from someone who is in front of the courts on a daily basis.

You will definitely be instructing a solicitor, as solicitors deal with the day to day running of a case; some do their own advocacy up to the FDRA (second court hearing) stage but rarely at a final trial (the third hearing). We explain the court process in detail in Chapter 10.

As most divorces involving a narcissist find their way into the court process at some stage, it is likely that 'Counsel' (a barrister) will be instructed to represent you in court at some point. Your solicitor will be able to advise you on this.

As the barrister is likely to be involved in the case for just a short period of time, but at a crucial stage, it is vital that your solicitor provides them with information about the facts and the assets involved but also about the personalities which they will be dealing with.

A barrister may not represent one party to a relationship if they have previously been instructed by the other.

Remember that a narcissist will want to drain you of funds as quickly as they can in order to make you nervous of the cost of legal advice, and to demonstrate that your proposed course of action is not in your best interests. They will want to make you fearful for your long term financial security, and make you believe that you were misguided to think that anyone could get the better of them on your behalf.

The right lawyer will be a guide, a source of strength, a reliable sounding board and, most importantly, will have the expertise to create the right team around you to take you through the process of removing yourself from your toxic and debilitating relationship. Remember that your lawyer is instructed by *you*. If you sense that they may not have a command of the situation you must say so, and if, on reflection, you feel they are not right for you, say so and terminate your contract immediately. You might even want to ask them for another recommendation. You might find this difficult to do, as you may have people pleasing tendencies, but you must put your own best interests first, and not be afraid of displeasing the lawyer by ending your contract with them – because the right lawyer, with the right approach, who the narcissist is unable to run rings around, could save you literally tens of thousands of pounds over the course of your divorce, as we explain later.

> " **A narcissist will want to drain you of funds as quickly as they can in order to make you nervous of the cost of legal advice.** "

Representing yourself without a lawyer

Although you most definitely will require legal advice, there may be times within the process when it is preferable for you to be a litigant in person (LIP). It is not advisable to start the off as an LIP, however.

But, further on in the process, if the narcissist is deluging your lawyer with pointless correspondence, probably just to increase your legal costs, it may be a good idea to take your lawyer off court record so that correspondence is no longer sent to them on your behalf. You can then deal with the letters yourself and refer to your lawyer only when necessary. One word of caution about this. You need to be emotionally able to deal with this correspondence yourself which may be quite vile in content. If you are not, you may want to agree with your lawyer that they will collect correspondence from your spouse/partner and only deal with it via one composite response, say once a week.

Understanding the divorce process

Most family lawyers will tell you that the divorce process is just a very straightforward paperwork exercise. It is something you can deal with yourself through the government portal should you choose to do so. However, it is a process which you need to fully and properly understand – especially when you are divorcing a narcissist.

In order to divorce you must be able to prove an 'irretrievable breakdown of the marriage' using one of the following five 'grounds':

- Adultery

- Unreasonable behaviour

- Desertion for two years or more

- Two year's separation with consent

- Five year's separation – no consent required

The 'no fault' basis for divorce has finally received the Royal Assent after over 24 years of campaigning. At the time this is being written it is not permissible by statute but it soon will be. It is intended for those couples who are in agreement that they should separate, but have not yet lived separate and apart for two years or more, and want things to be as conciliatory as possible.

The 'Petitioner' is the spouse who issues the divorce proceedings and the 'Respondent' is the spouse who receives them. What is called the 'decree proceedings' i.e. the divorce process, is completely separate to dealing with financial matters or child arrangements and will be charged separately. The two (or three) can run concurrently, effectively on parallel lines, but they are separate. If a solicitor gives you a costs quote for 'the divorce' this will just mean the decree proceedings and nothing else i.e. not dealing with finances or any issues regarding the children which might arise.

If financial remedy or children proceedings are issued the spouse issuing these proceedings will be described as the 'Applicant' and the spouse receiving these will be the 'Respondent'. So, you could be the Petitioner in the divorce and the Applicant or the Respondent in financial remedy proceedings or proceedings under the 1989 Children Act. (Do bear in mind that the expectation is that Children Act proceedings will only be issued if the parents are unable to reach agreement. Ideally there will be no order regarding the children.)

Although the divorce process is quite a simple 'procedure' there are certain points which you need to know and understand.

A   Adultery

It is important to note that in divorce proceedings the court is *not* more financially generous towards the spouse who was 'wronged' by their adulterous partner, but many people aren't aware of this. Some assume, incorrectly, that the issue of divorce proceedings under a 'fault based' ground such as adultery, will result in a better financial outcome for the Petitioner. Financial remedy proceedings are not fault based and the court does not provide any form of retribution. If you are going to petition under the 'adultery' ground you have a period of six months from the date when you became aware of the adultery to issue divorce proceedings.

The precise wording of the ground however, has two elements, the second being that the Petitioner finds it 'intolerable to live with the Respondent' and therefore each act of adultery causes the six month time limit to recommence. The Petitioner may turn a blind eye to an affair which they hope will fizzle out. When they realise it will not, the most recent act of adultery is the one which the Petitioner finds intolerable and which causes time to start to run. What this means is that if the adultery is continuing and you have been hoping that your husband/wife will end the affair but that doesn't happen you can rely on the most recent physical act of infidelity, i.e. the last time sex took place, to be the point when you found this behaviour intolerable and from which time starts to run.

It is also worth pointing out that the spouse who is having the affair cannot petition for a divorce on the grounds of their own adultery.

If you petition on the ground of adultery the other spouse has to admit this. If you think that they may not make such admission it could be better to issue proceedings under the 'unreasonable behaviour' ground stating that the Respondent is engaged in a new relationship which you find unacceptable. As indicated above, it doesn't matter which ground you use as nothing else will turn on the basis of the divorce – this is NOT a fault-based jurisdiction, and if the matter ends up being decided by a judge in court, it won't be affected by who cheated on who, or who abused who.

Surprisingly, this ground is *not* available if there is a new relationship with a member of the same sex. The definition of adultery is 'penetrative sexual intercourse *with a member of the opposite sex*'.

B   Unreasonable behaviour

The Petitioner will need to cite half a dozen reasons why they can no longer reasonably be expected to live with the Respondent. Those allegations of behaviour must be continuing or have happened in the last six months. If the alleged behaviour is more than six months old the Petitioner is deemed not to find it intolerable and the ground is lost.

Again, there is an assumption that the Petitioner under this ground will do better in the financial proceedings as a consequence of the other person's behaviour. This is incorrect. 'Fault' has no part to play at all.

This is currently the most common ground for divorce as it is the only ground available where the couple are still living together but neither has commenced a physical relationship with a member of the opposite sex. The argument for the new, much anticipated, no fault based ground actually emerged from this ground, because it was recognised that having to allege unreasonable behaviour in order to get a divorce hardly sat comfortably with resolving matters in a conciliatory way.

If the Respondent finds the allegations unpalatable, it is still possible for them to agree to the divorce petition, provided that the Petitioner confirms in open correspondence (i.e. in a letter which can be shown to the court), that they accept that the Respondent denies the allegations and will not rely upon them as fact, if the Respondent allows the petition to proceed.

This is called an 'undefended decree' of divorce, and it means that the allegations of unreasonable behaviour are not proved as true, but that the Respondent has simply agreed to them pragmatically because the marriage has clearly broken down.

The allegations of behaviour are very subjective; it is what this particular Petitioner considers to be unreasonable to be tolerated. It is important to remember the precise wording of the ground: '*The Respondent has behaved in such a way that the Petitioner cannot be reasonably expected to live with the Respondent*'. It is not the behaviour which is unreasonable but the expectation that the behaviour might be tolerated. Mrs Owens famously had her divorce petition rejected by the Supreme Court in 2019. The reason for this is that the Supreme Court judges agreed with the lower courts that the allegations of behaviour were just 'marital bickering'; the petition failed to explain why she found this behaviour intolerable or that it would be unreasonable to expect her to do so.

It is likely that this is the ground for divorce which you might use, especially if it is likely that your spouse may deny adultery. Also bear in mind that as it is not possible to commit adultery with a member of the same sex, this may well fall under this ground as behaviour which it would not be reasonable to tolerate.

C   Desertion for two years or more

This is now the least common of the five grounds for divorce. Historically it was not unusual for one party to a marriage to simply 'disappear' but now this ground is rarely used. A narcissist would, in any event, be unlikely to want to miss the drama created by the chaos which they can cause in the divorce process.

D   Two years' separation with consent

This is the most neutral ground for divorce. It's dependent on both of the couple being in agreement to divorce in two years' time, not just at the point of separation but also when the two year period has elapsed. Be wary of this if your spouse is a narcissist – they might seek to exploit this ground and waste two years of your life.

Occasionally a couple will enter into a 'Deed of Separation' at the time the relationship breaks down. This is an agreement to regulate financial and other matters and record an agreement to divorce on this ground two years later. It is important to remember that consent can be withdrawn; that consent must be given at the time the actual divorce petition is issued. Beware that your spouse might suggest a two year separation petition and then change their mind at the end of the two year period, refusing to agree to a divorce at this time. Financial circumstances may have changed and you could find yourself back at square one all over again. If you feel that the marriage is over it is far better to issue divorce proceedings straight away and get on with it. Otherwise you could find yourself manipulated into 'round two' of a toxic relationship, which has morphed into a pointlessly protracted separation.

It is possible to resume cohabitation for a period of up to six months after separation has taken place without losing this ground for divorce, but the two year period will be extended by the period of cohabitation (which cannot exceed six months).

For 'separation' to count for the purposes of this ground both of the couple must be clear that they are living apart because the relationship has broken down. For example, if one of the couple were working away from home, that time away would not count as 'separation' for this purpose, if the breakdown in the relationship had not been communicated to their spouse in clear terms.

As dealt with on page 148, sometimes a couple may have agreed to separate but can't live in different properties for financial reasons. It is possible to live 'separate and apart' under the same roof. You just have to live in the same way that people who house share do i.e. have separate rooms and each do your own cooking, cleaning, washing etc. This can be more difficult if you have children, especially as you can't take your meals together, but the best way around this is to divide the week with each parent being responsible for the children on the same days that they would if they had separated into two separate homes. This maintains the separation and also helps the children get used to the new routine even while under the same roof.

E   Five years' separation – no consent required

If there are no other grounds for divorce this final ground provides a 'catch all' situation. It is however a long time to wait and to have your life effectively 'on hold'. As most married couples can put together a petition on the basis of ground B, this ground is very much a last resort.

As the other spouse does not need to consent to the petition provided a period of five years' separation can be demonstrated, a decree absolute of divorce will not be granted until financial matters have been resolved, in order to give financial protection to the party who does not want the marriage to be brought to an end.

Again, the period of separation can be extended by up to six months if cohabitation is resumed.

Evidence of irretrievable breakdown of marriage

▶   **Adultery**

▶   **Unreasonable behaviour**

▶   **Desertion for two years or more**

▶   **Two year's separation with consent**

▶   **Five year's separation – no consent required**

The five years' separation ground can sometimes be used as an excuse for the spouse who does not want to commit to their new partner by marriage. If someone has left a relationship to be with a new partner and their spouse does not want to petition on the grounds of adultery or two years' separation with consent, it is open to the departed spouse to tell their new partner that there is no way they can divorce until five years have elapsed. This allows them to dodge new commitment and keep their options open – an attractive position for the narcissist.

Defending divorce proceedings

If you don't want a divorce, and your spouse does, there is always the option to 'defend' a petition for divorce by filing an 'Answer' with the court. The time limits for doing so are very strict and therefore, if this is a course of action you wish to adopt, you need to take legal advice immediately you are served with the divorce papers.

Filing an Answer can be a tactic adopted to simply cause delay (and increase costs for the other side – although this will inevitably apply for both parties). However, in reality it is likely that ultimately a divorce will be granted if all of the paperwork is in order and everything is properly pleaded in the petition (i.e. the grounds relied upon are accurate and enforceable).

It might be something you would do if you don't want the divorce and want to cause as much delay as possible. It is something which your narcissistic spouse might do if they are enraged by you having the audacity to issue divorce proceedings.

A defended divorce will simply cause additional legal costs. Realistically if one person wants a divorce the marriage is unlikely to be saved by attempting to defend the divorce. It is far better to direct resources to the important issues such as resolving financial matters and child arrangements.

The importance of pronouncement of Decree Nisi

The court will only have jurisdiction to regulate financial matters (except on an interim basis) once Decree Nisi has been pronounced. Getting to this stage is therefore important. You must have Decree Nisi in place before attending a Financial Dispute Resolution Appointment (FDRA) in financial remedy proceedings (see Chapter 10 for details regarding the court process).

'Decree Nisi' means that your paperwork is in order and the court accepts that you have grounds for divorce. You do, however, remain married until Decree Absolute has been pronounced.

Although Decree Absolute can be applied for by the Petitioner six weeks and one day after Decree Nisi has been pronounced, this can be, and usually is, delayed until financial matters have been resolved. If one party were to die before financial matters have been resolved it may be better to be the widow/widower than the former spouse. This is particularly the case where pensions are involved and on death the other spouse would have a widow or widower's benefit.

If you are worried that the other party may apply for Decree Absolute beforehand (the Respondent to divorce proceedings can apply for Decree Absolute three months after the date when the Petitioner could first have applied) you should ask for an 'undertaking' that they do not do so, or at the very least 14 days' notice of an intention to do so in order that you have time to apply to the court to stop pronouncement if to do so would be financially detrimental.

Do bear in mind that the court will not always refuse early pronouncement of Decree Absolute as the judge has to balance the need for everyone to get on with their lives.

Should you be the Petitioner or Respondent?

If you do not want your marriage to be over, issuing divorce proceedings may be the last thing that you want to do. Being the Petitioner, however, does bring a number of advantages which should be considered:

- You are in control of the process – that may be psychologically very important.

- You can choose the ground for divorce.

- You can control the speed of the process.

- It is harder for the Respondent to apply for Decree Absolute as they must wait an extra three months before being able to do so, and their application must be on notice so you will be aware of it in advance and have the opportunity to challenge it. As Petitioner, you just make the application in writing, with no advance warning to the other side.

If your narcissistic spouse gets wind of the fact that you may be intending to issue divorce proceedings they may do so first in order to retain control. This is something that you may need to be prepared for. Do remember that, in terms of outcome, nothing at all turns on who is the Petitioner and who is the Respondent so it really doesn't matter and is purely a control issue. Remember not to react over things that don't make any difference.

Divorce is a 'non fault based' system

To reiterate, it is a common misconception that if you consider that your relationship has broken down as a consequence of your spouse's adulterous relationship or, in your view, appalling behaviour, this should translate into some kind of advantage in the financial remedy or child arrangements proceedings. Unfortunately this is absolutely not the case.

> **"The financial remedy process is a pragmatic commercial exercise which has no regard to perceived 'blame'."**

Many matters proceed to court due to the unrealistic expectation that a judge will administer retribution. Such expectation can only give rise to disappointment and unnecessary expense. The financial remedy process is a pragmatic commercial exercise which has no regard to perceived 'blame'. This may be hard to hear, but it is the reality and accepting this fact early on will be important for your own well-being.

Costs of the Decree (Divorce) Proceedings

The decree proceedings, financial remedy proceedings and children proceedings are entirely separate so far as costs are concerned. Solicitors will give fixed cost quotes for the divorce side of the process to include the court fee. The VAT inclusive fee is usually around £1,500 to £2,000. You can also lodge the divorce proceedings yourself via the government portal where the only cost is the court fee.

Fees for financial remedy or children proceedings will be separately charged.

The Mediation Information and Assessment Meeting (MIAM)

When you are involved in the process of divorcing a narcissist, ending up in court proceedings is probably an inevitability, but you need to be sure that you have considered the other options that may be suitable before deciding that court is simply unavoidable.

Before issuing any court application it is necessary to attend a Mediation Information and Assessment Meeting or MIAM. This is an appointment with an accredited mediator to discuss not only the option of mediation but also all other forms of 'out of court' dispute resolution. No application to court should be issued without it first being explained exactly what alternatives are available.

It is important that the person conducting the MIAM is aware of any personality issues which are in existence in your case as this will help them look at which 'out of court' options might be suitable for your specific situation.

Here we consider each of these options in turn.

Out of court methods of dispute resolution

Those methods which are most likely to work where one party suffers from NPD are marked with '*'.

Mediation

The standard type of mediation is a process which is unlikely work in reaching a resolution where a narcissistic individual is involved. However, other more effective types of mediation exist which are more likely to be successful – these are described later in this section.

Going back to the standard type of mediation, there are various reasons why it is likely to fail when a narcissist is involved, even if shuttle mediation is proposed, where you and your spouse remain in separate rooms and the mediator moves between you.

Firstly, the mediator may not initially realise that your spouse suffers from NPD. And even if you or your solicitor inform the mediator of your suspicions at the outset, it might be that they do not have a good enough understanding of NPD to handle things effectively.

They may not fully understand that the narcissist, in reality, does not want to settle the case. They may not be aware that the narcissist will see them as a new and empathic professional who they can charm and manipulate in sessions, with the added benefit of you meeting 50% of the cost. They may not initially be able to see through the charming story telling or the narcissist's presentation as a victim, just 'trying to do their best for their family' in these difficult circumstances, but being presented with 'hostility' and 'unreasonableness' from you at every turn.

During the process, the narcissist will do their best to get the mediator 'on side'; to form an inappropriate relationship with them within the process in order to undermine you. This may start with them contacting the mediator direct either by telephone or email with an innocuous query, perhaps about the timing of the meeting, which then develops into exploring what sort of person the mediator is in order to use them to their advantage. They may arrive very early for a meeting in the hope of engaging the mediator in private conversation, or take a long time to pack their bag and put on their coat at the end of a meeting while you quickly depart, again in an attempt to have a private conversation. If the mediator appears pliable, they will pile on the charm and play the victim role, keen to cause the mediator to become tacitly sympathetic to their situation. If the mediator falls for their charm and appears to be forming something of an alliance with them the narcissist will be quick to report this irregularity to you, thereby forming an unlikely alliance with you through which to undermine the mediator, and therefore the process.

The narcissist may either insist on their own choice of mediator, thereby having the opportunity to imply to you that the mediator is on their side. Alternatively, they may accept your suggestion as this presents an opportunity for blame when the process breaks down.

Even if the mediator does have the measure of the situation, the narcissist will try to prove them wrong so that they question their own judgement. If the mediator is experienced and robust, the narcissist may seek to undermine and challenge them in order to make them feel uncomfortable; perhaps by challenging the mediator's GDPR compliance, or by referring to mediation process guidelines.

This may continue until the inevitable neutrality of the mediator rises to the fore, at which point the narcissist is likely to turn on them and metaphorically lash out. Either way, it provides for a highly toxic environment, and not one within which a reasonable outcome can be constructed.

Mediation as an option is likely to be welcomed by the narcissist. It brings a new player to their game, with the joy of spinning the wheel for three people, alternating the roles of victim, perpetrator and rescuer. It provides an opportunity for direct contact with you which will be particularly attractive to them if you are already living separately, and it will undoubtedly be an opportunity to cause delays, rather than a forum for constructive negotiation.

Furthermore, the narcissist will be aware that the discussions in mediation cannot be referred to outside of that context, and that nothing they say is legally binding. They may therefore delight in pretending to explore options and build up your hopes – only to constantly change the goalposts at the last minute and then suggest that the others involved in the process, including the mediator, did not properly understand what they had intended.

This is a process which is unlikely to result in a settlement of any kind. It would be wrong to say that a mediated outcome is an impossible achievement, but it would need to be extremely carefully managed by the mediator. The following factors would need to be in place:

- The mediator fully understands what NPD is and the consequential behaviours which are likely to manifest

- The narcissist has their eye on an outcome which they would like to achieve

- That outcome is within the bracket of that which the court would see as reasonable

In the majority of cases, though, the narcissist will see mediation simply as a forum through which to increase costs and wear you down.

Hybrid mediation *

This may be a good option where your spouse is narcissistic. It results in a settlement in the majority of cases involving narcissists (perhaps in as many as 80%), and works out to be significantly quicker and cheaper than the court process.

> **" In the majority of cases the narcissist will see mediation simply as a forum through which to increase costs and wear you down. "**

Hybrid mediation is a fusion of the family and civil/commercial mediation models, undertaken by specially trained mediators. When you are looking for a mediator to work with it is a very good idea to check if they are trained in the hybrid model as this method is more likely to be successful if your spouse/partner suffers from NPD. The reasons for this are as follows:

- The mediator will have undertaken an advanced level of training and is more likely therefore to have the skill set to deal with your situation.

- Meetings will be held separately with each of the couple so you do not have to face your spouse across the table if you would prefer not to. This will appeal to both parties – to the grandiose personality of the narcissist who can 'perform' to the mediator, and to the spouse who will be spared from watching and enduring the display.

- The mediator can hold confidences in order to assist the negotiation which can be very helpful in achieving a settlement. This can reduce the opportunity for manipulation by the narcissist, as the mediator is very much in control of the process. It means that the non-narcissist can tell the mediator what they would be prepared to give ground over so that the mediator can guide the couple towards an outcome which makes the narcissist feel like they have won – but at the same time the other party has achieved the outcome (or as close to it as possible) that they were prepared to accept all along.

- Lawyers can be in attendance at some or all of the meetings as appropriate which provides enormous support.

For all of the reasons set out above, if you are going to consider mediation, the hybrid model is the one which may work best for you.

In order to persuade your narcissistic partner to agree to hybrid mediation your solicitor may wish to appeal to their sense of specialness and importance. Explaining that this is a cutting edge new method, which 'only the forward thinking people are doing' may be enough. If your narcissist has a sense of snobbishness and superiority, then also implying that the courts are seen as very much a place where 'ordinary' people end up, and 'not for cases like yours' may help convince them to engage. This method of securing the co-operation of your narcissistic partner may seem underhand to you, but, as you are learning, logical communication is not likely to work with someone who is experiencing narcissistic injury.

Hybrid mediation, with the correct team involved, is likely to be a method which will be in both of your best interests long term. It works out significantly cheaper than going through all of the stages of the court process, potentially saving tens of thousands of pounds, and can take just a few sessions to reach a resolution, shaving months or more off the resolution process. As described later in this section, it can also be combined with another method to form The Certainty Project, another excellent option where a narcissist is involved.

Collaborative practice

Adopting the collaborative approach is something which also should be considered with extreme caution where one of the couple is narcissistic. It may, in fact, be much less appropriate than mediation.

Collaborative practice is a process where the couple and their respective lawyers will sign an agreement known as a 'participation agreement' confirming that they will work together to achieve an acceptable outcome for the couple. They will confirm that neither of the couple will issue an application to court. All negotiations will take place via 'four way' meetings between the couple and their lawyers and all advice by each lawyer will be provided openly to the couple.

If, however, the collaborative process breaks down for any reason and agreement cannot be achieved, both parties must change their legal representation. Narcissists are highly likely to change solicitor often and therefore this will not cause them a problem at all. For you, though, it brings in a very subtle and unattractive form of control. You may have formed a strong working bond with your lawyer, in whom you have confidence and from whom you gain support. This, in turn, may provide you with the strength to stand up to your narcissistic spouse/partner; perhaps something very uncharacteristic and which the narcissist really doesn't like. The perceived bond between you and your lawyer may be a bond which the narcissist badly wants to break. The collaborative approach provides the perfect opportunity to do that.

Collaborative practice may appeal to the narcissist for additional reasons:

- It provides an otherwise unusual chance to meet the solicitor on the other side at an early stage. The narcissist can charm and flatter them in the hope of creating a relationship of friendliness and 'banter' which unsettles their spouse/partner.

- Having met the lawyer on the other side they can be critical and undermining of that lawyer to their spouse/partner, pretending to be helpful.

- They can perpetually move the goalposts, prolonging the process and increasing the cost.

- By behaving badly, they can try to force the other side's lawyer to call time on the process. This makes their spouse or partner's lawyer look like the 'bad guy' for causing their own client the added distress of having to find a replacement lawyer.

For all of these reasons the collaborative approach should be avoided.

The Certainty Project *

The Certainty Project is a new method of working established in 2020. As such it is likely to appeal to the grandiose side of the narcissist's personality as being a new and forward focused way of resolving issues for the separating couple, and it may be a good option overall.

The court system is sadly in a very poor state, largely as a consequence of under-funding. The Certainty Project provides a means of private and cost effective adjudication, mirroring the benefits of the court process, but at the same time offering the couple the opportunity to create their own settlement with the assistance of their lawyers and an accredited mediator.

Having instructed solicitors the first step will be to appoint an 'arbitrator' whose role is to have overall control of the process, and who acts as a judge. You will find details of specialist arbitrators on the IFLA website (Institute of Family Law Arbitrators) where it will be clear which ones deal with finances and which deal with child related issues – some deal with both. The arbitrator will be the point of reference for the case. A preliminary meeting will be arranged with the arbitrator to discuss the scope of the case and to appoint a mediator. The arbitrator will be on board to deal with any issues of process or interim issues, and their instant involvement helps things stay on track.

The solicitors will deal with the provision of disclosure (in financial cases) and will then refer the couple to the jointly instructed mediator. For the reasons outlined above, where one of the couple suffers from NPD, the hybrid mediation process is likely to be the preferable option.

If the couple are able to reach agreement on all issues the mediator will prepare a Memorandum of Understanding. The couple will then each take advice on that document, which sets out the proposals from their respective lawyers. If both are happy to proceed the arbitrator will make an 'award by consent' in financial proceedings or a 'determination by consent' in child proceedings.

The last stage, in financial proceedings, is to apply for this to be finalised into a consent order by the court. In children proceedings a court order may not be necessary as it is preferred that there is no court order if the parents are able to agree arrangements. You might, however, want to set out those arrangements in a 'child arrangements plan' which would be signed by both parents as a binding and enforceable agreement. Child arrangements plans are discussed in detail in Chapter 11.

If some or all issues can't be agreed, the matter will pass back into the hands of the arbitrator who will make an adjudication, where they make the final, legally binding, decisions as to what happens.

The whole process is expected to last no more than six months, a very much shorter period than the duration of an application through the court. The cost, both in monetary and emotional terms, will be significantly less. It is also much easier for your lawyer to give you a 'worst case scenario' costs quote at the outset. If you settle matters at an earlier stage within the process then your costs will be less.

There is much to commend the structure and certainty of this way of working and it is certainly something which you should discuss both with your own lawyer and in a Mediation Information and Assessment Meeting as a possible option.

Neutral evaluation *

If your case involves some difficult legal issues such as how assets which were acquired prior to the marriage or inherited during the marriage should be treated, you may want to ask for the view of a neutral evaluator at the outset before both parties become positional and intransigent. Both parties would, through their lawyers, instruct a neutral evaluator who would probably be an arbitrator by qualification (although does not need to be) to provide their view on the issue or issues in order to assist the future negotiation. This can be used in advance of or during any of the processes referred to here. The cost would be borne equally between the couple or as otherwise agreed.

The private FDR

The point at which most cases, not involving a narcissist, settle within the court process is at or shortly after the Financial Dispute Resolution Appointment (the FDRA). This is described in detail in Chapter 10. This procedure can be replicated on a private basis. You would choose your 'judge', again probably from a list of qualified arbitrators (although they do not need to be so qualified) and each side will put their position across. The 'judge' will give an indication of what they think of the merits of the case of each party and try to help them to reach an agreement. Note that the judge can't impose a decision on the couple at an FDRA (whether privately held or not) – they can only give advice as to what they think would be reasonable. In other words, they can give their assessment of what they think a judge might impose upon the couple if the case could not be settled by negotiation, and had to be decided at a 'final' court hearing.

The benefits of the private process are that you can choose your time and venue and have a 'judge' exclusively at your disposal for the day. The cost of the 'judge' would be borne by the couple in equal shares. However, this is not the best route to take with a narcissistic spouse if you are hoping to agree a settlement at this stage, as the view of the judge as to the best solution is just that – a view, which the narcissist can simply choose to disregard. It is therefore potentially a way for the narcissist to rack up more costs and reduce the available financial marital pot. Arbitration, however, (see below) is a good alternative when a narcissistic party is involved.

Arbitration *

Arbitration is the private alternative to the final hearing in the normal court route, which is usually the third court hearing. In arbitration, an 'arbitrator' makes a decision as to the outcome of your case, essentially acting as a judge. If you decide to go down the arbitration route there is no need to have the first two stages in the traditional court process (FDA and FDRA) should you choose not to. If, however, you think you might benefit from a private FDR to be helped to reach your own decision without something being imposed you can do so, although, as detailed above, this may not work with a narcissist. Arbitration is an entirely bespoke process so you can do whatever you think is helpful to resolve the case. The rules are, however, that you would have to use a different arbitrator to preside over a private FDR to the one you use for the final arbitration.

In the traditional court process, the couple only pay for their solicitors and barristers – they do not pay for the judge's time. However, in arbitration, the arbitrator *is* paid a fee (shared between the couple).

Because of this additional cost, a common misconception is that arbitration is more expensive that the traditional court process. This is completely incorrect. One of the benefits of arbitration is that it is a much quicker method of resolution than the court process and legal fees will be less – usually by at least a third.

Aside from this obvious and important benefit the advantages of arbitration are as follows:

- You can choose your arbitrator from the list found on the IFLA (Institute of Family Law Arbitration). The arbitrator will be dedicated to your case. They will have the time to read all the papers properly – sadly, this is not always the case in the normal overstretched court system.

- You can choose your date and venue.

- The process is bespoke and will be tailored to best suit your particular case.

- The matter will be resolved far more quickly and cost effectively than can be achieved within the traditional court system.

- It is in the arbitrator's interests to do a good job of deciding what is fair and reasonable, as their reputation as an arbitrator and future work depends upon it.

If you are to arbitrate, both parties must be in agreement. (It should be noted that the narcissist may want to cause delay and unnecessary cost and therefore may not be prepared to agree.)

The first step is to arrange a pre-commitment meeting with the arbitrator. The purpose of this meeting is to discuss:

- The scope of the process and the issues in the case

- Whether the decision should be made 'on paper' or whether there should be an oral hearing

- The arbitrator's fee

You can undergo arbitration for both financial proceedings and children proceedings.

Firstly, the Arb1fs (financial proceedings) or Arb1cs (children proceedings) is drafted and signed by the parties, binding the couple to the process.

The arbitrator makes a decision based either on written submissions or following oral evidence at a formal hearing.

In financial proceedings an 'Award' will be provided by the arbitrator. The lawyers then re-write this as a consent order which they then submit to the court for a judge to approve. If they do, it is converted into a legally binding consent order. The judge ensures that the decision made by the arbitrator is fair and something which the court is prepared to ratify.

In children proceedings it will be a 'Determination' that is made by the arbitrator. With children proceedings it is preferred that there should not be an order of the court unless essential, so this Determination may or may not be submitted to the court. If, however, one party does not adhere to the terms of the Determination, it can be submitted to the court at a later stage for enforcement.

The arbitrator must be paid before the Award or Determination will be provided. If one party refuses to pay their share of the fee the other can pay in full and be reimbursed under the terms of the Award or Determination.

If, during the arbitration, one of the couple refuses to provide financial disclosure when required or to comply with any other direction an application can be made to court to deal with enforcement. It is likely that the party whose failing has necessitated the application to court will be ordered to pay the costs.

Arbitration is an integral part of The Certainty Project which combines the support of a mediator, to help the couple reach their own agreement, with the over-arching support and control of the arbitrator who can make a decision if required.

In summary, if your partner is narcissistic, you may wish to try to resolve financial or child related matters out of court. Classic mediation or the collaborative process are unlikely to be suitable in your case, and a private FDR may also not be the best option.

However, if you were to consider mediation, you may want to look at the 'hybrid model' which includes the protection of separate meetings, the ability to hold confidences and the support of your lawyer within the process. If it is inevitable that an agreement cannot be achieved by negotiation, and that a judge will have to make the final decision, 'arbitration' may be highly suitable. Finally, The Certainty Project, with its combination of formulating your own outcome through (hybrid) mediation plus having an adjudication on any issues where agreement cannot be reached, has much to commend it. Remember that the narcissist has to agree to undertake these methods, and appealing to their grandiosity and sense of specialness may be a necessary part of persuasion.

A brief look at the standard court method of financial dispute resolution

This is the route that most people who are involved with a narcissistic spouse find themselves taking in divorce and it is the most difficult and expensive option for all concerned. We discuss the court process in detail in Chapter 10, but summarise it here.

- **The Form E**. This is a form that is filled in by both spouses, to show the current finances. It includes everything including property owned, income, expenditure, pensions and company assets.

- **The Draft Questionnaire**. This is a list of questions raised by both parties to clarify financial information or ask for information that is missing from the other side's Form E.

- **The FDA**. This is the First Directions Appointment. It is the first court hearing. Here a judge decides which questions from your draft questionnaire can be asked of your spouse, and vice versa, and imposes a deadline for these to be answered by.

- **The FDRA**. This is the Financial Dispute Resolution Appointment. It is the second court hearing. Here your lawyer (often a barrister) puts your case forward to a judge, and your spouse's barrister does the same. The judge then tries to help you to reach an agreement. The judge can't impose a decision on the couple at an FDRA – they can only give advice as to what they think would be reasonable. In other words, they can give their assessment of what they think a judge might impose upon the couple if the case could not be settled by negotiation, and had to be decided at a 'final' court hearing. Many 'normal' cases settle at this point, or in the weeks after the FDRA, although narcissists tend to want to go all the way to the next stage, the final hearing.

- **The Final Hearing or Final Trial**. This may also be called an 'adjudication', a 'contested hearing', or a 'defended hearing'. It is the only part of court proceedings where you have to speak – here you will be cross-examined on the witness stand by your spouse's barrister, and your barrister will cross-examine them. A judge will then make the final decision regarding how your finances will be split. This is an expensive process to undertake, and can go on for more than a day.

"The court method of financial dispute resolution is the most difficult and expensive option for all concerned. "

A brief look at the court method of dealing with issues relating to the children

Rather than dealing with child issues through the court process, these are far better resolved via methods which maintain and support ongoing communication between parents, such as mediation (hybrid or classic). The main reason for this is that children's needs change as they get older, and therefore the rigidity of a court order can create more problems than it solves. It may simply give rise to ongoing litigation which may dominate the children's early life – and provide constant fuel for the narcissistic parent.

In some circumstances, however, the court process is the only option. This is dealt with in more detail in Chapter 10 but we set out the basics below.

The application

To make the application you will have to fill in a Form C100, with Form C1A if there is an allegation of harm. The applicant must attend a MIAM before an application can be issued except in exceptional circumstances.

You will be asked if you application is 'urgent'. Of course, anything which involves your children will be urgent, but it is important that this is put into context. The court is dealing with allegations of serious harm, abduction etc. Whether you can see your child on an extra midweek evening in addition to existing contact will not be seen as 'urgent'. Some applications i.e. those which involve a holiday or change of school may be time sensitive and therefore need to be dealt with ahead of a particular deadline.

The First Hearing Dispute Resolution Appointment (FHDRA)

At this first appointment the court will look at the issues, decide whether a fact finding hearing is necessary (where issues of disputed facts need to be determined) and order a section 7 report to be prepared by a CAFCASS officer. This will, among other things, consider the child 'welfare checklist' and the wishes and feelings of the children.

The Dispute Resolution Appointment (DRA)

This mirrors the FDRA in financial proceedings. The judge will try to help the parents reach agreement. This takes place in court.

Final Hearing

In the event that the parents are unable to reach a decision the court will impose an order.

Where you are dealing with a co-parent who has NPD, child issues may arise more often than usual. The most important thing is to ensure that you find a way to deal with these issues, which may arise regularly, in a way that best enables you to co-parent and protects the welfare of your children. Here, preparing a detailed 'child arrangements plan' is very important, as you want to cover every potential issue to provide clear guidelines for the future. We cover this in detail in Chapter 11.

Narcissistic divorce behaviours

8

I n divorce or separation, narcissists may behave terribly, but they behave *predictably* terribly. They cannot (even if they were the ones to end the relationship) accept any blame whatsoever, so instead they vilify their former partner. Everything has to be their partner's fault – they are suddenly seen as 'all bad' and they themselves are 'all good'. (Remember how narcissists aren't able to see others or themselves realistically, as a blend of good and bad traits, but can only see them as one or the other?).

Combine this with the narcissistic injury they have suffered at having lost one of their primary sources of narcissistic supply, and at having had their perfect life exposed as imperfect, and you have a recipe for disaster. Narcissistic rage will spew forth, and the narcissist will stop at nothing to try to annihilate you, in every possible way. They will try to punish you financially, emotionally, physically, mentally, spiritually and maybe even physically, depending on their particular brand.

Their sense of entitlement will be particularly evident, and they will expect *everything*, from the marital assets and money, to the children, pets and wedding china, and especially things with sentimental value to you.

Every abusive behaviour, if they were subtle to begin with, will now be ramped up to a level 10. You will certainly be in no doubt that narcissism is at play through the divorce process, if you weren't completely sure before. Because they are severely lacking in true empathy, they cannot care what this is doing to a fellow human being – even if you are the parent of their children.

Take note. Narcissists don't want a resolution of matters. They don't want a swift, fair conclusion. As soon as you think you may be getting close, they will shift the goalposts, and have you tearing your hair out. Why? Because they need their last giant hit of narcissistic supply from you for as long as they can have it. And then, once they've done that, they need to top it off by winning. These are *needs* for the narcissist, whether they realise it or not, but they will justify their behaviour on the grounds that you deserved it.

The two case histories that follow are typical of narcissistic divorce behaviours. They have not been exaggerated.

Case Histories

Martin

Martin, aged 45

My marriage of 12 years, to Natalie, unravelled in a way that I could never have imagined. Things started to really fall apart after ten years, although the warning signs had always been there, looking back. She started to openly conduct affairs, meeting men online and rubbing my face in it. Bragging to me about how great the sex was with these strangers, and staying out all night. At first she had the decency to pretend that she was staying at a friend's house, but later she didn't even bother to lie. It was as if she was trying to hurt me deliberately, to see how far she could push me. She seemed almost smug. She used to taunt me, sometimes in front of our 11 year old son, telling me that she knew I loved her far too much to ever leave her, no matter what she did. To make matters worse, she would go from cold heartless adulteress, to softly spoken and caring within minutes. I was in pieces, and found it hard to cope with her monstrous cruelty. I could barely eat, and my mind would race all day and night as I tried to make sense of it all.

As soon as I mentioned divorce, on the grounds of adultery, Natalie changed her tune, sometimes saying that she had been joking about the affairs and other times saying that she would never admit to them; that she'd make me wait two years to divorce her. I realised much later that she believed that admitting to adultery would affect how much money she would get in her divorce settlement. But also, everything had to be done on Natalie's terms. She always had to play the victim, and get her own way, and nothing, absolutely nothing, could ever be her fault.

I went to see a solicitor, and we decided on unreasonable behaviour as grounds for divorce as being the most likely thing Natalie would admit to. My solicitor and I decided to hold off until after my son's entrance exams for secondary school, a couple of months later. But the very next day, my own letter arrived. It seemed Natalie had beaten me to it, true to form, and was divorcing me on those same grounds, with no consideration of how the timing would affect our son's exams. She included the fact that I had moved to the spare room (due to her affairs) as one of my unreasonable behaviours, and that this had meant no intimacy between us, which made her feel unloved. It was quite ridiculous, but I accepted the blame and agreed to the divorce.

The next day, I discovered that she had cleared out the joint account, from which the mortgage was due to be paid. I confronted her immediately, and she claimed that she'd done it because she "knew I had thousands stashed away". When I told her that it wouldn't make her look good in the divorce, she returned the money. When it came to Natalie, I had already worked out that what people thought of her mattered, although I hadn't worked out why. For tax purposes, I had been putting money into accounts and an ISA in her own name, rather than into mine, as she wasn't earning. The irony was that all I had was the relatively small amount of money in the joint account. She had all the rest, tens of thousands, and I had no access to it. Over the divorce, she took to gloating about this, calling me 'an idiot' for setting up these accounts for her in the first place.

It transpired that Natalie had chosen an expensive divorce lawyer known for high net worth cases – something I definitely wasn't, even as a finance director for a moderately successful London firm. She was convinced that I was hiding money, and she would regularly tell me how her solicitor, who was 'the best', found the things I said 'ridiculous', and had nicknames for me. I look back and realise how silly that seems now, but I did believe her at the time, and it did unsettle me. She was good at ridiculing me, and undermining my confidence – she'd been doing it for years.

Martin

Natalie had decided that she was going to stay in our Georgian home, with our son, and that I was going to bankroll her for the rest of her life, as well as pay our son's school fees. There was no way, in her book, that she should have to work, especially with her back/knees/shoulder/tiredness (which she hadn't had a problem with before). She felt entitled to it. It was her due. She told me that her solicitor had told her that this would be the outcome, and I would just have to rent a small flatshare somewhere. I was shocked and scared, until my poor solicitor, who very kindly listened to my fears, assured me that this would definitely not be the case. My solicitor must have thought I was weak and pathetic – after all, this is how I felt. I cringe at how I must have appeared all through this time, looking back.

We had one mediation session but the mediator had quickly realised that mediation was not a viable option as Natalie had made a point of hissing accusations loudly at me every time I tried to answer a question. She rolled her eyes and called me a 'liar' over and over. When it was Natalie's turn to answer questions, she would simply rant about what she deserved, and how she wouldn't be able to work because of her various ailments. The mediator seemed pleased when the time came to usher us out of her office. I was deeply embarrassed. Natalie thought it had gone well, and that the mediator had agreed with her.

Natalie would treat our son as a confidant, and I would return from work to be met by him and his worries. "Mummy's been shouting all day. She says you are going to ruin our lives because you don't want us to live here anymore. She says that we are going to have to move to a small house and be poor. She says you meet girlfriends in the pub and you don't love her anymore... She says that you forced her to get divorced..." I knew then that moving out was not an option, and that I had to stay to protect my son.

It took two years to come to a conclusion. By the end, I was on my knees. Natalie would be out when I returned home from London every day at 8pm, and our son would be anxiously waiting for me, still in his school uniform, unfed, homework not done. On the rare occasions that I would go out, to vent to a male friend, she would shout after me, so our son could hear, "Don't forget to use a condom!" It was degrading, being

Martin

accused of all the things that she was doing, in front of our young son.

Natalie would terrorise me whenever we were in the house together. She would tell me that she was moving to Australia (where she had family) with our son, and would text me house details of places she was considering. She would excitedly tell our son of her plans, in front of me, and tell him how wonderful it would be. She genuinely didn't believe me when I told her that she needed my consent to move out of the country with our son, and more solicitors' letters were required to make her see sense.

Years of Natalie's out of control spending had taken its toll on our bank balance. Designer clothes, shoes and bags were a necessity to her, and she had developed a penchant for antique jewellery auctions. She decided that buying expensive wine for laying down as an investment would be a good idea as she fancied herself as an expert, but would often just open the wine for visitors to impress them with her knowledge. One year, she even spent all of my bonus on a two seater sports car for herself, without any consultation.

Natalie's Form E reflected her unrealistic expectations, and she stated her financial needs as being more than my annual income. At the FDA her legal team raised ridiculous questions, such as how many air miles I had, and whether she should be entitled to the cash equivalent of half the value. She even suggested that our son's trust fund, set up by my father with us both as trustees, should be counted as one of my assets, and suggested that a forensic accountant be employed to look into my finances as she thought I was hiding my true income.

The highly irritable judge gave the impression that I was at fault, and impatiently suggested I "talk sensibly with my wife around the kitchen table". He clearly had no idea how unproductive that would be, unfamiliar as he was with Natalie's screaming tantrums and plate smashing. Natalie rapidly nodded her head to this, whilst making a show of dabbing at her eyes, ever the victim. I felt like this man just didn't have a clue, and didn't care about those in front of him enough to look behind the show being presented to him. It was humiliating, being spoken to in this way. I quickly learned that in the court process you were handing over your fate to a judge who might have got out of bed on the wrong side that day, or not had enough coffee, or be tired or hungry. It seemed that those factors, as well as whether he or she liked your face or not could determine how you got to live the rest of your life. It didn't exactly inspire me with confidence.

When it slowly dawned on Natalie that our finances weren't as good as she had hoped, she decided to email the CEO of my company and tell her that I was terrible with money, a cocaine abuser, and a violent, abusive man. The CEO called me into her office and showed me the email. I was shaking as I read it. I don't know whether it was more out of fear or anger. I'd worked at the company for five years, and had restructured its finances in that time. Thankfully, the CEO didn't believe a word of it, and recounted the horrors of her own divorce a few years earlier. That email was forwarded on to Natalie's solicitor by mine, and she was asked to desist. It still did not stop her from making verbal threats to tell my professional body lies about me. It was only when I pointed out that her destroying my career would mean that I wouldn't be able to afford to give her maintenance that she stopped. By this time, things had got so bad that I was refusing to speak to her without openly recording her.

After the FDA, Natalie seemed to realise that she wouldn't be getting the family house, so she starting cornering me, trying to get me to agree to letting her stay there with our son until he was 18, whilst recording me. Eventually, after letter after letter, she accepted that the house would have to be sold, but even then she insisted upon making things difficult. She initially refused to agree to market the house at the middle valuation we had received, insisting that the wildly unrealistic top valuation should be tried first. More letters flew back and forth about this. She even made it difficult for house viewings to take place, saying that the timings proposed 'weren't convenient'. She was clearly under the impression that house prices would increase if she delayed the process.

One evening, I found Natalie in my bedroom, trying out different combinations on the safe I had bought to lock away my divorce-related paperwork. She didn't even seem embarrassed that she had been caught, instead asking me if I would forward her details of any houses that I would find acceptable to live in. She had been asked to find some by her solicitor, for court, but 'couldn't be bothered' and so expected me to do it for her. That was typical of Natalie. If it wasn't high drama or fun, she wasn't going to do it, and she turned her nose up at having to look online at the type of tiny, insalubrious house that she expected me to end up in.

As usual, Natalie kept everyone waiting for her. She had always hated paperwork, and so was delaying signing some essential forms required so that our pensions could be assessed for a pension sharing arrangement. Eventually, a junior solicitor from her firm turned up at the house with the forms, all filled in, and made her sign them on the doorstep so that the information could be released and the actuarial report written. It looked unlikely that the report would be ready in time for the FDRA, and my legal team were expecting to have to postpone the FDRA at the last minute as a result. The report arrived just the day before the FDRA, and everyone, except Natalie, let out a collective sigh of relief.

Her 'offer' at the FDRA was that she wanted 95% of the equity in the house, as well as double the spousal maintenance we had offered. She had included in her paperwork a letter from her GP surgery, stating that she was medically unfit for work. Conspicuously, the letter was unsigned, with no GP having put their name to it, and I still have no idea how she got it. Her barrister was shut down immediately by the female judge, who deemed the offer unreasonable, and the letter inadmissible. Natalie, who had turned up in a low cut top, figure hugging skirt and bright red lipstick, presumably expecting a male judge, was fuming, and stormed out of the courtroom muttering that at least it would be a better judge at the next hearing. Her solicitor and barrister shuffled papers, both bright red.

I was exhausted. Living with this, day in day out, was taking its toll on me, and even though I'd managed to stay strong for our son so far, I felt like the blood coursing round my veins was acidic at times; toxic. I felt like this was literally going to be the death of me, and a physical illness wouldn't be far away unless I got off this roundabout. I just couldn't face the idea of going to trial. After discussion with my solicitor we made a counter offer. Eventually, six weeks after the FDRA, we settled on Natalie getting 82.5% of the equity in the house, and substantial maintenance, so that she, unlike me, would be mortgage free.

Martin

Eventually, after some months, we got a reasonable offer for the house. Initially, and predictably, Natalie refused the offer, saying that it was too low, but she eventually relented. Of course, we weren't out of the woods just yet.

There were four houses in the chain, but Natalie refused to accept the proposed exchange date because the house she had decided to buy was still being built, and wouldn't be ready for another four months. She felt that everyone in the chain should either delay their exchange dates to fit in with her or agree to pay interim rent for her until her house was completed. Yet again, she was trying to control the process. An urgent court date was scheduled, and the judge ordered that Natalie accept the exchange date, and suggested she pay her own rent.

That night, she dialled 999 and the police attended the house. She told them that she wanted me out of the house as she 'hated' me. Our son saw the whole thing. Thankfully, she didn't make any allegations of abuse, and she received a stern telling off for wasting police time. But I was shocked, even after everything, at just how low she would go.

Even with the house sold, Natalie was still playing games. Just one week before we were due to complete on the house sale, I found some particulars for properties over 100 miles away on the hall table. It seemed that Natalie, having secured a financial settlement in order to buy a house locally (in expensive commuter belt Surrey) was, in reality, planning to take our son much further away. Yet again, letters flew back and forth, and Natalie brazenly defended her actions on the grounds that she would be able to buy much grander property in Somerset than she could in Surrey, and that our son was old enough to travel on his own on the train to visit me, provided I paid his train fare. My legal team decided that we would have to threaten to take her back to court on the grounds that she had made material misstatements at the FDRA, and my heart sank once more. Thankfully, she relented, and went back to the original plan to buy a house locally.

I cried the day I walked into my tiny new house on an estate just a mile away from my old house, the house I had once loved. But they were tears of relief. I was free of Natalie, although my son was not. It was only the following year that I heard the term narcissistic personality disorder, and everything slowly fell into place.

I continue to receive multiple texts from Natalie every now and then, threatening me with court, asking for more money, and telling me how difficult her life is. She regularly tries to stop our son from visiting me, according to him, but our father-son relationship remains good. She gets angry at me often, but I never see her face to face these days. Most recently, she accused me, by text, of not caring about her when I ignored her birthday. She occasionally still asks me to pay for her private health insurance, as she is the 'mother of our child'. She regularly threatens to tell my new partner what a terrible husband and father I am. I have learned to ignore all of this, with my new found understanding of her personality disorder, and am slowly rebuilding my life and finances. Two years post-divorce, the future finally feels full of possibility.

Annie

Annie, aged 42

It was only after 19 years of marriage that I realised that my husband had narcissistic personality disorder, through a book given to me by a friend who happened to be a psychologist. It was such an odd realisation – a combination of lightbulb moment after lightbulb moment coupled with long periods of disbelief. The confusion consumed me. How could these two versions of the man I had loved for so long both be true? Was everything I had believed just been a lie? We'd said in sickness and in health. Was NPD a sickness? What if his behaviour was a sign of something more sinister? A brain tumour maybe? What kind of a wife would I be if I left him in illness? Did he ever love me? The painful truth eventually dawned. He had not. He had loved what I could do for him, and how much I had adored him, but not me. The relationship I was deeply grieving hadn't even been real. I felt guilty for my own grief.

I had wanted to leave him for ten years. For the first five of those I had been too scared, as he had threatened to 'make my life hell' if I ever even thought about it. For the last five I had got close many times, but he had always drawn me back in with tender, heartfelt apologies, excuses that he was depressed (but with none of the tell-tale signs) and short lived promises that he would change.

In the end, I divorced him on the grounds of unreasonable behaviour, beaten down by years of being told that I was a bad person, unattractive, boring and a gold digger, and fed up with being a doormat. I didn't divorce him for adultery – he'd had several affairs with young impressionable girls from the office over the years, but he'd always blamed them on my failures as a wife, and I'd accepted the blame. We'd had an oddly calm discussion about it at the beginning of the divorce. He told me that as unreasonable behaviour made him 'look better', he wanted me to cite that instead of adultery. Bizarrely, the irony of how controlling that was was lost on me until much later.

What stood out to me was how surprised others were – it seemed to them that we'd had the perfect marriage. But their support didn't last long, as my rich, successful, debonair, charismatic husband played the role of victim, telling lies about me and my character. So many friends and family chose to believe him, and followed him, like children dancing behind the Pied

Piper, completely entranced. But those few who knew the real story, those closest to me, remained unfalteringly loyal. They could see through his false charm.

My husband had quickly withdrawn all the remaining money in the joint account after a few weeks of me starting proceedings. I was forced to cash in the small ISA I had in my name to spend on the basics and mounting legal fees. I applied for two 0% credit cards, forced to lie about my income to get them (which was nil) in order to get by.

My lawyers spent hours negotiating a figure for interim maintenance from him. Every time we seemed to be getting close he changed his mind, and he refused to pay any money at all for the duration of the court process, which lasted 18 months. He removed the home computer, so that I was left with only my phone for internet access and emails, and took all the utility bills, bank statements and financial information from the house. He also took all the family photos, including those from my own childhood, which I never saw again. He even cancelled Sky TV and the TV licence. His collection of five classic cars disappeared one night, never to be seen again, and he refused to provide my solicitors with information as to where they had gone until the final hearing when he explained that he had given three of them away to friends as thank you gifts for their support during the divorce. He calmly explained to my barrister that they hadn't been worth much anyway, as they were 'just old cars'.

Over this time, my husband lied to our twin 15 year old daughters, explaining to them that I had had a ten year affair with a good university friend of mine (whom they had known their whole lives). He claimed that that was the true reason for our divorce. They told me how he had sat them down individually and pretended to cry, telling them that he was suicidal, wiping away invisible tears from his dry eyes as he 'sobbed'. Neither one had been fooled.

In spite of his purported grief, he had found a new relationship with breathtaking speed, and moved into a rented flat in London with his new girlfriend after just a few weeks. This young girlfriend became pregnant alarmingly quickly, to my husband's expressed delight to his horrified daughters. They were even more shocked when he suggested that they live

Annie

with him and his new girlfriend full time. He expected them to leave their school, their friends and their mother. He even threatened to stop paying for their private schooling, unless they agreed to a new private school in London. He was true to his word. When they refused, not only did he stop paying school fees, he told them that he would be taking the family cat with him to London, as he had bought it, and so technically 'it' was his. Various letters from his solicitor about the elderly cat followed, wasting time and money. They only stopped when his girlfriend told him of her cat allergy. The situation was ridiculous.

My husband immediately proceeded to make claims of parental alienation against me through his solicitor instead. He claimed that I had guilt tripped and badmouthed our twins into not wanting to see him, failing to mention their distress when he had introduced his pregnant girlfriend to them without warning. It transpired that he had made them go shopping with her for maternity outfits in Harrods, telling them that this would be a bonding experience. The fact that the girlfriend was spending on his credit cards whilst his own daughters were being made to wear second hand school uniform didn't seem to register with either adult. The hypocrisy was not lost on the girls, however, and yes, they did pull away from him then, hurt and confused.

Just before the FDA, my GP rang me to tell me that social services had been informed that I was an abusive alcoholic and that I had been beating one of our girls. It wasn't hard to see who had made that claim, and thankfully it went no further, but I was frightened to death at what would be coming next, living in a permanent state of terror. My husband's solicitor simply denied it all.

I received so many phone calls from my husband that I disconnected my landline phone and blocked him from my mobile, one of the few pieces of advice I did receive from my solicitors. He would alternate between ranting and telling me how bad my lawyers were to how we should just settle things between ourselves, to how he hoped we could be friends. It was exhausting.

I'll be frank. My lawyers let me down through the divorce. I have no doubt that they meant well, and I know they felt for me, but I needed more than that. They would smile at me pityingly as I tried to explain what I was learning about narcissists, and how they were pathological liars, in their element in the court process. I would desperately try to get them to understand that this wasn't me being bitter, but rather that my husband had no respect for the rules and that he would bend them at every opportunity. They looked at me with kindness, but as if I was simply a hysterical woman, going through a difficult time.

They didn't know that who they saw was a far cry from the formidable tower of strength that I once had been – a rational, former Fleet Street political journalist. I felt so foolish. So embarrassed of the person I appeared to be to them. "He's just upset because you left him. He'll calm down soon" they said. "Of course he's got your daughters' best interests at heart - he's their father!" "He'd never do that! It wouldn't be in his interests!" "He's just a difficult man." "We don't find it useful to label people." These were refrains I heard so often that I ended up questioning my own reality, much as I had throughout my marriage.

I would send the lawyers information about NPD which I would insist they read so that they would be better equipped to deal with my case. I would then be billed for the time they spent reading it, but no adjustments to how my case was being handled seemed to result until we were a year down the line. By this point I had made prediction after prediction regarding my husband's behaviour, all of which had been met with slightly raised eyebrows by my legal team. All of those predictions had eventually materialised, and by the time the penny had dropped for my lawyers it was far too late for me. By the end, I was disillusioned and had lost all faith in the system. The fact that my lawyers had been 'nice' to me hadn't been enough. I had needed effectiveness. I had needed to be *believed*.

Throughout the divorce I was a wreck, utterly distraught – totally incapable of making the decisions that my lawyers kept asking me to make. What I needed was advice, or at least to be given some options with accompanying potential ramifications. I received virtually none, and the junior lawyer who was mainly dealing with my case explained to me that it was only her job to 'take my instructions'. It didn't seem to matter how blindly my instructions were arrived at, nor how reactive they

Annie

were on my part. I felt unheard, unsupported and helpless to change my fortunes – all feelings I had become very used to during my marriage. Feelings which, in retrospect, were being unwittingly perpetuated by my own lawyers.

I even felt judged. That because I had given up my job, at the request of my husband when we had had the twins, I somehow deserved this. That I should have known better. That as I had enjoyed the material benefits of his success as his wife but had chosen to leave after 19 years, even after years of abuse, I shouldn't be complaining now.

I didn't have the energy to fight. I was waking every night at 2am, unable to get back to sleep, terrified at the prospect of my blank future stretching out in front of me. A future which I had given away, in the name of love, to a man whose sole intention now seemed to be to crush me so that I would no longer be an inconvenience in his life. At times it was hard to breathe.

The letters from my husband's solicitor came thick and fast, and we spent hours upon hours responding to each point, every false accusation and every unreasonable demand. He was CEO of a big company – he was used to getting his way, and used to winning. He wasn't going to change now. He wanted answers to the pettiest of questions and I just thought that if I didn't give them, the judge would view *me* as the problem in court and this would affect my settlement. My legal bill, sadly, reflected this, and the financial pot waned further as a result. Of course, I came to realise that this had all been part of my husband's game plan. He would rather give the money to solicitors he didn't even know than to his daughters or their mother. It was very clever, how he managed to get my own solicitors to be the tools of his financial abuse.

Throughout the divorce, my husband came and went as he pleased, rifling through my paperwork when I was not around, taking things of sentimental value to me (including things that pre-dated our relationship), and suggesting when I complained through my lawyers that it would be illegal for me to change the locks of the family home. I eventually did so anyway, and received a threatening and bullying letter as a result.

My ex-husband refused to contribute to the upkeep of the marital home. He tried, through his solicitors, to get me to market it at below the market value, threatening court action repeatedly if I did not agree. He charmed the estate agent into agreeing to lower the asking price and told him to publicise that it was a divorce sale and that we would look at low offers. I suspect that he bribed him, but I had no evidence, and to have suggested so would have been in keeping with the mentally unstable picture my husband had painted of me. Again, my lawyers were unable to advise me as to the best course of action, but I held my ground, the house eventually selling for an acceptable sum. Needless to say, this all added to the stress I was under.

But it was when he sold the investment flat that we were renting out that things went from bad to worse. The flat had been in his name and he sold it completely without my knowledge. It was supposed to be our nest egg for our retirement, and I discovered, to my horror, that he had spent all £360,000 of the equity released by the sale in a matter of weeks. By the time I had realised it had gone, he had travelled to the Maldives with his pregnant girlfriend, bought her a new 4x4 Porsche and had sunk £100,000 into the stock market on bad investments, as well as paid off her debts and those of her mother. His solicitor would not be drawn on the subject, other than to justify the purchase of the car as necessary – as it was a safe vehicle with enough room for the paraphernalia required for a new baby. I don't know what sickened me more – the loss of all that money, or the smugness of that letter about my husband's new family.

My solicitors had the job of explaining to me that once the money had gone, that was it – it was out of the financial pot and there would be no recompense. They were surprised that my husband would waste money to his own detriment, and so had not anticipated it. None of us had fully appreciated the depths to which this man would sink to cause me pain.

It transpired that my husband was living in a flat in Notting Hill, with his girlfriend, costing him an eye-watering £7,500 a month, four times the cost of our mortgage payments. I was incredulous at how he could be allowed to run down our finances in this way. Even more confusing was how he would question every penny I spent in the supermarket, through his solicitor. A letter was sent just defending my decision to buy

Annie

a £35 toaster to replace one that had broken, that letter costing more than the toaster itself. It was sickening, and I could hardly bear to open my emails to see what correspondence my solicitors were forwarding on to me on a daily basis. I was haemorrhaging money that I didn't even have.

Suggestions had been made by his solicitor that I should reduce my outgoings by buying our daughters second-hand school uniform for the new school year – in fact we had already been forced to do this. My husband defended his decision to stop paying our daughters' school fees and letters flew back and forth about this, as I simply couldn't afford to pay. His solicitor suggested I asked my mother for money for school fees, and made the point that as she was old, she would probably die soon and leave me money in her will. It was suggested that this should be considered when determining how much, 'if any', spousal maintenance I should ultimately receive. Letters were sent in return explaining that my mother had no savings and did not even own her own house, which my husband already knew.

Three deadlines passed for exchanging our Form Es, and my husband's solicitor informed us on each date that we would have to delay as their client was a busy man and hadn't had time to complete his disclosure. On the day we eventually exchanged Form Es, I was shocked to discover that his financial disclosure was practically a carbon copy of mine, but with the amounts doubled. It seemed obvious to me that he had found my own Form E on one of his sneaky visits to the house and taken a copy. I asked my team whether this was legal, and whether we could do anything about it. They seemed flummoxed, and thought we had no real legal recourse – after all, I had no real proof. I had warned them weeks earlier that my husband didn't do the dull work of filling out forms, nor had he ever respected deadlines or rules, but they hadn't believed me. It felt as though the system that I thought would protect me was actually *allowing* my continued abuse. It was as if no one had a clue what to do with those who didn't follow their rules, so they did nothing.

I still wonder how my ex-husband's solicitor lives with herself, having sunk so low. How could she have spent 18 months barraging a broken woman like me with brutal letters full of threats and lies? Did she agree with his behaviour? She certainly enabled it. How was that even possible in a profession that was supposed to have standards? Was she a narcissist herself? What if she'd pushed me to suicide? A weaker person could easily have succumbed. Had that been her brief? It certainly seemed so. Would she have continued to sleep soundly through the night even then? Would she have been held accountable for her actions then?

My husband turned up an hour late to the FDRA, arriving just as both legal teams were wondering whether to leave. He refused to negotiate on all points, failed to provide his credit card statements, and left early as he was flying out to Dubai on holiday. He did, however, finally relent on paying our daughters' school fees, much to my relief. Even the judge seemed a little put out by his lack of engagement with the process. I was left reeling by the arguments that his team were making about my earning capacity, claiming that I just could walk back into my role as a broadsheet journalist, even though the landscape had changed completely in the 13 years since I had last worked. At one point, his barrister claimed that my husband knew I had a plot for a novel that was so excellent that it would be sure to be a bestseller, thereby reducing my need for spousal maintenance. I had to hand it to my husband – he had his whole legal team talking like him now, making ludicrous assertions of no substance.

By the final trial, I had lost two stone in weight, my hair was falling out, I was sleeping less than three hours per night, I was suffering from panic attacks and I was paranoid and on edge. Just two days before the trial, the gates of the house and the garage doors were rammed open in the middle of the night, but nothing was taken. I still don't know whether this was some sort of warning from my husband, and I never will, but it certainly had the effect of destabilising me even further.

I remember little of the trial, except how my husband played the victim, claiming that he had wanted to slow down at work for years, but that I had driven him to work so hard. He claimed that I had contributed nothing to the marriage at all, and portrayed me as a ruthless slavedriver. He was so convincing, even *I* felt sorry for him at one point, until I caught myself. He alternated between false tears and a chilling calm during his cross-examination. I wondered if anyone else found this odd. I remember noticing the contrast between my wedding

Annie

Annie

day and my own harrowing cross-examination. I found myself wondering how on earth I had got to this place, where I was having to fight for a percentage of the crumbs that remained of our finances – a shattered human, so very beaten down.

I remember walking out on to the street afterwards, squinting into the setting sun of the last day of my past, relieved. I thought that it was over, finally. But, of course, it is never really over with a narcissist, and he continues, to this day, to abuse our daughters, financially and psychologically. He remains emotionally unavailable to them, alternately blowing hot and cold, preferring one to the other at different times. They never really know where they stand with him, both torn between guilt and love.

The many people he turned against me by lying about my character have not returned, including some members of my own family, but I have come to terms with that and I have learned that trust is no longer something I freely give. Marriage is something I would never even contemplate again, not because of the concept of marriage per se but because of the realities of divorce.

What else have I learned? That there is no justice to be had, no fair outcome, when divorcing a narcissist. There is no winning, certainly not in a financial sense. But to be finally free of abuse is a win in itself – and, actually, that is enough for me.

Common narcissistic behaviours in divorce

Financial abuse

A high earning narcissist will happily reduce their own income and assets to punish their lower earning spouse. They will deliberately try to reduce what is left to divide up in the financial pot, even though it might also be to their own detriment - do not underestimate the lengths to which they will be prepared to go. The narcissist may:

- Spend excessively on luxury items and socialising.

- Give money away or buy unduly expensive gifts for others.

- Plunge money into unsuccessful business ventures.

- Sell assets, at vastly reduced prices, or give them away to friends or family.

- Delay taking drawings out of their own business.

- Forgo bonuses.

- Reduce their income. Note that successful narcissists, due to the nature of their personality disorder, are often self-employed, and so able to control their working hours and earnings. They will present this reduced income to the court as the amount any maintenance should be based on, and will increase earnings as soon as the divorce is finalised. Contemplating retirement is another oft used tactic.

- Overpay tax in line with their previous income (if they have reduced their income) so that a smaller amount is payable in the next financial year – effectively taking money out of the financial pot in the year of the divorce, to be returned to them post financial settlement.

- Claim illness and consequential inability to work.

- Encourage subordinates, staff, contractors or suppliers to make inflated financial claims, to increase their business outgoings.

- Insist on selling the family home at below the market value and encourage 'low ball' offers.

- Drive down the value of the family home by refusing to maintain it properly; publicise that this is a divorce situation so a quick sale is required; refuse to properly engage with an estate agent.

- Run up joint credit card debt.

- Withdraw large sums from joint accounts without explanation.

- Refuse to pay any form of financial support through the divorce process.

- Make false accusations against you so that you are forced to incur unnecessary legal fees defending yourself.

- Change goalposts when agreements have almost been reached, in order to run up legal bills.

- Stop essential payments, such as school fees, mortgage payments, utility payments, especially if you have no way of paying for these, or will have to eat into limited savings to do so.

- Use the children as tools of financial abuse e.g. by stopping paying for their activities in order to make the other, less affluent parent pay.

If the narcissist is the lower earner, a different pattern will emerge, although with some overlap. Their sense of entitlement will be pronounced, and their expectations will be enormous – to them, what's theirs is theirs, and what's yours is also theirs. They will also lie and manipulate in order to get their way. They may:

- Make wholly unreasonable financial demands, for example, expecting to be given the marital home mortgage-free without having to pay bills.

- Have inappropriate conversations with the children about possible future financial arrangements which unsettle them, in order to manipulate them into supporting them. This may include things such as saying that they will have to leave their school and move somewhere else, away from their friends; that they are going to be very poor due to the behaviour of the other parent; that they will have to move to a much smaller house.

- Make claims of ill health and inability to work.

- Run up joint credit card debt.

- Withdraw large sums from joint accounts without explanation.

- Make threats of blackmail (usually with lies, or twisted half-truths) in order to secure a better financial deal.

- Refuse to move out of or sell the family home or be obstructive with house viewings.

- Threaten to or actually stalk the other spouse, both online and in reality.

- Make false child support claims, perhaps claiming that an older child is in full time education when in fact they are working.

Emotional abuse

Narcissists need to be in control, and mentally destabilising their former spouse is a wonderful way to wield power and give them a sense of omnipotence. The drama that results is premium narcissistic supply. Tactics include:

- Stalking them both physically and online.

- Making threats of or actually carrying out surveillance by bugging the home, car or computer.

- Claiming that you have been abusive/violent towards the children as a way to reduce your contact with them or to limit your contact with them to supervised visits only, as a means to punish you.

- Claiming that the children do not wish to see you, are frightened of you, are adversely affected by contact with you (perhaps with allegations of bedwetting or nightmares after seeing you).

- Making claims of parental alienation against you.

- Enlisting the help of others ('flying monkeys' – called such from the helpers of the Wicked Witch of the West in the Wizard of Oz) to report on the activity of the spouse, or spread untrue and detrimental rumours about them to others.

- Intercepting mail or having it re-directed to themselves.

- Hacking emails or mobile phone.

- Removing all paperwork relating to joint finances from the family home or denying the spouse/partner access to any paperwork including the spouse's own.

- Refusing to move out of the family home, whilst continuing to engage in abusive behaviours.

- Openly conducting extra marital relationships during the separation process.

- Threatening to move the children far away/out of the jurisdiction of the court or even abroad.

- Threatening to blackmail the spouse, or their friends and family, if settlement terms are not accepted.

- Trying to manipulate their spouse into accepting reduced settlement/child arrangements plan through suggestions that the court will decide in their favour, perhaps claiming that their legal case is hopeless, and that they will 'lose'.

- Calling the police or social services with invented claims of abuse or alleged assault (this is very common indeed).

- Erasing or removing access to family photographs.

- Claiming that others are gossiping about them, or badmouthing them behind their backs, including claims that their own legal team are badmouthing the non-narcissistic partner.

- 'Hoovering' (trying to suck the partner back into a relationship with them by promising to change, threatening suicide or love-bombing).

- Threatening to destroy property, or even burn down the house.

- Threatening to ruin them financially.

- Threatening to badmouth them to their employers or report them to professional bodies if they do not agree to their settlement terms.

- Badmouthing their spouse's legal team to the spouse, in order to reduce their confidence in them, whilst inflating the brilliance of their own legal team.

- Messing around with the payment of school fees to render the children's future education uncertain and demonstrate that it is something of which they are in control.

- Threatening to have pets put down, or taken away.

- Conducting a smear campaign against the spouse/partner and attempting to isolate them from their support network by telling/writing lies to friends/ family/work colleagues and anyone else who features in the life of the spouse.

212

They may make extreme claims of secret unacceptable behaviour which they have had to silently bear such as affairs, drug abuse, alcoholism, violence, child abuse or mental health issues.

- Removal or destruction of property from the family home (particularly items of sentimental value such as photographs or jewellery or joint computers, televisions and essential furniture) without agreement.

- Removal of vehicles without explanation or agreement.

- Manipulative correspondence as 'scare tactics' or with undertones of blackmail.

Legal abuse

A narcissist will not conform to any rules or agenda other than their own. They do not expect to be told what to do and have no intention to conform. Don't forget that they do not want a quick resolution of matters; their intention is to punish you by dragging things out.

The narcissist will therefore make a mockery of the legal system, by refusing to play by its rules, *and by using it as a tool of abuse against you.* Bear in mind that you are highly likely to find yourself in the court process. Either the narcissist will have issued court proceedings against you because they want to be in control, or you will have found yourself with no alternative other than to issue proceedings through the court because the narcissist refuses to engage.

Even if the narcissist is the applicant in the court process, that does not mean that they will comply with their obligations within that process. Their desire to be in control will mean that they will behave abnormally. They naturally resist any kind of authority, including any court orders imposed on them by the court, especially if by doing so they are able to cause confusion and distress.

They will:

- Fail to provide accurate or complete financial disclosure to the court, starting with their Form E (see Chapter 10).

- Cause delays in whatever ways they can. They may use the mediation process to cause delays, with no real intention of resolving

"A narcissist will not conform to any rules or agenda other than their own. "

matters. They may ensure that they attend a mediation appointment having not done what they were asked to do at the last one, rendering the appointment a waste of time and money. Mediation costs are usually borne in equal shares and mediators cannot make one party pay for an unproductive appointment because that person has failed to do something, so here is an opportunity for financial abuse as well.

The 'collaborative practice' method of resolution is another perfect way to cause delay, also providing an opportunity to meet the other person's lawyer. In the meeting they can try to charm them and get them on side while denigrating and ridiculing them to their spouse or partner outside of the process. Better still, if they can cause the process to break down or the other person has to accept that it just isn't working both parties have to change lawyer, slowing down the process further.

- Ignore deadlines.

- Use your own legal team against you by finding ways to unnecessarily increase your legal fees. They will commonly bombard you with accusatory correspondence that you feel you have to defend through your solicitor, at your own expense, for example.

- Change goalposts just as you think you are reaching an agreement, to wear you down, increase your costs and perhaps make you more inclined to capitulate.

- Exploit any grey areas in the law, to waste more time and money. For example, if an agreement is reached at the second hearing – the FDRA – there may only be time for the lawyers to draft 'heads of agreement' (the main points) at court, leaving the actual consent order to be drafted later. This can however give rise to ambiguity over the precise detailed terms of the agreement, which the narcissist will delight in controlling for weeks or months, at great expense to your wallet and your mental health.

- Lie in court at the final hearing, even when under oath, in order to secure a poor settlement for you, and most likely get away with it. Unless it can be clearly shown that the court was misled to the point that an order was made to the detriment of the other party as a consequence (which is very difficult to achieve) nothing is likely to happen if one party lies on the witness stand. Bear in mind that an appeal is only possible if the judge made an error of law, not because they were taken in by a charming and plausible narcissist. And note also that the family court system does not provide any form of retribution for liars, again haplessly acting as a tool of abuse for the narcissist.

Communicating with the narcissist

9

I f there's one sure fire way to lose your mind, it's trying to have a logical, two way, productive conversation with a narcissist in the throes of narcissistic injury and rage.

Narcissistic communication is frustrating. Very frustrating, in fact. The narcissist will be accusatory (because you are deemed as 'all bad', and because they will be projecting their own faults on to you, so that they don't have to feel the shame of them themselves). They will gas-light you, denying your reality of what happened or how you are feeling, with gay abandon. They will justify their behaviour with head spinning pseudologic, which makes little sense, although it will be delivered with great conviction. They will lie about you and others, demean you, criticise you and devalue you. They will twist half or quarter truths into a semi-feasible sounding possibility, so that you are left wondering whether they are actually right, and they will contradict themselves even within single sentences. They will bombard you with multiple communications, ranting un-controllably. They will threaten, manipulate and scare you.

So what can you do to improve the situation?

Firstly, if you don't actually have to communicate with the narcissist, *then don't*. The gold standard is going 'No Contact' with the narcissist, and ensuring that you never have to communicate with them again by committing to it 100%. This starves them of narcissistic supply from you, leading them to shuffle off to find better sources of supply.

But of course, in the divorce process, even communication between lawyers keeps the narcissist topped up with quality supply, particularly as they now have extra players in their game. They can play one off against the other, and demonstrate their superiority and control of the situation, throwing chaos into the ring at every opportunity, and feeling smug, clever and superior as a result. And if you have to keep in touch with the narcissist because you work with them, have to share the same house, or have children with them then No Contact, sadly, simply isn't an option. Here's what you can do.

> **"If you don't actually have to communicate with the narcissist, then don't."**

- Stop all face to face or spoken (phone) communication as far as possible.

- Communicate only when *absolutely necessary* (trying to defend your position or explain how you feel do not count as reasons to communicate with a narcissist – you will be wasting your time, inadvertently feeding them supply and putting your mental health at risk).

- Try to communicate only via the written word, by email rather than any type of instant messaging, so that you can be less easily tempted to respond immediately.

- Give yourself at least a few hours, preferably a day, before you respond to their communications, allowing yourself time to see things objectively and to work out whether a reply to what is often a nonsensical rant is even necessary. Absolutely no knee jerk responses are allowed. None. Sit on your hands if you have to. Lock your phone in the car for a few hours so you can't respond. Distract yourself.

- Employ the 'Grey rock technique'.

The 'Grey rock technique'

The premise of this technique is simple, but if properly and consistently executed, the effects are profound. The idea is to simply become as interesting to the narcissist as a boring, large, grey rock.

Silent. Immovable. Dull. Unattractive. Bland. Inedible. A poor energy source. Devoid of emotion. Unreactive. Inanimate.

If you can do this effectively, you become a poor source of narcissistic supply, and the narcissist will skulk off in search of other sustenance surprisingly quickly. In other words, you will have *stopped feeding the beast of narcissism* with your attention and emotion.

There are various levels on which one must work with this, and they all feel very strange, and socially rude, at first.

- If you ever have to see the narcissist face to face, make *no eye contact* at all.

- If you have to speak to the narcissist, make your *tone of voice* very flat and uninteresting, a little like a robot. *Slow your speech* down, so that it sounds boring.

- Try to keep your facial expressions as neutral as possible, and become as unanimated as you can. Absolutely no raised eyebrows, shaking of the head in disbelief, looks of surprise or eye rolling, all of which will give the narcissist clues as to how you are feeling.

- When speaking or writing to a narcissist, use the *fewest number of words and syllables* you can. Answers should be monosyllabic – of the yes/no variety, with no justifications or explanations.

- Avoid being conversational. Do not use pleasantries or niceties. Just stick to the bare essentials. Imagine you are being extortionately charged for every word.

- Try not to ask questions (which could open up a discussion) but instead tell the narcissist what it is that they should do. For example, instead of "What time will you be dropping the children home?" write "Bring the children home at 6pm."

- Impart NO EMOTION AT ALL. We cannot overemphasise the importance of this one. Do not even allow the merest suggestion of irritation, frustration, sadness, passive aggression, happiness, cheerfulness etc into your communications. Do not try to appeal to the narcissist's sense of duty, morals or sympathy. You are opening yourself up to further unproductive communications if you allow even a chink of light through your grey rock armour. For the purposes of this, you are emotionally dead. *Think Mr Spock, only even more Vulcan.*

The key point with the grey rock technique is consistency. The narcissist will try to goad you into reacting emotionally once they sense that their supply from you is dwindling, and it is exceptionally difficult to refrain at first. But the quicker you are able to, the faster the narcissist will leave you alone, slinking off to seek alternative sources of supply.

How to manage the narcissist's written communications

A narcissist's style of communication, particularly when the narcissist has been 'outed', challenged, or abandoned, can leave one reeling in disbelief. It's common for written messages to be full of the following:

- Contradictions (even within a single message)

- Threats, which can be aimed directly at your Achilles' heel, or at the people you care about

- Character assassinations

- Unfounded accusations

- False justifications

- Blameshifting on to you or others

- False logic, or pseudologic, which often makes no sense, and can be used to justify certain behaviours

- Lying

- Rewriting of history

- Playing the victim

- Grandiosity (if the narcissist is an Exhibitionist Narcissist)

- Smugness and assertions of superiority

- Controlling dictatorial orders

- Projections, where you are accused of doing or being what the narcissist is actually doing or being

- Shamedumping on to you or another person (a form of projection)

- Devaluations

- Criticism

How to translate the narcissist's written communications

First, take a deep breath. The narcissist knows exactly how to push your buttons and you will, most likely, experience a sickening sense of dread when you see that there is a message waiting for you.

You may find your amygdala (the fight, flight or freeze part of the brain) being activated, and a sense of panic may ensue.

Before you've even opened the message, try to take a step back and notice how you are reacting. Do you become angry (fight)? Do you feel as if you want to run away (flight)? Or do you become overwhelmed and just freeze, completely unable to think (freeze)?

Notice whether your heart is pounding. Notice whether your palms are sweaty, or whether you feel breathless. You may feel a sense of heaviness or burning, or perhaps some other sensation, somewhere in your body. Again, just take a few seconds to notice where it is and what it feels like in your body. Just noticing these responses can help you to understand that your brain is simply reacting in a reflex manner to what it incorrectly perceives to be a threat to your life. This is not you, this is your outdated survival instinct, *and you, as a rational human can override it, with practice.*

If your instinct is to fight, and you become angry, modify the response by repeating to yourself a few times the following mantra: "I have rights".

If your instinct is to run away (flight), then give yourself a time out, and return to the message later, when your nervous system has calmed down.

And if you are a person who tends to freeze, and just surrender to the narcissist's demands, believing them to be right, then, before you open up their message, tell yourself that you are not to blame. "It's not all my fault". These strategies may help you feel more empowered when you do finally come to reading their message.

Remind yourself that the narcissist is emotionally just a child

As we've established, when a narcissist doesn't get their way, they will indulge in *toddler-style tantrums*, and rants and rages – behaviour which eerily resembles the throwing of toys out of the proverbial pram. If your narcissist hasn't exhibited this behaviour beforehand, they most definitely will during divorce.

The reason for this is that a large part of the development of the personality disorder resulted from the way in which the narcissist formed 'attachments' to his or her primary caregiver.

The future narcissist, as a child, was forced to orbit around caregivers (parents) who were unreliable, abusive, absent or neglectful. Sadly, this failure to attach in a healthy way to a caring, loving, stable parent causes big developmental problems for the child, who never learns to connect healthily with others and fails to develop empathy.

Developmentally, all normal children go through an essential, healthy narcissistic stage, during which they are all about the immediate gratification of their own needs, and are unable to consider or see the needs of others. This stage normally lasts from birth to around the age of seven to nine, when you will see empathy starting to develop in healthily attached children.

But the narcissist never emotionally develops beyond the normal narcissistic stage of childhood because the developmental foundations upon which the subsequent emotional stages are supposed to form are simply not there.

It's not uncommon for people to refer to the narcissist in their lives as 'Peter Pan', or within marriages as being 'as emotionally needy as one of the children', and there is a sound developmental reason for this.

Before reading written communications from a narcissist:

- Copy and paste the email or text into your word processor program; and then

- Change the font into a five year old font (there are numerous websites which have a variety of free children's fonts to choose from).

Whilst this might sound frivolous, it is actually a remarkably powerful, visual way of reminding you of what you are dealing with. It takes the heat out of the situation, and helps you to see that replying in an in-depth way, as if you were dealing with an adult, may not be relevant or useful.

The translation process

Now that you have the narcissist's communications in a child's font, you can begin the translating process.

Things to remember as you translate are:

- Do not take *anything* personally.

  When the narcissist accuses you of being anything at all, remember that he or she is probably *projecting*. It is never about you. It is always about them. They are batting off their own feelings on to you.

- Become thick-skinned.

  Ignore slights, frank insults and put downs. It is in the narcissist's nature to devalue others – it helps them to feel superior.

Here's an example email from a narcissist, which we have translated line by line below.

"Dear Margaret

Another disgustingly revolting, accusatory email from you I see. Frankly I'm surprised you could even send an email at one in the afternoon – aren't you normally comatose from the booze by then?

It's typical of you to try to turn the children against me when you know that I would do anything, anything at all, to see more of them. You have stolen my own children from me and I am devastated. Some days I can barely even face the day. I can't go on without seeing them. My whole world has crumbled and is meaningless without them.

I was late the other day purely because I have to go to work to earn money to keep you in shoes and bags. Tell me, are you and your sister spending my hard earned cash on cocaine, too? We all know how she used to be partial to a line or two. I suppose it's the stress of her high profile government job. She wouldn't want <u>that</u> getting out, I don't suppose. You should have waited for me to arrive instead of storming off – it's parental alienation, and I've noted it. You might think Amelia is too young at 11 to understand what is going on but I can tell you that she already understands how badly you treated me during our marriage – we've had many chats about it, and she is coming to understand the truth about you. You're going to lose her if you don't watch out. She can always live with me. My door will always be open for her.

How am I supposed to leave work early to pick up the kids when you expect me to keep funding your lifestyle? It's not my fault that I can't spend the time I want to with them. Isn't it time you got off your butt and actually did something? I always knew you were a loser – your mother was exactly the same, a leech. You should take a leaf out of your sister's book and start self-harming. And don't try to tell me that being a classroom assistant is work. You earn a pittance, and always will. You could have been so much more, why don't you become a proper teacher? What was the point of getting that supposed 'degree' if that's all you are going to do with it? You are clever and hard-working when you want to be. You could earn a fortune.

No self-respect, that's what my solicitor says about you. You're a classic apparently. She has a rather unflattering name for you, which I won't tell you – I'm sure you'd find it rather upsetting if you knew it. Oh ok then – it's 'Superbitch'. She's seen it all before. People like you never win, she reliably informs me, so you'd better watch out when the judge crucifies you next week. I've got one of the strongest cases she's ever had, by the way. And I think we both know that I am incredibly good under pressure, and extremely persuasive. I wouldn't fancy your chances much.

Taking Felix to A&E the other day without telling me was ridiculous. I need to be kept informed, and finding out by email is wrong. Everybody thinks so. You have Munchausen's Syndrome by proxy. FYI, I did what any sensible father would do when he fell off his bike. He was hysterical and needs to be taught how to be a man. I didn't believe that he had broken his elbow then and I still don't. I have texted him and told him to take the splint off as soon as he can, and to come and see me next weekend, when I will tell him in no uncertain terms that he is not to go to see any doctor without informing me first. You should do the same. If I have to protect them by getting custody of them then I will. If you can't act like a responsible adult then I will do that for them. Somebody has to. What a shame for them that it can't be their mother.

As to why Amelia feels the need to 'clean her room from top to bottom' when she comes to stay, well that's just a lie. Some of us have friends (unlike you), who want to stay over at mine because I, also unlike you, am a good person. One of the best people anyone could meet, actually, not that you could ever have appreciated that. It turns out everybody thought you were a vulture, preying off me after all. If Amelia doesn't like the fact that people have slept in her bed and used her room that's just tough. You are making her mad, and I wouldn't be surprised if she gets OCD, if she hasn't already got it. I've told her she can choose a new duvet cover if she wants to anyway. I would never remove her from her mother in any case – a girl needs her mother even if that mother has issues, and is money grabbing. I'm worried about her. You should get her counselling. Maybe you should think about putting what she needs first for a change.

If I were you, I'd sack your lawyers. They didn't exactly do well at the hearing, did they? I mean what was that? All that simpering to the judge. Where did you find that ridiculous little man? Are you sure he's actually a barrister? Next time, spend a little more money on one, if you want to win, that's my advice. I told you that mediation would have brought a better outcome for you. I mean, what is the point of us going to court? You should be able to discuss this rationally instead of giving all my hard earned money to your lawyers. You are being pathetic – can't you see that they are just taking advantage of you? They are laughing all the way to the bank at you. I wonder what their nickname is for you – they are bound to have one.

On the subject of mediation, I think you will do much better financially that way. You are simply throwing away your own financial security by going through the court system. I'm open to mediation, and think we should try it again. It'll be in your own best interests. This time we could go for someone really good – not that oddball your solicitor suggested last time who couldn't even add up. I have some names of people in London. Refusing to even try will only make you look bad to the judge. I tried ringing you about this, but I see you have blocked me. A little over the top, frankly, not being able to have a civil conversation with me. Pathetic, actually.

And no, I don't know where the TV remote control or the internet router is. I hope you are not accusing me of taking them? Why would anyone do that? I think you are becoming a little paranoid, but they say that alcohol can do that to a person. If you need internet so badly, just buy a new router – it's hardly rocket science, and I'll be paying for it anyway, so actually I can take what I want. You are losing it, clearly.

Please leave the Xmas decorations in the shed for me to collect. I will not come into the house for them, as you have accused me of doing, like some sort of stalker. It is my right to have them and get whatever I want whenever I want to from anywhere. It's my house, that you have the great privilege of living the Life Of Riley in. I suggest you change the locks if you are so worried about it. You'll be on thin ice if you do, as anyone who knows anything about the law will tell you.

I'm getting the children on Saturday afternoon. Have them ready by 2pm. I will be giving a very important talk in London to some world class financiers on Friday, and will be attending a dinner afterwards, so I don't know what time I'll be able to pick them up the next day. And before you suggest that I get someone else to do it, only I can deal with work of this nature, not that you have the slightest understanding of what it is that I do, and how highly regarded I am. You'd probably start treating me with the respect I deserve (and get from everybody else) if you did. I won't be kept waiting on Saturday, by the way.

Felix told me last week that you were late collecting him from school. How do you suppose that makes him feel? He told me that you were crying when you arrived. Hardly appropriate for a nine year old to see. Are you really ready to be dating – I presume that's why you were crying – dumped eh? Not surprising when there are seven single women in your age group to every man – most of them gym goers unlike you. Perhaps you should try for a 70 year old sugar daddy instead if you want to maximize your chances of success."

The translation

Dear Margaret
Translation: I am calling you Margaret because I know you have always hated that name, and no one calls you Margaret as a result. I hope it unsettles you, Maggie.

Another disgustingly revolting, accusatory email from you I see.
Translation: I hereby send you another revolting, accusatory email. (Note the projection here).

Frankly I'm surprised you could even send an email at one in the afternoon – aren't you normally comatose from the booze by then?
Translation: I'm accusing you of this in writing to make you fearful that I will say that you are an alcoholic to the court, so scaring you into thinking that I'm going to try to take the children off you. Clever, aren't I?

It's typical of you to try to turn the children against me when you know that I would do anything, anything at all, to see more of them.
Translation: I am trying to turn the children against you (projection). It's brilliant, this every other weekend thing. I get to do whatever I want the rest of the time, without having snivelling kids cramping my style.

You have stolen my own children from me and I am devastated. Some days I can barely even face the day. I can't go on without seeing them. My whole world has crumbled and is meaningless without them.
Translation: Come on Maggie. Take the bait. You always were a sucker for a sob story. Ring me. Or invite me round for a cup of tea... I need that supply... (Pity play).

I was late the other day purely because I have to go to work to earn money to keep you in shoes and bags.
Translation: It is your fault that I was late. I don't 'do' responsibility, in case you hadn't noticed. (Blameshifting)

Tell me, are you and your sister spending my hard earned cash on

224

cocaine, too? We all know how she used to be partial to a line or two. I suppose it's the stress of her high profile government job. She wouldn't want <u>that</u> getting out, I don't suppose.

Translation: I am threatening to blackmail you through your sister as a method of intimidation and control. Scared? I hope so. Look how powerful I am. How omnipotent. I can crush the people around you, and it'll be your fault. You should never have left me.

You should have waited for me to arrive instead of storming off - It's parental alienation, and I've noted it.

Translation: How dare you exert a boundary with me? You wouldn't have dared whilst we were together. Your job is to facilitate me. What gives you the right to have rights? Only I am entitled to rights. (Sense of entitlement, violating boundaries). I am trying to alienate the children from you. (Projection).

You might think Amelia is too young at 11 to understand what is going on but I can tell you that she already understands how badly you treated me during our marriage - we've had many chats about it, and she is coming to understand the truth about you. You're going to lose her if you don't watch out. She can always live with me. My door will always be open for her.

Translation: I can't have my own flesh and blood knowing the truth about me, do you hear me? I can't. I'm going to hate you instead. It's easier. I hate you. You are the bad one. You are rotten to the core. And I'm going to make the kids hate you too. (Shamedumping, seeing the other as 'all bad', badmouthing, parental alienation).

How am I supposed to leave work early to pick up the kids when you expect me to keep funding your lifestyle? It's not my fault that I can't spend the time I want to with them.

Translation: I'm not exactly going to leave work early now that my new secretary is there, am I? She thinks I'm great – full of admiration for me. I'd much rather be there than with the children. Zzzzzzz. (Driven by a need for narcissistic supply above all else).

And don't try to tell me that being a classroom assistant is work. You earn a pittance, and always will.

Translation: I can make you feel so small. It's strangely comforting. (Devaluation, in an attempt to inflate own ego).

You could have been so much more, why don't you become a proper teacher? What was the point of getting that supposed 'degree', if that's all you are going to do with it? You are clever and hardworking when you want to be. You could earn a fortune.

Translation: You are clever and hard-working. Dammit. And I've lost you. And everyone knows. Well, I might as well try and use that against you, saying you have enormous earning capacity in court. That'll teach you for leaving.

No self respect, that's what my solicitor says about you. You're a classic apparently. She has a rather unflattering name for you, which I won't tell you I'm sure you'd find it rather upsetting if you knew it. Oh Ok then – It's 'superbitch'. She's seen it all before. People like you never win, she reliably informs me, so you'd better watch out when the judge crucifies you next week. I've got one of the strongest cases she's ever had, by the way.

Translation: I care about what other people think about me, so, so much, so you must too, right? Bloody solicitor. She should just shut up and sign my letters to you. I'm not interested in her 'advice'. All this talk of 'what is reasonable'. You're going to win. Shit. Shit. Shit.

And I think we both know that I am incredibly good under pressure, and extremely persuasive. I wouldn't fancy your chances much.

Translation: Maybe I should have been a barrister. All that strutting around and being clever. The spellbound audience. The terrified woman in the dock. Right up my street, that. God, I am clever aren't I? I fooled you for all those years, after all. Feeling a bit more cheery now.

Taking Felix to A and E the other day without telling me was ridiculous. I need to be kept informed, and finding out by email is wrong. Everybody thinks so. You have Munchausen's syndrome by proxy.

Translation: I should have taken Felix to A&E the other day. Everybody thought I was an idiot. The shame of it. But you have to wait in A&E. It can take hours to be seen. Hours. I just couldn't be arsed. And now I look like a bad parent. But I can't be the bad parent. I can't. Ouch. You'll have to be instead. Ha! (Shamedumping).

FYI, I did what any sensible father would do when he fell off his bike. He was hysterical and needs to be taught how to be a man.

Translation: I have no empathy. And people were looking. And not in a good way. Bloody kids.

I didn't believe that he had broken his elbow then and I still don't. I have texted him and told him to take the splint off as soon as he can, and to come and see me next weekend, when I will tell him in no uncertain terms that he is not to go to see any doctor without informing me first.

Translation: It didn't happen. It didn't. There. That's better now. (Denial, in order to avoid feeling shame, gas-lighting the son).

If you can't act like a responsible adult then I will do that for them. Somebody has to. What a shame for them that it can't be their mother.

Translation: If I can't act like a responsible adult then you will have to do that for them. Somebody has to. What a shame for them that it can't be their father. (Projection).

As to why Amelia feels the need to 'clean her room from top to bottom' when she comes to stay, well that's just a lie.

Translation: It's true. She does. (Denial, gas-lighting).

Some of us have friends unlike you, who want to stay over at mine because I, also unlike you, am a good person. One of the best people anyone could meet, actually, not that you could ever have appreciated that.

Translation: I need friends. I'm starving. Not enough supply. The ones I have are rubbish. Living here in this empty flat on my own is killing me. No validation, you see. No distraction from myself. You, unlike me, are a good person. One of the best people anyone could meet, actually. I'm a bad person. Ouch. (Need for narcissistic supply, shifting Maggie's good qualities onto himself, projecting his own deficiencies on to her).

It turns out everybody thought you were a vulture, preying off me after all.

Translation: I was a vulture, preying off you. Not that I care. (Projection).

If Amelia doesn't like the fact that people have slept in her bed and used her room that's just tough. You are making her mad, and I wouldn't be surprised if she gets OCD, if she hasn't already got it.

Translation: Blah blah blah. I don't care if she doesn't like it. I have no empathy, remember? There must be something wrong with her, not me. And cleaning and doing laundry is BORING, and I hate it. I'm too important for all that menial rubbish, especially if someone else is going to do it anyway, even if it is an 11 year old. (Lack of empathy, sense of entitlement).

I would never remove her from her mother. In any case a girl needs her mother even if that mother has issues, and is money grabbing.

Translation: I'm rambling again, aren't I? I know I said I'd have her live with me earlier, but actually, those were just words. Parenting is dull. You can have her. (Contradiction).

I'm worried about her. You should get her counselling. Maybe you should think about putting what she needs first for a change.

Translation: I don't really care about her. Let someone else deal with her. Maybe I should put her needs first for a change. Nah. I'll let you do that instead – I'll just look after myself, thank you very much. (Responsibility shifting).

If I were you, I'd sack your lawyers. They didn't exactly do well at the hearing, did they? I mean what was that? All that simpering to the judge. Where did you find that ridiculous little man? Are you sure he's actually a barrister?

Translation: That hearing was a nightmare. My barrister was rubbish. (Devaluation, criticism, gas-lighting).

Next time, spend a little more money on one, if you want to win, that's my advice.

Translation: I bet I can get you to rack up even more legal fees, so there's even less left for you in the financial pot. You deserve nothing. I deserve it all. (Sense of entitlement, financial abuse).

I told you that mediation would have brought a better outcome for you. I mean, what is the point of us going to court?

Translation: Damn court. I'm going to lose, if I carry on down this route. (Manipulation).

You should be able to discuss this rationally instead of giving all my hard earned money to your lawyers. You are being pathetic - can't you see that they are just taking advantage of you? They are laughing all the way to the bank at you. I wonder what their nickname is for you - they are bound to have one.

Translation: She's got a good team there. Dammit. (Devaluation).

On the subject of mediation, I think you will do much better financially that way. You are simply throwing away your own financial security by going through the court system. I'm open to mediation, and think we should try it again. It'll be in your own best interests.

Translation. Oh come on. Be a good sport. Mediation will be great. I'll run rings around you and the mediator, who will think I am brilliant and right. You'll be a wreck, and like putty in my hands. And it'll delay things. And all the while, I'll get to look like the one who wanted to try to resolve things amicably. And you'll cave, and I will end up with all the money! I am, quite literally, a genius. Buhahaha. (Attempts at triangulation, manipulation, delaying tactics).

This time we could go for someone really good, not that oddball your solicitor suggested last time who couldn't even add up. I have some names of people in London.

Translation: It was the mediator's fault that mediation didn't work last time, not mine. This time we need the best of the best, because I am the best of the best, and I deserve it. (Blameshifting, devaluation, superiority, sense of entitlement).

I tried ringing you about this, but I see you have blocked me. A little over the top, frankly, not being able to have a civil conversation with me. Pathetic, actually.

Translation: For crying out loud. I need you. I need to be able to talk to you. I need the conflict. Can't you see, I'm starving without your supply here? I'm pathetic. (Need for narcissistic supply, devaluation, name calling, projection).

And no, I don't know where the TV remote control or the internet router is. I hope you are not accusing me of taking them? Why would anyone do that? I think you are becoming a little paranoid, but they say that alcohol can do that to a person.

Translation: Yep, I'm gas-lighting you. Convinced that you are going mad yet?

If you need internet so badly, just buy a new router. It's hardly rocket science, and Ill be paying for it anyway, so actually I can take what I want.

Translation: Everything is mine. Of course I took them. (Sense of entitlement, financial abuse/control).

You are losing it, clearly.

Translation: I am losing it, clearly. (Projection and gas-lighting).

Please leave the xmas decorations in the shed for me to collect. I will not come into the house for them, as you have accused me of doing, like some sort of stalker. It is my right to have them and get whatever I want whenever I want to from anywhere. It's my house, that you have the great privilege of living the life of riley in. I suggest you change the locks if you are so worried about it. You'll be on thin ice if you do, as anyone who knows anything about the law will tell you.

Translation: Another helping of word salad, Maggie? (Pseudologic, word salad, contradiction, sense of entitlement, intimidation).

I'm getting the children on saturday afternoon. Have them ready by 2pm. I will be giving a very important talk in London to some world class financiers on friday, and will be attending a dinner afterwards, so I don't know what time I'll be able to pick them up the next day.

Translation: Do as I say. And don't forget how important I am. And by the way, I'll be late again. (Superiority, grandiosity, sense of entitlement).

And before you suggest that I get someone else to do it, only I can deal with work of this nature, not that you have the slightest understanding of what it is that I do, and how highly regarded I am. You'd probably start treating me with the respect I deserve, and get from everybody else, if you did.

Translation: *DO YOU KNOW WHO I AM???* (Grandiosity, superiority). *Can I have some narcissistic supply from you please, in the form of admiration and awe?*

I won't be kept waiting on saturday, by the way. Felix told me last week that you were late collecting him from school.

Translation: *Only I am allowed to be late.* (Hypocrisy, sense of entitlement).

How do you suppose that makes him feel?

Translation: *I am morally superior to you. Ok, I'm not. But I'm not admitting it. Not to myself, or anyone else. And as to how it makes Felix feel – frankly, who cares?*

He told me that you were crying when you arrived. Hardly appropriate for a nine year old to see.

Translation: *Yesss. You are in pain! I wonder what else I can get out of Felix about you?* (Lack of empathy, taking sadistic pleasure from another's pain, criticism). *Keep on crying, Maggie!*

Are you really ready to be dating? I presume that's why you were crying. dumped eh? Not surprising when there are seven single women in your age group to every man, most of them gym goers, unlike you.

Translation: *I'm ridiculing you. God that feels good. And devaluing you at the same time. Bliss.*

Perhaps you should try for a 70 year old sugar daddy instead if you want to maximize your chances of success.

Translation: *Oh my God. What if she meets someone rich? And clever? And successful? And handsome? I'll look like a loser next to them. And everyone will realise that she's upgraded from me. What to do? I know – I'll destroy her confidence, like I did before. Simple. Phew. I will not be made to look like a fool.* (Manipulation, gas-lighting, demeaning, ridiculing).

Formulating your reply

The next thing to do is to look at which bits of the communication you actually have to respond to. Hopefully, the translation process has made you aware of what is important and what is not.

Work out what you have to respond to

Initially you might feel that you have to respond to all accusations in order to clear your name, especially should these communications find their way to being in front of a judge. In fact, you don't. The ranting nature of the narcissist's communications, might strike fear into *your* heart (because the narcissist knows which buttons to push with you), but actually, to a third party, they appear ridiculous. So, only respond to the bits of the narcissist's communications that you absolutely have to for legal or organisational reasons. *Ignore the other parts*, no matter how inflammatory and outrageous they may be.

"We" is a magic word

Research has shown that using words such as 'we', 'our' and 'us', rather than 'I', 'my' and 'me' seem to temporarily remind narcissists that other people and relationships exist, and makes them more empathic. Wherever possible try to use these collaborative pronouns, particularly when facing challenging situations. Never say "*I* need you to do X" – in doing this you are setting yourself up as being more important than the narcissist. Your needs are irrelevant to the narcissist and this will result in a knee jerk reaction where the narcissist feels that their authority is being challenged. Say "*We* need to ..." instead.

Be task focused

The narcissist's agenda is not the same as yours. They do not wish to find a resolution to problems or to move forwards. They wish to prolong your divorce proceedings for as long as possible, in order to punish you and gain supply from the drama. You were their most reliable source of narcissistic supply. It may seem counter-intuitive, but they do not want this aspect of their relationship to end, even if they ended the relationship. You must not feed this. Concentrate only on moving things forwards. Keep to the point, ignore any blame and focus only on solutions.

Do not start a sentence with 'no'

If a suggestion is being made that you do not agree with, or a question being asked to which the answer is 'no', do not start the sentence with 'No'. 'No' inflames a narcissist. It gives them the sense that you are seeking to take the control away from them, and that you believe yourself to be superior to them. Implicit in this is that you do not see them as special/clever/right/superior, which is a big challenge to their sense of self, and can cause even more narcissistic injury and rage. Indeed, you may not get any further than saying the word no, if you put it first in a sentence. Many narcissists, if told they cannot do something, will make a point of doing it anyway, just to prove you wrong and assert their superiority.

Do not react emotionally to the narcissist

To a narcissist, reacting emotionally is a sign of weakness, which will be used against you, if not immediately, in the future. The narcissist needs to get narcissistic supply out of every single interaction. That could come in the form of feeling important, clever, special, appreciated or nice, or it could come in the form of conflict and drama.

To keep things calm, you need to stay away from giving supply through drama and conflict. No matter how much they push your buttons, do not be drawn in. Like with the grey rock technique, *channel your inner Mr Spock*.

Be polite, but not friendly

Use as few words as you can

Employ the use of Fogging

If possible (and it isn't always), find something you agree with in the narcissist's communications. This technique is called 'Fogging' and it may be useful in disarming the narcissist to some extent. You do not argue back, but you give a calm response which is placatory but not defensive, whilst not giving in to their demands. It involves acknowledging any parts of the criticism that is true whilst not responding to the other parts. In other words, you acknowledge the *literal* truth in what the narcissist is saying, but you don't react to any implicit suggestions they are making, and you don't agree to do things they may want you to do.

As an example from the message above, you could simply say, "Felix did fall off his bike, yes." Then you would move away from the subject on to the bit that actually needs to be dealt with to move things forwards.

Here you haven't justified yourself, contested any criticism, criticised them in response or become defensive, and you haven't agreed to do what they say; you have merely agreed with the part of their statement which is true. This helps you to remain emotionally detached from criticism, whilst placating them.

Imagine that the narcissist's insult is a stone they are throwing at you. Instead of reflexly throwing it back, you envelop it in the fog that is surrounding you, so that it simply disappears.

Lay down your boundaries

Here, be polite but firm.

Do not be lulled into a false sense of security by the occasional reasonable sounding message

The narcissist is merely trying to engage you – if you fall for this trick and respond as you would to a non-narcissist, the accusatory, ranting, rageful messages will inevitably follow.

Do not fall for the narcissist's pity plays

This are just another way to draw you back in as a source of narcissistic supply – resist the urge to listen to or act on your natural empathy when dealing with a narcissist.

In the example above, an appropriate response could be:

"Dear John

Felix did fall off his bike, yes.

So, we are agreed that the children can be collected at 2pm on Saturday. If you have not arrived by 2.15pm, they will be unavailable for collection for the remainder of the day.

We can split the Christmas decorations between us. I will leave some in the shed.

Regards,

Maggie"

Note the laying down of a boundary regarding late picks ups, the deployment of 'we' and 'us' and the use of fogging. It may sound stilted and unlike how you would normally write, but you are dealing with a narcissist in full meltdown here, and you are trying to minimise the narcissistic supply you give them and keep things civil. The normal rules do not apply.

Once you have written an email or text, re-read it a few hours later, looking for even implied 'in between the lines' emotion, irritation, sarcasm or one-upmanship, and erase any you find before you send it. At first, it may be useful to enlist an objective friend to help you with this, to take any remaining heat out of your responses.

It's really important to remember that if you do get it wrong and lower yourself to the narcissist's level in your written communications, you will most likely find yourself reading your own words in court one day, and this could count against you. Be careful – these rules are for your own protection.

Some other things to consider when trying to communicate with a narcissist

These tactics may be useful at times, if you cannot avoid communicating with them.

Trying to get them back to the matter in hand

To get them back on task, and away from rants, tantrums, accusations, complaints, talking about themselves etc, try asking: "Can we work out what we need to do to collaborate effectively with the task at hand?" Or, "Can we focus on the current problem that we need to be solved, and how we best stay on track to solve it?' Or, "Could we prioritise what needs to be done so that we can sort out the current issue?

Note the judicious use of *closed questions* here – the narcissist has to respond with a yes or no. Open questions can work against you with a narcissist if you are trying to get them back on task, for example: "What do we need to do to move forwards with the task in hand?" could open up a whole spectrum of answers, wasting yet more time, especially as 'moving forwards' is far from what the narcissist really wants. Also note the use of the 'magic we.'

Praising the narcissist

If you need the narcissist to do something, this is worth a try, but not if they are in the middle of a rage.

Try to appeal to the narcissist's sense of importance, cleverness, specialness, or niceness to keep things civil. It may feel wrong, pandering to them in this way, but this is not the same as being sycophantic. Simply praise things that are true, and no more. (Overdoing the praise where it is not warranted, with constant flattery, will only feed their unhealthy narcissism). Make sure your praise is in line with how the narcissist likes to see themselves.

Avoid hyperbole, and words such as incredible, amazing, wonderful etc. Be measured and proportionate in your praise. "You have always been good at encouraging Felix with his football. Would you take him to his match on Wednesday?" "You are good at persuading people to do things. Would you be able to speak to Amelia's teacher about letting her drop Drama?"

When praising a narcissist, you are trying to point out their real strengths.

Praise goes a long way to disarming a narcissist, even when they are being downright rude. You may have to learn to swallow your pride and overcome your natural resistance to offering it, however.

Positively reinforce the narcissist's good behaviour

For example, if the narcissist arrives on time to pick up the children, you could say: "Thank you so much for making sure you are here on time today – it's very helpful in keeping us all on track."

Note that here we are using the 'you' pronoun at the beginning of the sentence. This should be reserved for when you are giving the narcissist ownership of their good behaviour, in order to reinforce it.

Contrast current bad behaviour with past good behaviour

Start with the good behaviour first, using the 'you' pronoun. Then insert the behaviour you want changed, using the collaborative 'we' pronoun. Finally, sandwich it in another piece of praise, using the 'you' pronoun.

Bear in mind that if a narcissist is in the stage where they want to make everything as difficult as they can for you, then this won't work, but some can respond well to this method of persuasion.

Think of it as a hamburger – compliment, confront, compliment. For example: "It was so helpful last week when you were able to sign your bit of the house sale paperwork and get to me quickly. I've noticed that this week it's been a bit harder. It would be great if we were able to go back to completing paperwork quickly, so that we can be as effective as possible. I really appreciate all the effort you put in with this."

Let them feel they have won, or let them have the last word

Narcissists need to win at all costs, regardless of how big or small the issue is. And if they can't really win, they *must believe that they have won*. You and your lawyer will need to bear this in mind when communicating with them. At the very least, they will need to have had the last word, so swallow your pride and let them have it.

Advice for your solicitor when communicating with the narcissist's solicitor

Don't give deadlines

There is absolutely no point in imposing deadlines upon a narcissist in correspondence as, to them, rules are made to be broken. They will definitely not want to do as you insist. A narcissist will understand that you have imposed a deadline because you want them to make a decision quickly, and they will understand, if you are making an offer to them, that you will not withdraw that offer just because a deadline has passed. Ignoring deadlines is just another way to give the narcissist a sense of control and resulting narcissistic supply, and once a deadline has passed and been ignored, you and your team end up looking powerless and foolish. Polite *suggestions* of timescales are fine, but deadlines end up being disempowering to you and your lawyers.

Dealing with difficult correspondence

When your solicitor receives correspondence from the narcissist's solicitor, hopefully they will realise that the narcissist's solicitor is merely acting as a mouthpiece for them. It is more than likely that the narcissist is writing letters and insisting that their solicitor just copy and paste them on to their letter headed notepaper, and then sign them as if they have been written by themselves in their role as legal advisor. In fact, the narcissist's solicitor is probably trying to give the narcissist sensible advice, but is being ignored. At the end of the day, their solicitor is being paid by them, and therefore has to follow their instructions, even if those instructions are clearly morally wrong. Remember that narcissists abuse everybody, including their own solicitors.

> **"There is absolutely no point in imposing deadlines upon a narcissist in correspondence."**

It may be useful to arm your solicitor with some useful written responses to defuse the situation when they receive outrageous, accusatory, ranting correspondence from the other side. The following work well:

- The allegations made by your client are denied, but we do not consider it beneficial to go through the points made in turn. We prefer to focus on the future and a settlement rather than dwell on past issues which are not relevant to the key issues between our clients.

- We do not propose to argue a different perspective of past events in correspondence. Our client does not accept your client's version of events, but we would encourage both to move forwards and put the past behind them.

- Reference to the issues raised does not serve any useful purpose and, save to confirm that your client's position is not accepted, we are not instructed to comment further.

- If there are matters which do require discussion, we believe the most cost effective route would be to engage in hybrid mediation, with lawyers present. Our three suggested hybrid trained mediators are X, Y and Z. Please take urgent instructions.

The Court Process

10

I n this section, we walk you through the court process, stage by stage. Sadly, divorcing through the courts is an adversarial process, and there is no room for forgiveness, especially when you are up against a narcissist. You will have to be prepared to fight, even it goes against how you see yourself.

The financial court process begins with the applicant making an application to the court by filling out a 'Form A'. However, before they do this, (except in very exceptional circumstances) they must attend a Mediation Information and Assessment Meeting (MIAM) with an accredited mediator. The purpose of this is to see whether the case can be dealt with via some form of 'out of court' process. The mediator will explain what the alternatives to court are and will write to the other party inviting them to attend a similar meeting. The obligation to attend a MIAM was put in place due to the court system being over-stretched and under-funded in an attempt to move those cases which are capable of being dealt with in a different way out of the court process.

In Chapter 7 we have already explained that mediation and some other 'out of court' alternatives are unlikely to be successful where one party suffers from NPD. This is something which you should explain to the mediator at the MIAM. When arranging a MIAM it is important to consider the level of training which the mediator has had. Only an accredited mediator can conduct a MIAM but you may want to consult with a hybrid trained mediator who will be able to explain this option and conduct the mediation in accordance with the hybrid model. This form of mediation which involves separate meetings and lawyer support is far more likely to succeed in a situation where one of the couple suffers from NPD than the classic form of mediation which simply involves the mediator and the couple.

A court fee is payable when submitting Form A – £255 (at the time of going to print).

The court will issue a 'notice of hearing', which sets out a timetable of steps that need to be taken ahead of the 'first appointment', also called the 'FDA', which will be your first day in court.

The financial court process deals with two issues:

1. What is there?

2. How should it be divided?

The 'directions' set by the court will be:

1. A date for completing Form E (35 days prior to the date allocated for your first appointment in court).

2. A date for providing a draft questionnaire (asking questions to further explain the content of Form E, see below); statement of issues (setting out in brief terms the issues for the court to decide); and Form G (a document stating whether a first appointment (FDA) is required or whether – by agreement only – that stage can be skipped because disclosure is complete and the case can go straight to the First Dispute Resolution Appointment (FDRA)).

In all cases a legal costs estimate (Form H) must also be filed with the court and exchanged with your spouse's solicitor a couple of days before the hearing date.

If you are represented by a solicitor, they will arrange all of the above, and walk you through it.

The Form E

The standard method for providing financial disclosure is the completion of a document known as Form E. You both have to do this regardless of whether you are planning to resolve matters through the court process or in another way, like mediation. The two Form Es provide a complete picture of the couple's finances including property values, other capital, pension provision and income from all sources. The documents which are to be produced with Form E are listed on the final page of the form. If you are not going through the court system, the two solicitors will set a date to exchange your forms with each other. If a court application has been made an exchange date will have been set by the court. The idea of exchange is that your Form E is sent to your spouse's solicitor *at the same time* as they send your solicitor theirs.

It is not unusual for Form Es not to be exchanged on the date set because one or both parties are not ready, but they should be exchanged early enough to ensure that you and your solicitor have sufficient time to work out your questionnaire (see below) and put together your 'statement of issues'. If you are going through the court process, this needs to be done well before the date set for the First Directions Appointment (FDA), your first day in court. So, exchanging your Form Es in time is an important part of the process.

When it comes to filling in the Form E, a narcissist is very likely not to provide all of the required information, particularly if they are self-employed. This will be a nightmare for their own solicitor who is likely to receive information and documents in dribs and drabs. It is highly likely that it will be late, incomplete and possibly inaccurate.

At section 4.4 of Form E it is possible to include a section about "bad behaviour or conduct by the other party". The form itself stipulates that "bad behaviour or conduct by the other party will only be taken into account in very exceptional circumstances when deciding how assets should be shared after divorce/dissolution." This means exactly what it says. It is extremely unusual for this section to be completed at all. However, it is not unusual for the narcissistic spouse to set out here a detailed analysis of the behaviour which they believe to be relevant in order to intimidate the other party to the marriage. It is important not to be unsettled by the inclusion of irrelevant detail in this section and similarly important to steer away from completing this section except in the most exceptional of circumstances.

A narcissist will usually consider deadlines to be something that apply to other people, and will feel aggrieved at having to follow someone else's rules. It is highly likely that they will miss deadlines for exchanging Form Es, prolonging your agony and the process. This approach will be designed to undermine and infuriate you, and intentionally so. Unfortunately, the failings of the court system serve to compound this.

Within the court process it is unfortunately very difficult to make people do things. If deadlines are missed it is possible to make an application for a 'penal notice' to be attached to the order for directions. The aim of this is to compel the narcissist to do what they are required to do by the court (i.e. provide their Form E to you). Unfortunately, the court administration system is so slow that it is easy for them to do what they were supposed to do *after* your application for penal notice has been issued but *before* it has been dealt with by the court. In theory, making an application for a penal notice means that you are applying for them to be sent to prison if they do not do what they are supposed to do, but this rarely actually happens. This all adds to the infuriation, and your costs may increase unnecessarily.

The questionnaire

You may be told by your lawyer not to worry about the incomplete Form E provided by your spouse because you can fill in the gaps at the next stage via your questionnaire. Here, you decide with your lawyers which questions you wish to ask of your spouse in order to clarify their financial situation, and you put together a 'draft questionnaire'. The narcissist will also raise questions on your Form E, putting together their own draft questionnaire.

The purpose of the questionnaire is to ask for information and documents which provide evidence or clarification of the financial disclosure. Typical questions to find in a questionnaire are as follows:

- Missing bank statements

- Credit card statements

- Contract of employment

- Correspondence relating to redundancy

- Tax returns

- Information relating to share options

- An explanation about particular debits or credits on a bank account

The above list is not exhaustive but gives an indication of the sort of information which might be requested. Questions which can be described as 'cross-examination', i.e. asking for a justification of expenditure items or setting out rhetorical questions which are intended simply to make statements are not appropriate for the questionnaire and are likely to be removed by the judge when the document is considered. Questionnaires should not be unduly lengthy. Only relevant questions should be asked i.e. where the answer will assist the court in understanding the financial position of the parties.

When you receive the draft questionnaire it is important to remember that the judge at the FDA has the final say as to which questions are relevant and which are not. The document which you first receive may not be the list of questions which you are actually required to answer.

As indicated above, what are known as 'first appointment documents' (draft questionnaire, statement of issues and Form G) should be exchanged 14 days before the date allocated for the FDA hearing. Often this deadline is missed, but this doesn't matter too much as long as they are exchanged in sufficient time to be considered by both parties and their lawyers before the FDA hearing, which could be just three or four days beforehand.

If you have a solicitor instructed this should be sufficient time to enable them to consider the documentation. If, however, you are acting in person bear in mind that the rules say that these documents should be supplied 14 days prior to the date of the FDA hearing. If they have been provided late you are within your rights to apply for an adjournment of the FDA either via a court application (using Form D11) ahead of the hearing or, if there is insufficient time to file this with the court, at the FDA hearing itself. The other party ought to have complied with the time deadlines and you should not be disadvantaged if they have not done so. The provision of full and frank financial disclosure is one of the most important aspects of the financial remedy process – it is impossible to identify how financial matters should be resolved if the actual amount and value of the resources involved is not clearly identifiable.

Before each court hearing, the applicant's solicitor has to prepare a 'bundle' of relevant documents for the hearing in a prescribed format. If the applicant is not represented by a lawyer the job will pass to the solicitor instructed by the respondent. The 'index' (which is a table of contents, showing what documents are included in the bundle) must be agreed by both sides in advance. The bundle is sent to the court electronically, to be officially 'filed' by them. (If you are the applicant, and neither you or your spouse are represented by lawyers, then preparing these documents and sending them to the court will fall to you).

The FDA

The first court appointment is called the First Directions Appointment or FDA. This takes place in a courtroom, with both parties, their lawyers and a judge present. You may have instructed a barrister, on the advice of your solicitor, to represent you here. Be guided by your solicitor as to who should represent you. Just because the other side is represented by a barrister doesn't mean that you shouldn't be represented by your solicitor.

You do not speak at this hearing – your legal representative will speak on your behalf.

At the FDA the judge decides which of the questions raised in your questionnaires are reasonable and should be answered, and then makes an order giving a date by which those answers must be provided. The questions must be relevant to the issues set out in the 'statement of issues'.

It is important that valuations of major assets are agreed. If property values are not agreed the judge will set a date by which they are to be agreed and, in the event that agreement cannot be achieved, make provision for an independent valuer to be jointly instructed. The same will apply for other assets which need to be valued, such as a company. Other possessions (known legally as 'chattels') are not likely to be valued unless they are extraordinary.

It may also be necessary to have a pension sharing report. As a guide, this is likely to be the case where the couple are over the age of 40 and/or pensions are collectively worth more than £100,000.

If a formal valuation and/or pension sharing report is required, the costs of this report will be shared. Sometimes the financially stronger party will be required to pay the full costs initially on the basis that they will be reimbursed later when financial matters have been resolved.

The requirement to provide a mortgage capacity report for each party is a standard direction at the FDA, as is the requirement to produce a limited number of property particulars for you and the other party showing suitable future accommodation for each.

If the stronger financial party is the narcissist, they commonly refuse to financially support their spouse (and children) as soon as separation begins. In situations like this, where interim financial arrangements cannot be agreed, an application for 'maintenance pending suit' may need to be made by a separate court application. The court appointment allocated for this can be combined with the FDA. (Maintenance pending suit is temporary maintenance paid by one party to the other until the divorce becomes final).

Answering the questionnaire and complying with other directions

The narcissist is likely to provide obtuse or incomplete answers to your questionnaire, and not respond on time. Just because an answer is obtuse or unhelpful doesn't necessarily mean that the question has not been answered. The narcissist may play on this. Again, the penal notice option is available if the narcissist does not provide their replies to your questionnaire on time.

When you are dealing with a narcissist it is actually worth making repeated court applications for a penal notice. Although they feel a bit futile because, in reality, a judge is extremely unlikely to send your spouse to prison if they do not comply with them, they do paint a picture of wilful non-compliance. This can be important if the matter reaches a final hearing. You could also achieve a costs order (where the other side is ordered by the judge to pay the costs of your penal notice application). However, costs orders are discretionary and not all judges will make them.

A narcissist may also fail to provide a proper mortgage capacity report but rather just a vague figure provided by a broker. They may also be difficult over obtaining valuation evidence, especially of companies. These are things which you need to stay on top of as, if this information is not available in advance of the next court appointment (the FDRA) the process may be delayed.

> **"The narcissist is likely to provide obtuse or incomplete answers to your questionnaire, and not respond on time."**

Although a costs order may be made against the party whose fault it is that delay has occurred, this might be hard to prove, and delay may be highly undesirable in a process which is already excruciatingly slow.

The FDRA

Once you've managed to get through the financial disclosure process, showing all of the resources available or at least highlighting areas of dispute between you, you then move into the negotiation stage. This happens at an FDRA or Financial Dispute Resolution Appointment. Only in very rare cases where it is absolutely clear that a negotiated settlement cannot be achieved can an FDRA be sidestepped, and the case goes straight to a final trial.

The FDRA is a hearing which takes place in court. Usually both sides will each be represented by a barrister (Counsel), unless you have a solicitor who does their own advocacy to this level. Ideally, your solicitor should also be present, although they might send a junior from their firm to make notes on the day and provide your Counsel with information, especially if it is very unlikely that an agreement is likely to be reached at this court appointment.

The FDRA is rather like a mediation appointment with a judge. Neither you nor your spouse speak at the FDRA, unless not represented by lawyers (i.e. if you are a litigant in person). You are not cross-examined at an FDRA. The judge might ask you a direct question for clarification, but this is unlikely.

The judge will listen to both side's proposals, put forward by their respective barristers. They then give their view of what they might do if they were the judge at a final hearing i.e. the order which they would impose. At an FDRA the judge can only give guidance – they cannot impose anything other than an order for a final hearing to take place in the event that the couple are unable to reach agreement.

At the FDRA you:

- Do not speak.

- Should not show any emotion – eye rolling or gasps at what the other side or the judge is saying are out.

- Should be respectful of everyone who is present.

- Should listen carefully to what the judge has to say.

- Are allowed to write and pass a brief note to your barrister, who you will be sitting next to, if there is something of relevance to point out (but don't overdo this as it makes it hard for your representative to concentrate).

- Should appear outwardly confident. Your narcissistic spouse will not like this, as they were used to manipulating and controlling you. They won't like the uncertainty this will cause them to feel, and it might encourage them to settle.

Once the judge has given their view, you then go back into the room with your legal team who will advise you on what they think should happen from there. The barrister will leave the room to meet the barrister from the other side and try to negotiate with them on various points, and will come back to discuss what they have achieved, and what the other side are prepared to give or agree on. There may be much to-ing and fro-ing as they negotiate with the other side. You will not be present during these negotiations.

Points to consider before and during negotiations

The need to win or have the last word

Narcissists do not negotiate in the way that you might expect. They must win at all costs. Their agenda may not be to resolve the dispute but rather to retain control of the person who had the audacity to stand up to them, perhaps at any price. And if they can't really win, they *must believe that they have won*. You and your lawyers will need to bear this in mind when negotiating with them. At the very least, they will need to have had the last word. Make sure you let them think they have. It may be that if the narcissist realises that you may be prepared to accept less than they have been advised by their own lawyer that you *could* achieve at court, they may be prepared to accept this – because it makes them feel that you have capitulated, or because they think they have 'got one over on you'.

The best financial deal might not be what is important to you

During the divorce process you may have come to realise that you are not looking for the best financial 'deal' because the cost of trying to achieve that, on a personal level, might be too great. You may want your life back. You may want an outcome that you can live with and which the court will see as 'fair' or 'reasonable'. You may wish your legal costs to remain proportionate and affordable, especially as all legal costs incurred will only reduce the funds available for your future. It may even be that the legal costs of having to go to a final hearing will be so large that it makes more financial sense for you to make a significant financial compromise at the FDRA, which the narcissist might agree to. You may need to explain these points to your lawyer.

> **"If the narcissist can't really win, they *must believe that they have won.* "**

Work out your bottom line

Decide what your bottom line is at an early stage – perhaps with the assistance of Counsel (your barrister) as well as your solicitor, keeping this in your team's back pocket during the negotiation process.

Find your leverage

When you come to negotiation you will realise why it was so important to provide your lawyer with as much background information as possible. They will need to ascertain where your leverage lies; what is it that will attract the narcissist to settle before a final hearing? Perhaps agreeing to let the narcissist keep an asset that they want which a judge at final trial would probably order be sold? Or perhaps finding something that will trigger their shame (which they are unable to take on board, as part of their condition, and so will not wish to face)?

You will have the final say as to what you agree to, although you may find yourself making life changing decisions under extreme time pressure, albeit with legal advice on hand.

Your own legal team will not put pressure on you to settle. The other side may, however, make an offer which will be withdrawn if a deal is not done on the day. It is for this reason that you want to have in mind where your bottom line lies in advance of the hearing.

It can be very useful to have a supportive friend with you at the FDRA – they will not be able to come into the courtroom with you, but can be in the room with you and your lawyers beforehand and during the negotiation process, and can run out for coffee and food for you when necessary. They can also undertake the invaluable task of holding a consultation room for you while you are in court, to ensure you have somewhere private to go back to. Otherwise the only alternative is the court corridor, which is not the best place to listen to advice or make important decisions.

If the narcissist settles

The narcissist, if they are inclined to settle, may do so at the very last minute of the FDRA day, causing you to feel unsettled and rushed when agreeing to offers.

Once agreements have been reached, a consent order detailing the agreements reached on that day will need to be drafted. If there is time to do so, this may be done at court. The applicant's legal team will do the drafting, and this will be checked and approved by those representing your spouse. This will then be signed by both parties, and the judge. This will be the order setting out what you have agreed so that it is legally binding and enforceable.

If agreements have only been reached at the very end of the day, it is often only possible for the lawyers to draft the so called 'Heads of Agreement' which will be signed by the parties and the judge. This is a document that sets out the agreed settlement in principle so that it is enforceable.

This means that the consent order is left to be fully drafted by lawyers later. The problem here is that any ambiguity in the Heads of Agreement gives the narcissist immense scope to nitpick and change as much as they possibly can in their favour in the following days or weeks. The narcissist will look for loopholes to exploit, and will find them. It is vital that your lawyer is aware of this and does everything possible to close them down in the initial Heads of Agreement.

Often the consent order will be drafted by Counsel as part of their brief fee for the FDRA hearing. They may be pleased and relieved to have achieved settlement and see the drafting of the consent order as a relatively simple and straightforward task. However, if one party is a narcissist, that could not be further from the truth. Counsel's involvement in the case may have only been over a matter of days, and they may not fully understand how important it will be to leave no grey areas in their consent order, which will have to be extra clear and detailed. Your solicitor will have to make sure that Counsel understands the reasons for this, and ensures that they are one step ahead of the narcissist and aware of anything which might give rise to confusion in the future.

Some areas that narcissist's commonly exploit, and which you should be prepared to draw to the attention of your lawyers on the day, are:

- **The termination date for child support**. The usual order will say '*until the child attains the age of 18 or ceases full time secondary education whichever shall first occur or further order*' but when does secondary education come to an end? Is it their last day of school? The day of their last exam? Or the end of the summer holidays? The month needs to be stipulated in the order. If maintenance is to continue to the end of tertiary education, when exactly is that, and what happens if there is a gap year? If maintenance is to conclude at the end of secondary education you may want to stipulate that this should mean 31 August of that year. The same might apply if the conclusion is tertiary education.

- **The duration of spousal support**. This may also be tied to the termination of child maintenance, so clarity becomes doubly important. How long the maintenance goes on for is known as the 'term' of the maintenance and, crucially, it may or may not be extendable. This may be something you want to discuss with your lawyers when the consent order is being drafted. If the term is extendable, the recipient of the spousal maintenance can seek to extend it some years down the line, so that their maintenance continues past the original term. They would have to demonstrate that, through no fault of their own, they have been unable to become financially self-sufficient during the term and therefore it is appropriate, based on 'need', for that term to be extended. The extension would have to be agreed by the parties (or an application to the court would have to be made by the recipient of the spousal maintenance) *before* the term has come to an end. To prevent the term of spousal maintenance from being an extendable one a 'Section 28(1A) bar' would have to be included in the order – an important consideration in a narcissistic divorce, particularly if the narcissist is the party receiving spousal maintenance, as they may well feel entitled to try to extend the term of the maintenance in later years.

- **The sale of the family home**. A sale order does not mean a sale. Conduct of sale will be joint and this can give the narcissist another opportunity to play games. They may not agree to a future reduction in the sale price even if recommended by the estate agent. An unrealistically high valuation may have been agreed, for the purposes of an FDRA, which the narcissist may want to hold on to, locking you into living arrangements which need to be brought to an end. Or the narcissist may insist upon driving down the sale price of the family home prematurely in order to punish you, especially if you are receiving a larger percentage of the equity in the house than your spouse, meaning that any future price reductions affect you proportionally more than them. It may be wise to make sure that the agreed estate agent is nominated in the consent order and also confirm that both parties will follow their written advice on price. Perhaps you should also insist upon a fixed lump sum figure if you are the weaker financial party, or at least a floor (minimum figure), rather than a percentage of the equity, so that there is no scope for the narcissist to reduce what you actually receive from the proceeds of sale.

- **Any interim financial arrangements, such as interim child and spousal maintenance, bills, mortgage payments and payments for the upkeep of the house and garden, whilst awaiting the sale of the matrimonial home.** Often consent orders only kick in once the house sale is completed, but what happens in the run up to that? What is the status quo? Who should be paying for what and for how long? Again, make sure that your lawyers ensure that there is no room for ambiguity here.

A common post-court ploy by the narcissist, to continue to rack up your costs with yet more goalpost changing, is to refuse to agree to the precise wording and drafting of the consent order. If, however, you can't agree on the drafting, you can submit this to the court showing the areas of disagreement and the judge who dealt with the hearing will decide on the wording on paper.

It may be appropriate at this time, if you are suffering from such drafting issues, for your solicitor to come 'off the record' and just provide advice to you in the wings. This makes the narcissist think that you have reduced their ability to financially abuse you by making you engage in further legal correspondence with them. This may well give you the upper hand, and result in them agreeing to the wording of the consent order and to signing much sooner than if you were officially represented. You would have to be prepared for their solicitor's letters to come to you directly, though, and you might have to be quite mentally tough to deal with them, but this is well worth considering.

If the narcissist does not settle

A narcissist will not settle a case unless it suits them to do so. An FDRA can be an expensive day out – especially if it appears that nothing has been achieved. The hearing provides another opportunity for the narcissist to waste time and costs, wearing you down and perhaps making you inclined to capitulate. Although most cases settle at or shortly after the FDRA (the second court appointment), this is not true in narcissistic divorces, even in cases which 'cry out to settle' in the eyes of your legal team.

So, you may find yourself in the situation where nothing has been agreed at the FDRA. But, as you have been told that often negotiation between solicitors leads to an agreement in the weeks *following* the FDRA, you may not be too worried at this point. At the FDRA a timetable is set to prepare for trial – for a final hearing. You might not take it too seriously at the time, expecting that the narcissist will see sense and an agreement will be imminent. And of course, they might.

But the narcissist will only settle if it is in their own interests to do so. Narcissistic rage is difficult to overcome and, if it has not subsided, the overwhelming desire to annihilate and take control is likely to continue. When someone has NPD, although you may think that self-interest is the only thing that drives them, they are in fact prepared to put their own best interests to one side if it means hurting, even destroying, the person who has inflicted narcissistic injury upon them. The longer the duration of the relationship with that person was, the stronger the desire to inflict pain will be. Sadly, the desire to inflict maximum anxiety and misery will be overriding.

An adjudicated, final trial also provides the opportunity to take centre stage when they give evidence, and at the same time gives them the chance to have highly paid legal brains fight their corner; do their very best for them and only have eyes and ears for them for the duration of the trial. All great narcissistic supply.

It is likely that deadlines to sort things out before a final trial will be looming, but every time you come close to an agreement regarding what the narcissist is prepared to offer you, or accept from you, the goalposts are moved by them. The gap between you may suddenly seem insurmountable and you find yourself thrust headlong into a final hearing. You may feel ill prepared, both financially and emotionally, for the cost that is about to be inflicted upon you.

When it becomes apparent that the other side intends to fight, make absolutely sure you prepare for it. You may still be clinging to the hope of settlement, and avoiding the final hearing, but at this point you will have to tell yourself that is not going to happen. You must now be fully focused on the forthcoming trial.

We now take you through the final hearing stage and what to look out for, but something always to bear in mind is that, even when under oath, people, especially narcissists, will lie in court. And they, very probably, will get away with it. Although this is no reason to give up the fight, you may have to adjust your expectations of the outcome.

The Final Hearing

If the couple are unable to negotiate, agree and settle at the FDRA or afterwards, then the case will move to the third stage in the court process; an adjudicated hearing. Here, a judge listens to the evidence and will impose a decision. It cannot be the same judge that dealt with your FDRA because that judge heard your 'without prejudice' proposals.

Only a very small percentage (perhaps around 5%) of divorce cases find themselves resolved via an adjudicated final hearing. However, the percentage in narcissistic divorces is significantly higher than this, because narcissists often relish dragging their spouses to this final stage. It may even be that the majority of divorces that end up at trial involve a narcissist.

We have already looked at what you would need to do to achieve a negotiated settlement, in order to avoid a final hearing:

- Be prepared to accept less than you might be entitled to

- Find a way to make the narcissist feel like they have won

- Stay one step ahead

It is important to understand that the court process rarely achieves 'justice' or 'fairness', whatever your perception of the meaning of those terms might be. The judge will do their best to make an order which falls within the bracket of what is reasonable. *An appeal against that decision is only possible if the judge made an error of law, not because they exercised their discretion in a way you don't like as a result of being taken in by a charming and plausible narcissist.*

"The court process rarely achieves 'justice' or 'fairness'. "

The family court system does not provide any form of retribution for lying in court. Unless it can be clearly shown that the court was misled to the point that an order was made to the detriment of the other party as a consequence (which is very difficult to prove), nothing is likely to happen if one party lies on the witness stand. Sadly, that is very likely where there is a narcissist involved.

Affording the legal fees for a final trial

Remember that the rules state that each party pay their own legal fees. It is highly unlikely that a costs order will be made in your favour (where your spouse is made to pay your legal fees) even if it is entirely clear that you only find yourself at a final hearing due to the stubborn approach taken by the other side towards negotiation and the legal process.

At the FDRA you will have been informed by the judge that an adjudicative final hearing is likely to double your costs. Your narcissistic spouse may have borrowed money to meet legal costs, having been informed that commercial debts are likely to be discharged from the capital of a marriage, effectively reducing the financial pot. You need to think about how you are going to pay for your legal fees.

Borrowing money from family ('the bank of Mum and Dad') can be seen as a 'soft loan', i.e. something that doesn't need to be repaid. If you are going to borrow money from family or friends make sure that you have a written and signed loan agreement with a repayment plan and interest if applicable. Otherwise a commercial loan may be preferable. Ask your lawyer about a litigation loan if necessary. Interest may be high but it may help you with legal fees. If you find yourself in this invidious position you probably don't want to capitulate just because you can't afford to fight.

Remember, however, that you can settle at any time, but that may mean accepting what is on offer. You need to be sure that for every £1 you are spending on legal fees you are as sure as you can be that you will be getting at least £1 back.

If you simply can't afford legal fees, but don't want to back down, don't be afraid to be a litigant in person (LIP), where you represent yourself without lawyers.

"You need to be sure that for every £1 you are spending on legal fees you are as sure as you can be that you will be getting at least £1 back. "

The judge will be kind to you at the trial (but the actual outcome will not be affected). If you are the applicant but the other side has legal representation, their lawyer will have to prepare the trial bundle. (It normally falls upon the applicant's lawyers to prepare the trial bundle).

Because you are no longer legally represented your spouse's lawyer now has a duty to play with a 'straight bat' and to explain every stage to you in an understandable way. You may find that the tone of their communications improves as a result of this. Don't be afraid to ask them questions. We shall deal with how to be a litigant in person below.

Preparing for a final trial

You have reached the moment where you are going to ignore what the other side does. You are only interested in you.

If you are represented, your lawyer will be making the preparations for trial. If increasing legal fees have caused you to represent yourself as a litigant in person you will need to deal with the preparation yourself. In either case, you should pay attention to the following:

1. Check the directions order made following the FDRA; that will provide you with a timetable. Make sure you adhere to it. It is a good idea to pay proper attention to this document when it is first produced. Many of the dates by which you must do things will be calculable back from the date allocated for final hearing. This date may not be known at the time the order is prepared by the court office but as soon as it is confirmed work out these dates and put them in your diary.

2. Deal with everything in timely fashion.

3. You will by now have realised the need for the provision of updating financial disclosure, such as up to date bank statements, etc. Keep a folder and put your disclosure documents into it as soon as they arrive so that you can deal with updating disclosure requirements.

4. If you know you are going to be asked to provide property particulars, both for you and the other side, keep an eye on Rightmove so that you can talk from an informed position about the property market. Take the trouble to actually drive past (or even visit) the properties which are on your list, especially the ones you are saying might be suitable for your spouse.

5. If you are seeking to argue that pre-relationship or post-separation resources should be ring-fenced and left outside any sharing calculation, make sure that your figures are up to date so the resources can be clearly identified.

6. The most important document is your section 25 statement. Have a look at section 25 of the Matrimonial Cause's Act and the section 25 factors for which the court must have regard. They are:

Section 25(1) requires the court to have regard to all the circumstances of the case, with the first consideration being given to the welfare of a minor child of the family who has not attained the age of 18. A child of the family is defined as a child of both parties to the marriage or civil partnership, and any other child (not being a child placed with those parties as foster parents by the local authority or voluntary organization) who has been treated by both parties as a child and their family. This will therefore include step children.

Section 25(2) contains the following checklist of factors:-

a)   The standard of living enjoyed by the family before the breakdown of the marriage.

b)   The age of the parties to the marriage and the duration of the marriage.

c)   Any physical or mental disability of either of the parties to the marriage.

d)   The contributions which each of the parties has made or is likely in the foreseeable future to make to the welfare of the family, including any contribution by looking after the home or caring for the family.

e)   The conduct of each of the parties, if that conduct is such that it would in the opinion of the court be inequitable to disregard it.

f)   In the case of proceedings for divorce or nullity of marriage the value to each of the parties to the marriage of any benefit which, by reason of the dissolution or annulment, of the marriage, that party will lose the chance of acquiring.

Don't fall into the trap of thinking that the standard of living while married must be maintained. Of course two people can't live separately in the same way as they can together – finances simply will not permit this. The reference to standard of living just identifies the relevant cost bracket. It doesn't mean that it must be maintained at the same level, as this would be impossible

Make sure you understand the difference between your 'without prejudice' position and your 'open' position. A letter which is marked without prejudice cannot be disclosed to the court except at the FDRA which is a without prejudice hearing (unlike the final trial). Also, nothing which is discussed at the FDRA can be referred to at any other time, including at the final trial. (Anything which is marked without prejudice is privileged between the author and recipient and may not be shown to the court or referred to openly i.e. in a different communication which is *not* marked without prejudice. So, generally speaking, if without prejudice protection applies to a situation, whatever is said in that situation cannot later be relied upon by any party or used as evidence (whether it was said in a meeting, a letter or an email, for example). *Any* discussions undertaken under this without prejudice cloak of protection are confidential between the parties and, if the case goes to a final hearing, the without prejudice item cannot be mentioned to the judge).

Your previous without prejudice offers will therefore have been set out for the judge at the FDRA which is why your FDRA judge must not conduct your final hearing, as they must know nothing about these proposals. In the run up to the final trial you may still be making without prejudice proposals, as may your spouse, to try to reach an agreement. *Remember that these proposals should be more advantageous to your spouse than your 'open' position.* You must make an open offer within 21 days of the FDRA.

It is your 'open' position which will be set out in your section 25 statement, i.e. that which will be put to the trial judge as to what you think the outcome should be and what you are asking for. This is what you are going to fight for. Make sure that you clearly understand the terms of your 'open' position and how it differs from your most up to date 'without prejudice' proposal. Don't mix the two up.

> " **Make sure you understand the difference between your 'without prejudice' position and your 'open' position.** "

Note that the trial judge will assume that you have made a better offer on a 'without prejudice' basis even though they don't know what it is.

At the final hearing you will be represented by a barrister if you are not a LIP. You may already have had a barrister involved in your case. The person who will represent you at the trial will have been booked by your solicitor as soon as the final hearing date was known. They may have represented you at the FDRA.

There will be a date by which the brief to Counsel for the final hearing is 'deemed to be delivered'. This is usually 14 days before the date of the final trial. If the case settles after this date but before the trial date you will be obliged to pay Counsel's fee for the first day of the hearing no matter what. The fees for a hearing over two or more days are divided into a 'brief fee' and a 'refresher fee' for subsequent days. The brief fee is much higher than the refresher fees and it will be the refresher fees only which are saved if the hearing doesn't go ahead.

When negotiating on a without prejudice basis time may start to work against you as the brief delivery date looms, after which Counsel's fees will be payable for the first day of the hearing no matter what. Your lawyer might want to say that once Counsel's fees are payable (i.e. the brief delivery date has passed) your offer will reduce by that wasted cost if it is accepted after that date but before the trial date. Accepting an offer at such a late stage is not an uncommon approach adopted by a narcissist intent on costing you as much money as possible.

You may have already had a conference with Counsel to discuss the merits of your case. However, if you haven't and you feel it is important to you to have a meeting with your barrister in advance of the hearing, don't be afraid to say so. Your solicitor may be keen to save costs and may think it unnecessary for you, but if it is something you want and are prepared to pay for then insist. You are the client. You will have spent a lot of money up to this point and therefore, by comparison, the cost may not be significant.

It is vital that Counsel understands the mentality of the client on the other side. You may want to satisfy yourself that they know what they are dealing with before the date allocated for trial.

You may find that your chosen barrister is unable to deal with the final hearing at the last minute. Whilst continuity of representation is important for you, do remember that a barrister is just doing their job. They will rarely read the papers earlier than the day before the hearing and therefore it is relatively easy for someone else to step into their shoes. Certainly, this is the view the court will take. If it happens don't worry. The replacement will do just as good a job.

The trial bundle

The bundle is a collection of documents that is sent to the court in advance of the hearing, containing certain essential documents. It contains everything that the judge will see on the day of the final hearing, and you will need to become very familiar with how to work your way around it so that you can refer to it if you need to when you are being cross-examined on the witness stand.

It is the job of the lawyer of the applicant to prepare the trial bundle (unless the applicant is a litigant in person and the respondent is represented by a lawyer, in which case the obligation will pass to their lawyer, at their cost). If you are an LIP and your spouse is also an LIP, preparation of the bundle will fall to whoever is the applicant, but what is included in it will have to be agreed between spouses in advance of it being submitted to the court.

The timetable for the production of this bundle will be set out in the directions order arising from the FDRA. The bundle will contain the following documents:

- All court orders and notices

- All statements (which will include Form E and Replies to Questionnaire – both **without** supporting documents and your section 25 statement **with** exhibits

- All expert reports (valuations and pension sharing report)

- Any other relevant documents

The index (which is a paginated table of contents, in order, of what is included in the bundle, with page numbers to each document) is agreed in advance between the lawyers (or, if both you and your spouse are LIPs, agreed between yourselves).

If either side wants to include documents which are not agreed by the other side (this is usually correspondence), a small supplementary bundle will need to be prepared and the judge may have to decide whether they will read it as a preliminary issue on the day.

The bundle will be prepared electronically. If you are not preparing it yourself as an LIP, make sure that you receive a copy in advance (this will be a few days before the hearing) and familiarise yourself with it. If you want to receive a printed version, ask for one. There may be a small printing cost.

Previous 'without prejudice' offers, such as those made at the FDRA, cannot be in the trial bundle as the judge is not allowed to see them. You may feel that the judge will not, therefore, see how reasonable you have been and how hard you have tried to reach an agreement. However, these are the rules. This aspect will please the narcissist, who has forced you to reach the final hearing as a result of their unreasonable approach to negotiation. However, you can be sure that the judge will be of sufficient experience to pick up a flavour of what has been going on from the papers which have been disclosed, so don't worry too much about this.

The day itself

If you are still sharing a house with your spouse you may want to stay somewhere else overnight if the case takes place over more than one day and you do not want to be under the same roof during the time of the hearing. A narcissist will take every opportunity possible to devalue you and your legal team; to make you feel anxious and vulnerable. The stakes are high now, and you will need to feel confident.

The judge will hopefully have had a chance to read the hearing bundle. They will definitely have read the position statements filed by either side and will listen to oral evidence. Once the hearing is going ahead focus just on your role which is to give your evidence as best you can. Don't worry about what the other side does – your legal team will deal with that. Don't allow anything said or done by your spouse to take your attention away from what you need to do on the day which is to give your evidence truthfully and clearly.

What to wear at the final trial

This is always an important consideration for anyone on a day which is significant. In reality it probably isn't as important as you might feel it is, but presentation does matter, and it is important to feel confident. Whether your hearing is remote or in person make sure that you dress:

- for yourself; and

- for the impression you want to create for the judge

No one else matters. Wear what feels comfortable but looks smart. If you want to create an impression for the judge and you think your clothes can contribute to that, then do so. Don't over-think it or over-do it. You want the people that matter to be on your side.

What do you call the judge?

This is a really basic question but so important to tick off a list of things to remember. It's either Sir or Madam. If you forget – follow the lead of the lawyers.

Settlement 'at the door' of the court

By the time the day of the final trial arrives, the narcissistic spouse may have fulfilled their desire to punish and to control you by having compelled you to incur the financial and emotional cost of attending a final hearing. The uncertainty of the outcome of the hearing may, however, not be a risk they are prepared to take, especially if they have been advised that their case may not be that strong. It may, therefore, suit them to try to settle on the day.

The desire to win might, then, transfer to a desire to control the outcome of the day instead, and they might want to believe that, thanks to their negotiating skills, they have avoided an adjudication and settled on their terms, at the eleventh hour.

Be aware that this may happen on the day and make sure you have thought in advance what you might be prepared to agree to. Bear in mind how important it is for a narcissist to win when considering how to proceed. Think also about whether, having come this far, you now want to have your 'day in court.' Listen to the advice of your legal team – but bear in mind they can't give any guarantees. The court environment is a very uncertain place in terms of outcome, and family law is a very discretionary area of law – the outcome will be very dependent on the discretion of the final trial judge, so no one really knows how things will play out.

The decision will ultimately be yours, should the narcissist try this tack, so have a plan ready for settling, just in case.

You may want to also consider that an unsuccessful trial will be narcissistic injury for a narcissist, with all the repercussions of that. If you have children to co-parent, you may not want to be responsible for yet more narcissistic rage.

Your cross-examination

At the final trial, you will be put in the witness box and cross-examined by your spouse's barrister. Be warned – cases are won and lost from the witness box. How you perform has a huge bearing on the outcome of this trial.

If you are the applicant in the proceedings you will go first, which is sometimes easier. If your spouse is the applicant try not to listen too hard to what is being said by them. That is the role of your legal team. Try not to let it affect your ability to give your evidence well.

The order of 'play' is as follows:

1. Opening submissions by Counsel for the applicant

2. Evidence in chief applicant

3. Cross-examination applicant

4. Re-examination applicant

5. Evidence in chief respondent

6. Cross-examination respondent

7. Re-examination respondent

8. Closing submissions respondent

9. Closing submissions applicant

10. Judgement

> **Be warned – cases are won and lost from the witness box. How you perform has a huge bearing on the outcome of this trial.**

During your 'evidence in chief' your Counsel will ask you some simple questions to get you used to giving evidence.

Your spouse's barrister will then cross-examine you.

Re-examination, by your own Counsel, follows to undo any damage achieved in cross-examination.

Listen carefully to your legal team about how to give your evidence. There are three golden rules:

*   Answer the question

*   Tell the truth

*   Don't get emotional

Keep your answers short and succinct – just a sentence or two at most. If you are on your fourth sentence, you have probably said too much. Avoid the inclination to 'tell your story' from the witness box. It can be incredibly tempting to do this during cross-examination, but it will not work in your favour. Accept points against you if you have to – your barrister will deal with the fallout from this on your behalf. That is their job.

Don't argue with Counsel for the other side from the witness box. They may want to antagonise – in fact they are likely to have specific instructions to do so. Don't rise to that. Answer questions calmly and don't be afraid to pause when you give your answers. A pause in your head feels much longer than it is in reality.

The three golden rules

Whatever you do, try not to cry. Tears will not gain you any sympathy and will be a huge source of supply for your narcissistic spouse.

► **Answer the question**

If you are giving evidence over any break (lunchtime or overnight) you may not talk to your legal team about the case itself until your evidence is concluded.

► **Tell the truth**

► **Don't get emotional**

If your spouse is acting in person

It is possible that your spouse will decide to deal with the hearing in person – hoping that the fact that they will then be able to cross-examine you themselves will frighten you into capitulation.

If you find yourself in this situation remember that the judge is there to prevent abusive use of the court process. Just focus on your case in exactly the same way you would if both parties were represented by lawyers, as described above. Remember:

- Do not show your fear. If fear wells up in you, try to recognise that it is just an emotion and do not allow it to pull you into a series of negative thoughts.

- Appearing quietly confident (whether you feel it or not) will destabilise your narcissistic spouse.

- Be strong and resolve to do your very best for the duration of your cross-examination, which may go on for a couple of hours.

"Don't argue with Counsel for the other side from the witness box. They may want to antagonise – in fact they are likely to have specific instructions to do so. Don't rise to that."

- Make sure your answers portray you as a rational, reasonable person to the judge. What they think is all that matters here, not what the narcissist thinks.

- Do not play the victim.

- Be calm and polite to your narcissistic spouse, even as they ask you outrageous questions which are designed to frighten you, hurt you or portray you as a liar.

- If you can sound level headed and rational this will infuriate the narcissist, and they will more than likely start to ask more and more abusive and accusatory questions, in order to devalue you and criticise you further. This will hopefully be noticed by the judge, and will have the effect of discrediting the narcissist, rather than you.

- The narcissist without legal representation may show their true character much more readily than one who is represented.

Judgment may be given orally on the day but more often is handed down in writing a few days later.

The court process in Children Act proceedings

The welfare of the children of a separating couple is, one might say, very much more important than the resolution of financial matters. As we have stated previously, it is far better for parents to find ways to resolve issues relating to their children via a communicative and discursive route – not least because they may be co-parenting children for many years to come. This can be particularly tricky where one parent suffers from NPD.

Children Act Proceedings should really be an absolute last resort. The Children Act is actually legislation 'without teeth' and applications can be quite futile as, even if an order is achieved, the other parent can still refuse to comply with it and very little can be done – orders under The Children Act can be difficult to enforce. In circumstances where there is no alternative, however, a court application may have to be issued. An application for a 'specific issue order' is to require something to be specifically *done* in relation to children, such as being permitted to go on holiday or attend a particular school. An application for a 'prohibitive steps order' is to *stop* something from happening such as a medical procedure. As a parent, it is also important to consider the effect such litigation will have on the children themselves, if they become aware of it.

The welfare of the child is the first consideration of the court. The welfare checklist is set out at section 1 of the Children Act 1989 as follows:

1. The ascertainable wishes and feelings of the child concerned

2. The child's physical, emotional and educational needs

3. The likely effect on the child if circumstances changed as a result of the court's decision

4. The child's age, sex, background and any other characteristics which will be relevant to the court's decision

5. Any harm the child has suffered or may be at risk of suffering

6. Capability of the child's parents (or any other person the courts find relevant) at meeting the child's needs

7. The powers available to the court in the given proceedings

> **"The welfare of the child is the first consideration of the court."**

Before making a court application, the applicant must first attend a MIAM and the accredited mediator will write to the other side to invite them to attend a similar meeting. If no response is received or the response is negative the mediator will sign an FM1 to enable the application to be made via a Form C100. The court fee at the time of going to print is £215.

In the event that the applicant also wishes to allege 'harm' a Form C1A is lodged with the court at the same time, setting out in detail the allegations made.

The court will allocate a date for the first appointment within about four to six weeks of the issue of the application.

The First Hearing Dispute Resolution Appointment (FHDRA)

The purpose of this first hearing is for the court to ascertain what the issues are. There will be an opportunity to meet with and discuss the case with the CAFCASS Officer to see if agreement can be reached at this early stage. The CAFCASS Officer is a representative from the Children and Family Court Advisory and Support Service. It is the CAFCASS Officer who will have the opportunity to meet with the children. It is unusual for the judge to make any decision at the FHDRA, save to order that a section 7 report to be prepared by the CAFCASS Officer. As well as having an opportunity to meet with the children they will speak to both parents and any other relevant parties and will provide guidance for the court. The view of the CAFCASS Officer can be challenged at trial under cross-examination but it is likely that the judge will be heavily influenced by what they have to say.

It can take over 20 weeks for the CAFCASS report to be prepared.

The court may also order statements from each parent. The purpose of these statements is for each parent to set out their position. However, consideration needs to be given by the court as to whether the production of statements *before* the CAFCASS Officer's report would be helpful, or whether the statements should be delayed until after the report has been prepared. It is likely that both you and your narcissistic ex will be critical of each other in your statements, in order to present your own cases – but this could polarise you even further and impede agreement. Once things have been said it is difficult for them to be 'unsaid' and the adverse effect can be significant, so trying to resolve the issues without such criticism being set out in written form may be the best way forwards (especially when narcissistic rage is likely). And bear in mind that, although court paperwork should not be shown to the children, it is not impossible for them to have sight of such documents, even by accident, and potentially by design with a narcissistic parent. Of course, this could be damaging to the child in itself. So, the ideal would be an agreement being reached without the need for your statements, with the assistance of the guidance of the CAFCASS Officer in the section 7 report. However, it may be that, with good reason, statements from you are needed *by the CAFCASS Officer* before they commence their work. In this case the statements would be ordered to be provided first.

Where there are allegations of harm, the court may order a fact finding hearing, where the court will decide, on the balance of probabilities, what view would be taken by the court on the allegations raised if the matter were to reach a final hearing.

The Dispute Resolution Appointment (DRA)

This hearing very much mirrors the FDRA in the financial proceedings. The purpose is for the court, assisted by the CAFCASS report, to try to help the parents reach an agreement. Nothing is imposed by the court at this stage.

The Final Hearing

If parents are unable to reach agreement the court will impose an outcome. As happens in financial hearings (see above), the applicant will present their case first and give their evidence. They will be cross-examined and re-examined. Then the respondent will do the same. Both parents are likely to be represented by Counsel. The respondent's Counsel will make their final submissions first, followed by Counsel for the applicant. The judge will then make a decision, which may be provided orally on the day or later in writing.

Costs orders are rarely made in Children Act proceedings as parents are entitled to raise issues about their children, so you unlikely to recoup your legal fees from your former spouse. If, however, repeated applications are made, the court may prevent further applications being made without first obtaining the leave of the court.

The court will be heavily influenced by the views of the CAFCASS officer so very careful consideration should be given at or before the DRA to the content of that report.

The following points are worthy of consideration in connection with Children Act proceedings:

1. It is possible to represent yourself in Children Act proceedings.

2. It is not possible for the court to compel a parent to spend time with their children.

3. A court order can be inflexible, which may not work well in the longer term, as the child grows older and their needs change.

4. Orders, especially in relation to contact arrangements are, in reality, difficult to enforce if one parent refuses to adhere to the terms. There is an inaccurate belief that they will be enforced by the police. This is not correct.

5. A judge will always exercise caution when making decisions, which can mean that significant delay will be inevitable, especially when waiting for a

CAFCASS report. This may play into the hands of a parent who is unreasonably withholding contact.

6. 'Shared care' does not necessarily mean an equal division of time.

7. Except where there is a 'live with' order (which means that the parent with whom the children 'live' can take the children abroad for 28 days in any 12 month period without the written consent of the other parent), neither parent can take the children abroad without the written consent of the other parent.

There is no such thing as a 'custody' order, 'access' or 'residence'. The court will make a 'child arrangements order' which deals with where a child will live and how much time they will spend with each of their parents.

Where parents would prefer a private adjudication, the arbitration process has been available since 2016 (see page 185). From 2020 arbitration can also be used to decide applications to take a child out of the jurisdiction of the court, including applications regarding foreign holidays or external relocation (i.e. an application to move a child to permanently reside in another country).

The Certainty Project, which offers the opportunity to construct a child arrangements plan with a mediator, or an adjudication by an arbitrator if that doesn't work, is an excellent process model for dealing with all child related issues without going to court.

The weaknesses of the court system

Unfortunately, the court system suffers from inefficiency as a consequence of government underfunding. This is a reality which is unavoidable. The judiciary are diligent and committed to providing a fair outcome. They are, however, human and entitled to exercise their personal discretion. They may be taken in by a charming narcissist. They may be in a bad mood on the day of your trial. They may even have not had time to read your court papers before your trial. Avoiding a final trial, or the court process altogether, may well be in everybody's best interests. But if you do end up in court, do not have any expectation that the court will provide retribution or warn your spouse against treating you in the way they perhaps have throughout your relationship. The role of the court is either to regulate child arrangements in a Children Act application or to divide resources in accordance with the law in Financial Remedy proceedings – no more than that.

Post-divorce **11**

You've probably endured years of abuse, either of the subtle, low level, wearing kind, or the overt bullying sort or even a combination of the two. You've gone through a horrific divorce, during which the narcissist has completely decompensated and shown their true colours in no uncertain terms, driven by narcissistic injury and rage. They have shown no mercy and tried every trick in the book to annihilate you.

You are exhausted, and as your Decree Absolute arrives with a thud on your doormat, you feel a sense of relief – that now, surely, the abuse will be over.

Post-divorce abuse

But as your friends appear with champagne and toast your new-found freedom, we have to tell you that it may not be all good news. Unless you are one of the few people who are fortunate enough to not share children with the narcissist, and to have secured a clean break financial settlement (which is very often not financially possible because of lack of funds), the abuse will, to some degree continue. This is particularly the case if you have children with the narcissist, who will use them as tools of continued abuse. Narcissists are effortless manipulators. They will use whatever they can to get at you, for as long as they can, and the quicker you can completely uncouple from them, the better. If you still own joint assets for example (perhaps you are waiting to sell your house or other assets) the narcissist will view these as areas ripe for exploitation, and they will continue to cause mayhem until you have disposed of them. It is common for narcissists to drive down the price of assets to punish you if they are the higher earner, or to refuse to sell assets at an acceptable price if they are not. They will not go quietly, and anything that ties them to you is a potential weapon.

Things are unlikely to be as bad as they were through the divorce, but there will be times of frustration, pain and worry ahead, for as long the narcissist has to be in your life to any degree at all.

Remember that the narcissist will be unable to see you as a combination of good or bad traits, as all people really are. Because of their problem with 'whole object relations' as described earlier in the book, you will always be seen as 'all bad'. Not only that, but they will be cluelessly projecting their own flaws and bad behaviour on to you, genuinely believing that you are a villain, and they, a victim. You will continue to be badmouthed by the narcissist to all who will listen – they will never be able to wish you well, nor hope for your future happiness, as a healthy person might.

The ideal scenario is to go "No Contact" with the narcissist, and everyone they know, for ever more – it is by far and away the best way to minimise any opportunities for them to manipulate situations and people to your detriment. But if you can't do this because, for example, you share children with the narcissist, there are still ways to lessen the potential pain.

If you are the party paying maintenance to the narcissist you can expect continued attempts at financial abuse with:

- Complaints that they are unable to survive on the money they are receiving from you.

- Court threats or actual court action against you to seek an upward variation (increase) in maintenance.

- Intrusive surveillance from the narcissist of your living circumstances, with comments about how much you are spending on holidays, your car, your house. Remember that to them, what's yours is theirs, and what's theirs is theirs, due to their sense of entitlement.

- Online stalking for the same reasons as above.

- Claims that they cannot work due to ill health.

If you are the party receiving maintenance from the narcissist, they will be deeply resentful that they have to pay you anything. Again, to them, what's theirs is theirs – you have no entitlement to anything at all, even if a court order says differently. As they do not respect the rules or the law they may:

- Make late payments.

- Miss payments.

- Claim they cannot afford payments.

- Claim illness or needing to retire early after the financial settlement has been made.

- Threaten to or actually make applications to the court to downward vary (decrease) your maintenance, even after just a few months or years.

- Insist that you take up extra work, usually of their choice, in order to give them the ability to reduce their payments to you.

- Badmouth you or have inappropriate conversations with your children regarding money, casting you in the villain's role.

- Refuse to contribute to extras for the children such as gifts or school trips, using false justifications such as telling them that they cannot afford them as they give all the money to you.

- Manipulate the children into wanting certain items by encouraging them, and then insisting that you, the weaker financial party, will have to pay.

- Refuse to financially help to the children as they grow older with non-court ordered things such as driving lessons or university costs, so that you, if you are the lower earner, find yourself paying so that the children do not miss out.

- Stalk you online or in reality in order to ascertain what you are spending on, to use as ammunition against you.

You might expect that once the narcissist has a new partner, things will improve for you, and often they do, as the new partner is a fresh and exciting source of supply through the adoration and attention that they give the narcissist. However, the drama and conflict that they can get from you, as a reviled figure, will always have some pull for the narcissist. The new partner, who will invariably have heard about you as a cruel and vindictive monster, may even enable the narcissist's post-divorce abuse of you. And if you are really unlucky, they might even be enlisted by the narcissist as a flying monkey, and join in with their tactics. Bear in mind also that not all new partners will be aware of the narcissist's behaviour towards you post-divorce. Narcissists are pathological liars, and may well be able to completely compartmentalise things, especially if their partner is someone who they know might disapprove of their actions, and call them out on it. The last thing the narcissist will want is to be abandoned, after all.

The narcissist's harem

Many narcissists like to keep their old sources of supply on hand for when they need a top up of validation, adoration, drama or conflict in times of low narcissist supply. Narcissist's often have a harem full of these past love interests, and may wish to recruit you into it, possibly many years down the line.

If your ex is the type who has remained friends with his or her former flames, just be aware that one day, when you least expect it, this might happen to you. Don't fall for it.

The narcissist's children and you

In Chapter 4 we discussed how narcissists behave towards their children, and the reasons for this. Post-divorce, the children are the narcissist's biggest remaining weapon – and they will ruthlessly aim them at you and take fire, with no concern at all for their well-being.

If you have an expectation of being able to peacefully co-parent with a narcissist, you may well be disappointed – to a narcissist there is no such thing.

Sadly, not only will they exploit the children in order to abuse you, but they will also abuse them directly. To recap, they may:

- Parentify the children – requiring them to take on adult tasks such as becoming their confidante, or roles that they themselves find too boring or important to do themselves such as house cleaning and cooking.

- Cast them into the roles of the golden child, the scapegoat and the invisible child, alternately swapping the roles at their own whim.

- Directly financially abuse the children, even taking away their presents or their own money.

- Offer them gifts, special days out or holidays and then change their minds, shifting the goalposts. When the child is disappointed, they then shame them, for example calling them materialistic or spoilt.

- Indulge in calling them cruel names e.g. "Fatty" or "Thicko", often under the guise of joking.

- Violate their boundaries by reading diaries, walking into their rooms without knocking, checking their phone messages and even answering messages, from you, on their behalf.

" Post-divorce, the children are the narcissist's biggest remaining weapon. "

- Fail to engage with the children's schools, nor encourage or facilitate homework or revision, or do the opposite and be over involved and controlling.

- Exhibit controlling behaviours such as choosing their friends, school or university courses, how they dress, whether they can go out.

- Fail to provide or oversee the basics for smaller children such as clothing, tooth brushing and medication.

- Engage in neglectful behaviours such as failing to provide medical care when needed, such as for asthma attacks, suspected broken bones, etc due to their lack of empathy, or fail to acknowledge health conditions at all.

- Fail to take into consideration the wishes of the child regarding all sorts of things, as they view their children as extensions of themselves, who must therefore want and need the same as them.

- 'Love' the child purely in a conditional and transactional way.

- Shame the children.

- Be late for the children or fail to turn up at all for them.

- Carry out the repeating cycle of idealise (love-bomb) and devalue.

The narcissistic parent, having weaponised the children against you, will delight in finding all manner of ways in which to abuse you or cause you frustration through them. As they carry out these tactics, they love-bomb the children, who, grateful for the attention and pleased to be back in their good books, are unable to see the situation as it really is. Their brains learn the technique of cognitive dissonance as a survival tactic, where they deny, minimize or justify the less than salubrious behaviours of the narcissist, so that they are not in mental discomfort. Sadly, you are at risk of looking like the crazy parent in the eyes of the children when you (rightfully) get upset or annoyed by the narcissist's manipulations of them, and you. One such commonly employed area is financial abuse, but another particularly disturbing area is that of parental alienation.

Parental alienation

The term 'parental alienation' describes a process through which a child becomes estranged from a parent as a result of the psychological manipulation of the other parent. The child's estrangement may manifest itself as fear, disrespect or sometimes even hostility towards the distant parent.

In a situation where one parent suffers from NPD, it is not unusual for that parent to accuse the other of 'parental alienation' as part of their 'smear campaign' or in an attempt to undermine or devalue the non-narcissistic parent. This could be in a situation where child arrangements are entirely child focused and the narcissistic parent does not like them, or they are simply intent on causing mischief and upset.

It may also be that the narcissistic parent, through badmouthing the other parent, is the perpetrator of the parental alienation themselves. And it could actually be that the narcissist is doing a combination of the two – alienating the children from the other parent themselves, whilst actually 'projecting' this behaviour on to the other parent, accusing them of it (see page 83).

It's crucial, if any of these situations arise, that you bring them to the attention of your solicitor. This is yet another reason why it is so important for your solicitor to understand the features of NPD, so that they can work with the solicitor on the other side to carefully consider the motives behind any accusations made, whilst focusing firmly on the welfare of the child. In cases like this, you may need to jointly instruct (with the narcissist) an Independent Social Worker. This would need to be done at a very early stage, before the situation escalates to something which may be damaging for the child.

In accordance with the welfare check list set out in section 1 of the Children Act 1989, the welfare of any child/children is of paramount importance to the court. Documentation is crucial if you have genuine concerns about the adverse influence which the other parent may have on the children, so be sure to document everything. You will need to carefully monitor any adverse effects of behaviour you see upon your child, and a thorough understanding of how narcissists behave towards their children is crucial, so that you can point these specific behaviours out to the court, without mentioning the 'narcissist' word. Clear and cohesive evidence will need to be presented to the court if any application to limit, suspend or terminate contact is to be successful, and this will largely be down to you.

It may be appropriate for you to work with a family consultant or coach who may be able to provide guidance as to when the narcissist's behaviour is such that contact with the children should be limited or brought to a conclusion, especially as expert evidence will always be extremely important to the court in deciding whether it will be in the interests of the child to limit or end contact with the narcissistic parent.

However, you need to understand that the court is likely to consider it important for any child to have some form of ongoing contact with both parents, even if a parent has a personality disorder or other issues. The court will attempt to achieve a balance between the interests of the child and the benefits of an ongoing relationship with both parents, considered against the damage which the ongoing relationship may have on a long term basis.

Parental responsibility

If you have children with a narcissist, it is vital to understand the concept of parental responsibility. Narcissists look for loopholes in everything they can, and love grey areas. You need to be clear on this area of the law, and know your rights, and theirs, especially as you cannot expect the narcissist to be able to calmly and rationally share information and make joint decisions about the children with you of their own volition.

Those with parental responsibility have rights to:

- Access children's medical records

- Be involved with the choice of the child's school

- Be involved in decisions regarding medical treatment

- Be involved with the religious upbringing of the child

- Be involved when to comes to naming a child or changing their name

- Be involved in decisions regarding holidays abroad and trips away with non-family members

- Know where their child/ren are living unless there are safeguarding reasons which means that an address must be withheld

They are also responsible for:

- Disciplining the child

- Looking after the child's property

Parents have to ensure that their child is supported financially, whether they have parental responsibility or not.

If you have parental responsibility for a child but you don't live with them, it doesn't mean that you have a right to spend time with your children. However, the other parent must include you when making important decisions about their lives.

You do not always need to get the consent of the other parent for routine decisions, even if they also have parental responsibility.

If it's a major decision (for example, one of you wants to move abroad with your children) both parents with responsibility must agree in writing, but if you cannot agree you can make an application to the court, by applying for either a Specific Issue Order or Prohibited Steps Order. A judge will then make a decision which is in your children's best interests.

Who has parental responsibility?

A mother automatically has parental responsibility for her child from birth.

A father usually has parental responsibility if he's either:

- married to the child's mother; or

- listed on the birth certificate (after a certain date, depending on which part of the UK the child was born in).

You can apply for parental responsibility if you do not automatically have it.

For births registered in England and Wales

Married parents

If the parents of a child are married when the child is born, or if they've jointly adopted a child, both have parental responsibility.

They both keep parental responsibility if they later divorce.

Unmarried parents

An unmarried father can get parental responsibility for his child in one of three ways:

- Jointly registering the birth of the child with the mother (from 1 December 2003)

- Getting a parental responsibility agreement with the mother

- Getting a parental responsibility order from a court

For births registered in Scotland

Married parents

A father has parental responsibility if he's married to the mother when the child is conceived, or marries her at any point afterwards.

Unmarried parents

An unmarried father has parental responsibility if he's named on the child's birth certificate (from 4 May 2006).

For births registered in Northern Ireland

Married parents

A father has parental responsibility if he's married to the mother at the time of the child's birth.

If a father marries the mother after the child's birth, he has parental responsibility if he lives in Northern Ireland at the time of the marriage.

Unmarried parents

An unmarried father has parental responsibility if he's named, or becomes named, on the child's birth certificate (from 15 April 2002).

For births registered outside the UK

If a child is born overseas and comes to live in the UK, parental responsibility depends on the UK country they're now living in.

For same-sex parents

Civil partners

Same-sex partners will both have parental responsibility if they were civil partners at the time of the treatment, e.g. donor insemination or fertility treatment.

Non-civil partners

For same-sex partners who are not civil partners, the second parent can get parental responsibility by either:

- Applying for parental responsibility if a parental agreement was made; or

- Becoming a civil partner of the other parent and making a parental responsibility agreement or jointly registering the birth.

Applying for parental responsibility

If you're not the mother, you can apply to court to get parental responsibility.

You need to be connected to the child, for example as their father, step-parent or second female parent.

More than two people can have parental responsibility for the same child.

Scotland has its own set of rules, covered under 'ordinary cause procedures'.

You can apply in one of two ways:

- Sign a parental responsibility agreement. If you're a father who wants parental responsibility and the mother agrees, you can fill in a parental responsibility agreement, and have the agreement signed and witnessed at your local family court.

- Apply for a court order. If you want parental responsibility but cannot agree on arrangements with the mother, you can apply for a court order.

Parallel parenting

As we have established the only way the former partner of a narcissist can heal from narcissistic abuse is to, first and foremost, disengage from them. The ideal here is to go 'No Contact'; to cut all ties and communication of any sort completely. But when joint children are involved other measures have to be employed to ensure the well-being of that parent and by extension, the children.

We have already discussed the sad truth that co-parenting is not an option with a narcissist. Given half a chance, a narcissist's preferred option is instead to 'counter-parent' – to disagree with as many things as they can, and to throw as many spanners in the works as possible. Narcissistic supply is, once again, the key motivator here, and the drama, the conflict, the havoc, the need to win, the superiority, the "I know best" mentality all plays into this. Trying to battle it is pointless. This is where 'parallel parenting' comes in.

Here, contact between the parents is very limited indeed, allowing them to disengage from each other as much as possible whilst remaining connected to their children. The aim is also to shield the children from being placed in the middle of parental conflict. Communication between parents only occurs when absolutely necessary.

> **"Co-parenting is not an option with a narcissist."**

In parallel parenting, everything is separate – extracurricular activities, school meetings and doctor's appointments are not attended together. Generally speaking, unless otherwise agreed, the rules of whichever household the child is staying in at the time are followed.

Absolutely key to establishing parallel parenting is to create, with your lawyer, a child arrangements plan, which must be as detailed as possible; no stone must be left unturned, and no potential eventuality left unconsidered. This will be dealt with in detail later in this section.

Parallel parenting communication tips

We have already looked at specific communication strategies in Chapter 9.

It is also very important indeed to agree on a *single method of communication* between you and the narcissist – being bombarded with multiple ranting phone calls, texts, WhatsApps and emails is likely to be the result of not establishing such a rule. *It is generally better to communicate only by email,* where you can be more considered in your reply than with more intrusive methods such as text. At least with email you are less likely to respond in the heat of the moment and so inflame tensions further.

However, if the email route is not enough to keep your narcissistic ex in check, it may be beneficial for you to communicate only using a specialised parenting app, such as OurFamilyWizard. These apps enable all necessary child related communication, including schedules, calendars and appointments, and communication cannot be retrospectively edited. There is even a 'tonemeter' which encourages less inflammatory communication. Narcissists don't generally like such apps as they find them to be controlling, but if they can be persuaded to agree (perhaps by being persuaded by their own lawyer, or by being made to think that it was their own idea, and a means to control *you*) they can be very effective all round. Notably, these records are admissible as evidence to the court. They are well worth considering for the sake of your sanity. You may wish to split any annual fees between you or, if you pay for the narcissist, it may encourage them to agree to it.

Remember to be very careful how you communicate with the narcissist:

- Refrain from rising to any baits, under any circumstances. Narcissists know exactly which buttons to push to elicit a response which you may then find used against you in court, making you appear unstable or unreasonable.

- Refrain from speaking to them on the phone or in person if at all possible.

- Insist that if phone conversations have to occur, they will be recorded using a phone app. This may help to keep things civil.

- Give yourself a few hours to cool down before responding to the narcissist's communications.

- Decide whether there is anything to be gained from responding to the narcissist's communications *at all* and only respond if absolutely necessary.

- Use the 'grey rock' method of communication. If you have to see the narcissist face to face (not recommended) limit all facial expressions, speak in a dull monotone voice, and make reduced or no eye contact with the narcissist. Use as few words as possible, and give the narcissist no energy, moving away as soon as they can. This is in order to ensure that you are not a source of narcissistic supply, and are as boring to the narcissist as a grey rock. It may feel rude to you, but you will soon see how effective it is at forcing the narcissist to move on to more rewarding climes, narcissistic supply-wise.

- Know how to respond to a written communication, as described in detail in Chapter 9. Do not engage in any arguing. Do not try to defend or justify yourself, or respond to or make any accusations. Use the fewest words possible, for example: "Yes, 8pm", or "I do not agree to this", or "Pick up will remain at 5pm", or "Noted." Only the absolutely essential points regarding child related arrangements should be responded to. Add no niceties (they count as giving the narcissist narcissistic supply). This is 'grey rock' but in the written form.

- Be aware of what to do in situations where the narcissistic parent sends a written communication (such as by email), falsely claiming that an agreement was reached verbally when it wasn't. Respond in writing that no conversation ever took place, and document everything. It is common for a narcissist to try this tactic – they are highly manipulative and lie without a guilty conscience. Emails of this nature are common, e.g. "Further to our spoken conversation just now, I am writing to confirm that we agreed that I could have the children for the entire Christmas holiday this year..."

Documentation

Set aside a short amount of time every week to ensure that all your records of communications with the narcissist are kept up to date.

All communications should be downloaded, printed, and filed.

If telephone conversations do occur, they should be recorded and downloaded using a recording app on your phone. The recordings themselves may not be admissible in court but they will be useful for keeping track of what was said.

Keep a dedicated log detailing late pick-ups, cancellations and injuries sustained by the child etc. You never know when you might need this down the line, as narcissists have a habit of returning to court.

The child arrangements plan

If you want to avoid returning to court regarding issues to do with the children, it is vitally important that you agree a child arrangements plan, or parenting plan, which is almost 'over-detailed'. You need to pre-empt your narcissistic ex's tendency to look for loopholes and exploit any grey areas as their way of exerting control, causing chaos and abusing you and the children. Bearing in mind that a narcissist can have the emotional response of a small child, they may actually respond well to a clear set of guidelines which are indisputable, just like a child might.

It's really important to be particularly careful if your lawyers are negotiating an agreed child arrangements plan *at court*. The euphoria of having reached an agreement in court can sometimes lead to the lawyers rushing the drafting of the detail of the child arrangements plan. This is particularly likely if Counsel

> **"It is vitally important that you agree a child arrangements plan which is almost 'over-detailed'."**

does not fully understand the situation regarding your ex-spouse's personality. Here, it is essential that the solicitor in attendance stresses to Counsel the need for detail when drafting the child arrangements/parenting plan. A junior solicitor should not be left on their own attending court with Counsel in this sort of case, as they simply may not be up to the job.

You may be one of the lucky ones who reached an agreement out of court and the drafting is taking place at your solicitor's office. Again, crucial attention must be paid to the detail – your narcissistic ex may query the cost of such dedication, but getting this done effectively at this early stage will be key in helping you to avoid unnecessary litigation or disputes in the future.

If the narcissist and their legal team are resistant to a detailed child arrangements plan, make sure your lawyer has any information and documentation to hand to support your requirement for it.

These are some of the topics which you should consider having included in a child arrangements plan.

General parenting guidelines

a)   The importance of providing a united front for the children. How will the parents behave in front of the children? Is it important for the children to see that decisions are made collectively?

b)   Might it be important to agree to discuss any parenting issues by email as and when they arise, or should a regular (perhaps monthly) email exchange be agreed to this end? If so, which date of the month will this occur?

c)   How do the parents ensure that the children have a voice within the process? Might it be appropriate to arrange for them to speak with a grandparent or other relative?

d)   How will the parents communicate to the children the arrangements which they have made?

e)	How will the parents make sure that the children stay in contact with supportive relatives from the other side of the family, or friends?

f)	Are there any important rules that the parents consider essential for the children (for example bedtimes, when homework is done, computer games or films, staying out late)? Is it agreed between the parents that 'house rules' should be imposed in both homes? If not, why not and how will this be explained to the children?

g)	How do the parents work together to make significant decisions (for example school, course selection and careers advice)?

Communication

a)	Deciding on one form of communication, preferably email or a parenting app such as OurFamilyWizard.

b)	What is a reasonable time frame for responding to emails (for example 72 hours maximum)?

c)	What communication with the children is acceptable between the child and other parent when they are not staying at their home? Should specific times be agreed or a level of frequency during a period of time?

d)	Should the children have a mobile phone? If so, who should pay for the contract? Who pays for a new phone if it is lost/damaged?

Education

a)	What are the arrangements for 'pick up' and 'drop off' at school? How might these be altered in exceptional circumstances?

b)	Who will attend parents' evenings? Will the parents attend together or separately? (It is likely to be better for you to agree to attend separately, or for only one parent to attend, so that you can minimise contact with the narcissist, and prevent manipulations and triangulation involving the teachers).

c)	How is information from the school shared between the parents? Is the school happy to accept an email address from each parent or does some mechanism need to be in place?

d)	How are agreements to be achieved regarding extracurricular activities? Who will ensure that the children attend?

e) Are any other third parties allowed to collect the children from school or any other activity? If so, who and in what circumstances?

f) How does the school/parent portal for the child get set up so both parents have access to read school reports, activities etc.? Should there be one account with a shared password or is it possible for the school to set up two linked accounts, one for each parent?

g) Who pays for each extracurricular activity?

h) What extracurricular activities are acceptable and how is this agreed?

i) Who should attend school events (sports days, plays, concerts etc.)? For the mental health of the non-narcissistic parent it may be best, if both parents have to attend, that they agree to sit separately and not to communicate. Is the child permitted to speak to both parents on these occasions if the parents attend separately and how is this managed to ensure minimum embarrassment and awkwardness for the child?

j) How should information regarding the children's friends be shared e.g. possible friends who may be a bad influence etc.?

k) Who pays for school trips and how are these agreed?

l) Who pays for instrumental lessons and examinations or similar?

Medical issues

a) Which parent attends medical appointments? Is one parent responsible even if an appointment falls in the other's parenting time or is this responsibility shared?

b) Who is responsible for taking the child to the opticians? Who pays? Who holds any prescriptions? How is information about this shared?

c) Who is responsible for dental appointments and treatment? Or the orthodontist? Who arranges and takes the child to appointments and who should pay?

d) How is medical information shared?

e) Should medication be held at both homes or taken between the two? Where inhalers, Epipens or similar are required, how should it be ensured that they are retained at both homes, and are up to date? Can the parents agree how and when medication is administered?

f)   Agreements regarding diet – is the child vegetarian or vegan in their primary residence? Should the rules of each home regarding diet be respected, and the child eat whatever is considered normal in the home in which they are currently staying?

g)   Agreements regarding allergies and food intolerances etc. – where a particular diet is required to support treatment for other conditions, how can it be ensured that this is uniform in both homes?

Holidays

a)   Who should hold the children's passports? Will the other parent always retain a copy? Who has the obligation to renew (and pay for) passports? If this is shared how are funds reimbursed in a timely fashion?

b)   Who holds EHIC/GHIC cards for European travel? A time frame for these to pass from one parent to the other ahead of trips needs to be agreed.

c)   In advance, with an agreed time frame, each parent should inform the other of the location of any holiday including flight details, destination address and a contact telephone number for the duration of the trip.

d)   A framework needs to be agreed for permission to take the children abroad.

e)   Agreement to organise and take the children for travel immunisation needs to be sorted in good time if you are the parent taking them abroad.

Introduction of a new partner

a)   Agreement as to how and when (after how long) new partners should be introduced to the children needs to be sorted as well as consideration of whether this introduction to the children will also be communicated to the other parent.

General contact arrangements

a)   How will the parents inform the child about arrangements that have been made?

b)   What will be done in the case of an emergency?

c)   What happens if one parent is going to be late either collecting or returning the children? What is an acceptable period of time to wait and what might mean that the visit should be cancelled? What is the agreement as to how and when the late party will communicate this to the other parent?

d)   Where should 'pick up/drop off' take place? Can this involve the home of each parent or does it need to be a neutral place? If so, where? Can the children walk up the path to their parent's home unaccompanied? Must the other parent stay away from the property?

e)   What is the arrangement if one parent has consumed alcohol and is unable to drive? Should a taxi be involved? If so, which company and who should pay? Can a third party collect and return the children without the parent?

f)   What activities are deemed unacceptable at the other parent's house? For example, cycling without head protection etc. Can these guidelines be agreed?

g)   Should clothes/toothbrushes etc. be kept at both homes or packed and taken from home to home?

h)   Who provides and launders school uniform/games kit if contact takes place over a weekend and into the school week? Should there be two sets of school uniform/games kit and does each parent pay for one set?

i)   Do the parents have uniform guidelines for discipline? What discipline is deemed acceptable?

j)   What happens on the other parent's birthday/Mother's day/Father's day? Do the parents agree that they will each enable the child to get a present for the other or agree not to do so?

k)   If forms need to be signed by both parents how will they be returned to the other parent? What is the time frame for this?

l)   If a weekend needs to be swapped, is the main schedule retained or does that parent then have two weekends in a row?

Preventing the children from getting caught up in parental conflict

Unfortunately, even with a detailed child arrangements plan in place, there will be times when disagreements and conflict will be unavoidable. You may have to accept the likelihood of this, as well as the fact that it will largely fall upon you, as the non-narcissistic parent, to shield the children from such conflict as far as you are able.

The narcissist is likely to:

- Treat the children sub-optimally, because they know no other way.

- Badmouth and lie about you to them, in order to punish you.

- Use the children as a means through which they can legitimately maintain contact with you and keep some form of control. The children are likely to be your 'Achilles heel' and therefore an excellent button to repeatedly press.

- Use them to cause pain to you with no regard whatsoever to the consequences of the children being caught in the middle.

- Make numerous court threats via the children.

You have a very difficult line to tread – between enabling the narcissist's bad behaviour and openly denigrating it. Neither is ideal, and in truth, there is no perfect answer to these dilemmas.

What you can do

- Try to avoid a 'knee-jerk' reaction to the narcissist's behaviour in front of the children. Count to ten, go into another room, rant in your journal or to a friend. Only once you've got things off your chest and returned to a place of rational thinking can you respond logically and calmly.

- Pick your battles carefully. What you definitely do not want to do is give your children a childhood of which the predominant memories are friction and litigation between their parents over them.

- Accept that the court system is unlikely to be your salvation. It might be the only option in extreme situations but in most cases court action will only fuel narcissistic supply and make matters worse.

- Carefully consider whether discussing the narcissist's behaviour directly with them will have any positive outcome or whether it will just feed the drama. There are many occasions where you may just have to accept things as they are. You can only be responsible for your own parenting, and asking the narcissist to cooperate with you in adopting a certain parenting style is most likely to be met with deliberate opposition.

- Shield the children from the disputes between the two of you as much as you can, by not offloading on them, or trying to get them to see your point of view rather than the narcissist's. Stick your nose in the air and try to take the moral high ground.

- Try as hard as you can not to allow the children to become aware of how annoyed you are by the narcissist's manipulations via them. The effort required to maintain an outward image of calmness may well be Herculean. Again, offload on your friends, not on them.

- Expect times when your children will be unfairly turned against you, and run with it. If the children are old enough, you can simply suggest calmly to them that if they would like to know anything about you they can ask you directly. An explanation that if a person is angry with another person, they sometimes do not tell nice stories about them may also be helpful to younger children here. It is fine to contradict stories that are being told about you without specifically accusing the narcissist of lying – clarify what is *actually true about you* rather than directly labelling the narcissist's lies as lies.

- In situations where you can see the narcissist manipulating children against one another, try to provide support and reassurance but again, don't involve the narcissist. This will be exactly what the narcissist wants – to create chaos within the family and, as a consequence, be firmly placed back in the centre. If you can demonstrate equality between children and show no favouritism, you will be teaching them by example that no one child is better than the other in your household. Again, showing empathy, encouraging them to talk about their feelings and taking those feelings seriously, will be of benefit here – something that the narcissist will not be able to do. All you can do is lead by example.

- If the narcissistic parent refuses to pull their weight as Mum or Dad, for example not turning up to the school concert, sports day or parents' evening, try not to leave the children feeling that the other parent doesn't care, but at the same time avoid making excuses for the narcissist. Whilst you might want to avoid discussing the *behaviour* of the other parent with children, even if they are teenagers, you can still discuss with them their own reactions and feelings about it. You can treat the situation very 'matter of factly' without using it as an opportunity to highlight to the children how useless the other

> **"Compensating for or excusing poor behaviour is a no no, and so is exploiting it and using it to work in your favour."**

parent is. A response such as "That's a shame for you – I understand that you are disappointed" doesn't judge the other parent but does acknowledge that the child is allowed to have feelings (something which, of course, the narcissistic parent will be invalidating or ignoring).

When it comes to poor behaviour, compensating for it or excusing it is a no no, and so, of course, is exploiting it and using it to work in your favour. But completely ignoring it, or pretending that it is ok, when the risk is that the behaviour may be normalised by the children, is also not ideal. Perhaps the best course of action is to act consistently in a way which naturally contrasts your behaviour with the poor behaviour of the narcissist, without specifically talking about it. Be on time, show empathy, encourage the children to develop their own interests, celebrate who they are as individuals, support them in their ambitions and dreams, and teach them how to have boundaries. Listen to them, talk to them and get to really know them. Be a grown up. All things their narcissistic parent patently will not do.

As they grow up they will form their own view and develop their own adult relationships with both parents. They may decide not to have any relationship at all with one or other parent, but that should be left to their own adult judgement.

There is, sadly, an element of crossing your fingers regarding the amount of emotional and developmental damage that will be done to them whilst not in your care. But remember that even the 'best' parents inflict some damage on their children. It is part of everybody's life journey to overcome that damage. This is something you have limited control over – some acceptance, and self-compassion may be necessary here.

Practical tips for coping 12

First, let's talk about you

By now you will be aware that divorcing a narcissist is not the easy route, but you will also understand the severe limitations involved in staying in the relationship. There is no true empathy, no true connection, no true love and no true authenticity. There never will be, and there never can be, no matter how perfect the narcissist once seemed to you. The narcissist is *careless*, in that he or she *cannot* care about you, or anyone else. This was only ever a relationship of take and take.

And, because of the nature of the abuse you have suffered, whether it was of the chronic, low level kind, or the overt bullying sort, or a combination of the two, you have learnt, as a survival tactic, to walk on eggshells, whilst orbiting the narcissist constantly, never breaking away from that incredibly strong gravitational pull. You have subjugated your needs to the narcissist's needs, tiptoed around their fragile ego, given up your hopes, dreams and ambitions, put your life on hold, and fallen prey to the narcissist's 'future faking' (false promises about the future, which fail to ever materialise).

You have felt like you are 'not enough' for them, and you have tried harder to do better, to be better and to do more and to give more. And more. And more. You took on the responsibility of the failure of the relationship single-handedly – believing that it was your fault, that you should have felt lucky, that you were ungrateful. You have been gas-lighted, invalidated, criticised and demeaned, and your confidence is low. You may feel transparent, invisible, unheard. You may feel like only half a person. You definitely feel unfulfilled. You may have retreated into your shell, hardly recognising yourself anymore.

You may have been isolated from friends and family, and your support network may be small. You now know it will get even smaller as the beguiling narcissist picks off those who believe his or her tales of woe and victimhood. This is not a happy prospect.

You are used to thinking about the narcissist all the time. What they want, how to make things easier for them, how to facilitate their lives. It's now a reflex autopilot, thinking about them, and you can't get them out of your head, even though the thoughts are now not so positive. You are effectively addicted to them, as a result of trauma bonding.

You may be sideswiped by flashbacks as your brain finally allows you to see all the things it was previously suppressing in its bid to keep you safe from the discomfort of cognitive dissonance – the red flags of narcissistic personality disorder that you now realise were there all along.

You are grieving a loss of love that was never even real, and feeling the double anguish of that. It's debilitating at times, this pain.

As if this isn't difficult enough to cope with, once the divorce is underway the narcissist will fly into retribution mode, seeking to punish you for everything they can. Remember that they are wired to be unable to take the blame for anything – even if *they* left *you* for someone else, it will be your fault, and you will have deserved it. The venom with which they seek to bring you to your knees may be unlike anything you have previously experienced from them, and any doubts as to whether they truly do have NPD are likely to now vanish.

What follows are some survival strategies to help you cope during the divorce process and beyond. They are also the very first steps you need to take to begin the journey to healing from narcissistic abuse.

Dealing with thoughts about the narcissist

It's no wonder your mind is constantly pulled back to thoughts about the narcissist – after all, you have been a bit part in their show, most likely for years, and have lived to keep them happy and put them first. The trauma bonding that resulted from their emotional abuse tactics means that you are literally neurochemically addicted to them – these are difficult bonds to break. Add to this any flashbacks you may be experiencing, together with previously suppressed or denied realisations and memories popping into your head at inopportune moments, and it is easy to see why your mental space may be full.

Of course, some of these thoughts are useful to have – they are helping you to become aware of what happened to you, and why. But when they become ruminations, circular patterns of thinking, where the brain goes round and round the same subject matter, trying to solve an unsolvable problem, then you have an issue. Just like any other thoughts – if you think them enough, they become stronger and stronger, and more and more habitual, as the brain recruits more and more neurons to the thought pathway. Eventually, what started out as a tiny downtrodden path in the grass becomes a superhighway of ingrained thought, which you can be hurled down at great speed, so fast that you barely even noticed how you got there.

Scientists now understand that *every feeling, every emotion, is preceded by a thought*. Whether it's one you are fully aware of or not. Bear in mind also that memories are thoughts, as are daydreams.

In order to be able to cope in the divorce process, it is important to reclaim your mental space for yourself. It is time to stop these emotional hijackings resulting from uninvited thoughts about the narcissist, for once and for all. In order to do this, you first have to become aware of the thoughts that you are having.

Counting

This method may help you to become aware of just how often you actually think about the narcissist. You simply commit to counting the number of times you think about them in a day, as you go about your daily life. To start with, you may be thinking about them so often (literally hundreds of times a day) that it may be easier to set a timer, perhaps to go off every half an hour, during which you count each time you catch yourself in a thought or memory involving the narcissist. The aim is to record the number of times in each set period, and add them up to give a total number in the day before you go to sleep. This is usually a shockingly high number to begin with.

> **Scientists now understand that *every feeling, every emotion, is preceded by a thought. "***

Letting go of thoughts

It's really important, when you catch yourself in a thought, to not chastise yourself for having the thought – it's not your fault, and it is just the first step in training your wayward mind out of this unconscious habit. It's also important to understand that very often you will only realise that you are thinking about the narcissist after you have had several thoughts about them, one having led on to the next; the proverbial train of thoughts. Again, do not be harsh or judgemental with yourself. Instead, actively congratulate yourself for noticing the thought, no matter how far down the line you noticed it, count it as one (if you are doing the counting method), or just note it mentally to yourself if not, and then let it go.

It's vital to realise that when you have a thought about the narcissist, you also have a choice as to whether you engage with the thought – whether you allow yourself to board the train, and be taken on the 'Journey Of Subsequent Thoughts'. You have the power to stand at the station platform, and just watch the train pass through without climbing aboard. You have the power to let the thought go, so that you do not have to suffer the pain that such trains of thought will inevitably cause. This is not about stopping the thoughts. It's about noticing them, noting them, and letting them pass by without engaging with them. It's easier said than done, but a great first step in awareness.

The rubber band technique

This is a tried and tested two-step technique that can be used for a variety of problems. First, you place a rubber band loosely around your wrist, to wear throughout the day. You commit to noticing when you have thoughts about the narcissist in much the same way as in the counting method. As soon as you notice the thought, you jolt yourself out of it by snapping the rubber band around your wrist to cause a bit of discomfort. This has two effects – first, you learn to associate thoughts about the narcissist with immediate physical displeasure, and secondly, the discomfort helps you to stop yourself from re-engaging with the thought, snapping you out of it.

The next crucial bit is deliberately replacing the thought about the narcissist with another, more empowering thought, which has been prepared in advance. A thought about you that you know to be true would be a good example of something to try as a replacement thought. So, for example, you might say or think something like "I am creative" or "I am kind" – whatever you know to be true for you. If you find that difficult, you can simply say to yourself, every time you ping the rubber band, "It doesn't matter."

In order for any habit to become ingrained, including thought replacing habits, one must repeat the action consistently for around 30 days.

Becoming immune to hoovering

You already know that you are, quite literally (from a neurochemical perspective) addicted to the narcissist, and this is why you are a prime target for being sucked back into the relationship, against your better judgement. Only *you* can stop yourself from going back again. Only *you* can make this the final time you leave your narcissistic partner. Portia Nelson's poem, below, is an incredibly powerful metaphor that beautifully describes the process of disengaging from your addiction to a narcissist. How much do these words resonate with you?

There's a hole in my sidewalk *(Portia Nelson)*

Chapter 1
I walk down the street.
There is a deep hole in the sidewalk.
I fall in.
I am lost … I am helpless.
It isn't my fault.
It takes forever to find a way out.

Chapter 2
I walk down the street.
There is a deep hole in the sidewalk.
I pretend that I don't see it.
I fall in again.
I can't believe I am in this same place.
But, it isn't my fault.
It still takes a long time to get out.

Chapter 3
I walk down the same street.
There is a deep hole in the sidewalk.
I see it is there.
I still fall in … it's a habit … but, my eyes are open.
I know where I am.
It is my fault.
I get out immediately.

Chapter 4
I walk down the same street.
There is a deep hole in the sidewalk.
I walk around it.

Chapter 5
I walk down another street.

Dealing with the 'But Why's?' and the 'But Surely's?'

These thought types will come into your mind over and over again through your divorce, and will also come up repeatedly in conversation with those who do not understand NPD and are discussing the narcissist's behaviour with you. Here are some examples:

"But why would they steal all the money?"

"But surely they wouldn't want the children to suffer?"

"But why would they refuse to move out of the house when it is clearly just up-setting for everyone?"

"But surely they must have loved you at the beginning?"

"But surely it is not in their interests to give all the money away as they will suf-fer themselves financially too?"

"But why would they use the children as pawns?"

"But why would they want to punish you – they were the one that had the affair?"

When you come across these questions, in your own mind, and in the minds of others, do not waste any more time trying to justify, rationalise or understand the narcissist's behaviour. The answer is simple. They are not wired like you. If an alien had odd non-human behaviours, (e.g. regurgitating food and then re-eating it) when asked by others why they do that, you would respond with "because they are an alien".

The same is true for our non-alien narcissists. They do these things "*because they are a narcissist.*" That's it. That's all. That's why. *Because they are a narcissist.* No further thought required – spare yourself the mental energy. You are going to need it for other things.

Dealing with fear about the future

Fear of the future is one of the biggest fears that victims of narcissistic abuse have. They have often become reliant on the narcissist in certain ways (which the narcissist has used as methods of control) and they wonder whether they will be able to cope without them. Of course, the years of criticism and demean-ing has eroded their sense of self-confidence and self-esteem, and this heavily plays into this fear.

Will I be able to afford to live? Will I be able to afford a decent house? Will I be able to pay the bills? Will I be able to cope with the children? Will I be able to be a good mother/father? Will I make any new friends? Will I find a support net-work? Will I ever find love? Will I ever trust again? Will I ever really be free of the narcissist? Where in the country will I move to? Which country will I move to? What will happen job wise? What do I want to do with my life? Will I be able to go back to college? The list goes on.

Looking to the future at this stage, during the divorce process, can be incredibly frightening for many – a completely blank canvas is all they can see. This might sound exciting to those who don't understand the impact that narcissistic abuse has had on a person's mental health, but it most assuredly is not, to the victim. If the victim is someone who had given up work to look after the narcissist and the family then this is even worse, and there isn't even the routine or stability of a nine to five job to keep them grounded as they move from being married to divorced.

This fear can hit you like a freight train, and panic and terror can ensue. It can wake you up in the middle of night, and get you hyperventilating. A feeling of the deepest, darkest dread about the future can chronically sit heavy on your chest, in your gut and in your head. It can cause exhausting ruminations, as your mind works overtime seeking a solution to ease your suffering. When it fails, it can pull your mood downwards in a spiral of circular thoughts. Here are some tips for coping.

De-programming your negativity bias – gratitude.

Part of the reason you are feeling this fear is because, as a human, you are wired to focus on the negatives in life. This 'negativity bias' is a somewhat outmoded evolutionary survival tactic – a relic of days of old. Back then, focusing on the negatives – on what *could* go wrong – was essential to the survival of the species. But we are no longer hunting or foraging for food, whilst trying to avoid becoming prey ourselves.

It has been proved that it is much harder to get rid of a negative thought than a positive one – negative thoughts are 'sticky', like Velcro, and positive thoughts are not, like Teflon. It has also been shown that negative thoughts are harder to change into positive thoughts than the other way around.

If you think about it, you are bound to be able to remember a day when, say, five good things happened, but the day was completely ruined by just one bad event, which really got under your skin and you couldn't shake off. That was the negativity bias at work.

Thankfully, you no longer have to be at the mercy of the negativity bias, now that you are aware of it. *The practice of daily gratitude is the single most powerful coping technique in this book, and it has the power to change your experience of your divorce for the better*. It literally rewires your brain to see things as they really are, and not through the lens of doom. We urge you to try it.

There are various ways to incorporate gratitude into your daily routine, but a great start is to simply *become aware* of all the little things that you are grateful for through the day, in real time, as they are happening – and the smaller they are, the better. Feel grateful that when you open the tap to wash your hands that you are met with lovely warm water, which feels good on your fingers. Feel grateful for that first sip of tea in the morning. Feel grateful for the birds singing as you make your way to the car. For the dog greeting you with enthusiastic tail wagging upon your return. For the fact that you have a working oven in which to cook your dinner. For the nice conversation you had with the shop assistant. For the warmth of your winter coat. For the children you saw giggling together as they got off the bus. For the smell of that scented candle you lit.

Then, last thing at night, think back over your day and find ten things to count, on your fingers, that you were grateful for that day. As you think of them, re-member the feeling of them, and actually engage with the feeling of gratitude you had for them at the time.

The practice of gratitude, carried out every single day in the way described above, has the power to turn your thinking around within just a few days. It is likely that once you start it, you won't want to stop.

Becoming aware that no one actually knows what the future holds

It's so easy to feel sorry for yourself when you are going through a breakup with a narcissist and are scared every day. You may look at your friends and family, with their picket fences and stable relationships, their pension funds and their smiley happy faces, and feel more than a tinge of jealousy. That they are able to make plans and know what they will be doing in the future. But the truth is that, although they may appear to be living your ideal life at the moment, they also have no idea what lies around the corner. *In fact, they can be no more certain of their futures than you can be of yours.*

Future stability and security is just an illusion – anything can happen to anyone at any time. Yes, humans like to be able to feel that they have some control over their futures so they plan accordingly and, of course, it is wise to do so. But no one knows what the future really holds. It's largely the *loss of control* over one's life that is scary. Think about the stockpiling of toilet paper and food that occurs when a worldwide pandemic strikes – people justify it on the grounds that they may not be able to get supplies because of the pandemic, even though, in reality, they know that the supermarkets are able to keep supply chains open. They are not really doing it to stock up on food – they are doing it to give themselves a sense of security and stability, and a feeling that they have some control over the situation. It is this loss of perceived control that is scary, not the future itself. Realising this, and the fact that no one really has control of the future anyway, may help you to see that it is your *mindset* that can be your greatest enemy, or your biggest ally in this journey. And, now you are narcissist free, *you* get to make that choice.

Stop labelling things as good or bad – the story of the Chinese farmer

Once upon a time there was a Chinese farmer whose horse ran away. That evening, all of his neighbours came around to commiserate. They said, "We are so sorry to hear your horse has run away. This is most unfortunate." The farmer said, "**Maybe**." The next day the horse came back bringing seven wild horses with it, and in the evening everybody came back and said, "Oh, isn't that lucky? What a great turn of events. You now have eight horses!" The farmer again said, "**Maybe**."

The following day his son tried to break one of the horses and, while riding it, he was thrown and broke his leg. The neighbours then said, "Oh dear, that's too bad," and the farmer responded, "**Maybe**." The next day the conscription officers came around to conscript people into the army and they rejected his son because he had a broken leg. Again, all the neighbours came around and said, "Isn't that great!" Again, he said, "**Maybe**."

> " You are not your brain, nor its thoughts. Your brain is just a complex machine. "

The point of this story is that we can never really tell whether the things that happen in life are 'good' or 'bad' – we can only really know in retrospect, as we join up the dots. So next time you catch yourself labelling a situation as 'bad' (or 'good'), just check yourself, keep an open mind, and wait to see what happens instead, with curiosity.

In the words of the late philosopher, Alan Watts, "The whole process of nature is an integrated process of immense complexity, and it's really impossible to tell whether anything that happens in it is good or bad – because you never know what will be the consequence of the misfortune; or, you never know what will be the consequences of good fortune."

This is definitely worth bearing in mind as you move through your divorce, and your post-narcissist life.

Trusting in life

Again, this is another mindset choice that is related to the points above. If you are currently believing that the world is against you, and that bad things always happen to you, could you embrace the notion that perhaps things are happening *for* you, and not *to* you? Could you believe, even though things seem awful at the moment, that the universe is a benevolent one? Could you believe that 'everything happens for a reason' and that it will all become clear in the fullness of time? Could you even accept everything that has happened to you, as if it was a choice, rather than resenting it? Is it worth a try, given that you have absolutely nothing to lose?

Thoughts are not facts (even the ones that tell you that they are)

Thoughts are just that – thoughts. When we are in stressful situations, we tend to believe what our thoughts tell us, unquestioningly. In fact, our brains are constantly on, generating thousands upon thousands of thoughts, mostly in the background. When a thought reaches our consciousness, and we become aware of it, we tend to make the assumption that because we thought of it, it must somehow be true. You are not your brain, nor its thoughts. Your brain is just a complex machine.

Next time you have a thought that threatens to throw you into fear about the future, STOP and take stock. Could it be that this thought, that feels so real, is just a thought, and therefore not a fact? Could you challenge the thought, and come up with the opposite thought, which might be just as plausible? For example, "The judge is going to believe that the narcissist needs to retire on the grounds of ill health and I will therefore receive no spousal maintenance." Could there be an alternative version of this that is just as likely? Perhaps, "The judge is going to see through the narcissist's pity plays, not believe them, and I will receive a fair settlement as a result"?

Noticing when you are catastrophising

Fear has a habit of taking you to straight the worst case scenario, in the blink of an eye.

Imagine that something has happened – for example you have received a written threat from the narcissist's solicitor telling you that if you do not drop the selling price of the marital home, they will be taking you to court in order to force you to do so. Here you are at point A.

Your mind, working on overdrive, immediately takes you to the situation where you have been forced to lower the house price by a ludicrously large amount. You are now, in your mind, at point B.

You have had an offer for the house which is even less than the new lower asking price you were forced to market it at. Before you know it, you are at Point C.

The narcissist has accepted the firesale offer, but you have refused. Quick as a flash, you find yourself at point D. But not for long.

The narcissist has taken you back to court and the judge has ordered that you sell at the lowball offer. You are at point E, and your head is spinning as you are hurled along towards point F.

You have sold the house, and have been unable to find anywhere that you can afford to live in with the children and the 4 cats, other than a studio flat in a really unsavoury part of town, with drug dealers who leave empty cans of lager and used needles at your (shared) doorstep. You are at point F.

You are now reacting as if you are at Point F, scared and upset, worried about how you will all fit into the studio flat, wondering where you will re-home the cats, planning how you will break the news to the children, wondering whether you will need to find the local soup kitchen, imagining how your friends will react when they see you in your new reduced circumstances, contemplating hanging versus overdose versus carbon monoxide as a method of suicide. You are now dead, the children are being brought up by the narcissist and they have become narcissists themselves. All is lost. You are at Point G.

You, as a result of your mind, think you are at point G, the worst case scenario. Your heart is pumping, you are hyperventilating and tears are streaming down your face. But really, you are still only at point A.

It's really useful to be able to catch yourself catastrophising, and bring yourself back to the reality of just being at point A, so that you can respond in the most effective and logical way.

> **" It's really useful to be able to catch yourself catastrophising, and bring yourself back to reality. "**

Focusing on what you want, not on what you don't want

Fear of the unknown can so easily take you over, so you find yourself imagining all sorts of terrible outcomes – that you will be homeless, that you will lose the children, that you will not be able to find a job, that the narcissist will take everything. This will be enough to strike terror into your heart. When this happens, it may be helpful to make a plan to disengage from those thoughts, and replace them with thoughts of what you *do* want instead.

Of course, if you have been in a very long term relationship with a narcissist, you may have no idea of what it is that you want as you will have spent many years simply pandering to what they wanted. You may even *think* you know what is important to you, but in fact be unconsciously taking on the narcissist's preferences. And in thinking that these are things that you want and need, you may be putting yourself through unnecessary worry regarding your divorce, and what you will end up with. The things you think matter to you, may actually not. The wedding china and Uncle Frank's leather pouffe may not be as important as you thought.

This is where the Rocking Chair Test may help you.

The rocking chair test – working out what you want from your future

The premise is simple. With your eyes closed, you imagine yourself aged 95, sitting out on your verandah rocking on your chair; warm, safe and happy. You really connect with the feeling of having lived a life you have loved, and with the idea that you could die happy, right now. You take a few moments to engage all your senses, noticing exactly what you are seeing (perhaps the brightly coloured bougainvillea petals fluttering in the breeze), what you are feeling (maybe the warm sun on your face, a calm sense of contentment, the coolness of the iced drink in your hand), what you are hearing (possibly birds chirping overhead, the sound of the ocean waves crashing nearby) and what you are smelling and tasting (perhaps jasmine, honeysuckle and cloudy lemonade).

And now, from this wise place in the future, you look back on your life, and all the things that brought you to this state of near bliss. In other words, *all the things that really mattered*. You write them down, as if you are writing in a spindly hand, a foreword to your memoirs, for your eyes only. You write *with a sense of gratitude* – for your longevity, for all the things you have learnt, for this precious life you have been given. You may wish to organise your thoughts by writing within categories: Relationships, Love, Work, Finances, Health, Spiritual matters, Hobbies, Leisure time, to name a few.

> " **By bringing yourself back into the present you have the opportunity to escape from your worries.** "

When you read back through your stream of thoughts, you may find yourself surprised by how few things you thought you wanted would actually matter to you in the long run, and how some of the goals you thought were important were actually complete red herrings. You may discover that many of your goals were actually borne out of the expectations of others. Perhaps a few were goals you felt you should be aiming for in order to not waste certain inbuilt strengths and talents, even though you didn't really want them; perhaps others were obsolete goals, no longer needed to prop up the formerly fragile self-esteem of the old you. And of course, some may not have even been your goals at all, but those of the narcissist, or others in your life that you'd taken on unquestioningly.

This exercise can bring into sharp focus what you *really want* out of life. Could it be that *these* are the things you might want to focus on achieving when working out what a successful outcome from your divorce looks like?

Taking refuge in the present

Worrying about the future (or thinking about the past) happens when we allow our minds to wander. But research carried out by two Harvard psychologists, Killingworth and Gilbert, has shown that people spend 46.9% of their waking hours thinking about something other than what they are doing, and that this mind wandering makes them unhappy. This is especially interesting as it appears that mind wandering is actually the brain's default mode of operation.

Of course, many philosophical and religious traditions teach that happiness is to be found by living in the moment, and science has now shown this to be correct. When you find yourself worrying about the future or hijacked by the past, you actually have a choice as to where you can go. After all, the past is over, it has gone, and is therefore not real, and the future hasn't happened yet, and therefore also isn't real. When you find yourself getting lost in these thoughts of past and future, and the negative emotions that result from them, you could ask yourself, "Am I unhappy if I don't think about it?" And the answer is likely to be no. The situation itself isn't necessarily entirely responsible for your negative feelings – your *perception* of the situation and the thoughts related to it are what are causing your distress. In other words, you can actually blame a lot of how you are feeling *on your mind*.

Only the present moment is real, and so by bringing yourself back into the present you have the opportunity to escape from your worries, and also be in the real world as it actually is, in the present. This is the essence of the practice of mindfulness, and is one of the most powerful tools you could use to gain control of your wayward mind, and actually, in the long term, find happiness. We highly recommend that you consider finding a mindfulness course, joining a group or downloading a meditation app to help you to become a master of your thoughts instead of a slave to them.

Dealing with acute anxiety

There will be times when, despite your best efforts, you will be thrown into a state of anxiety, even if you are not 'the anxious sort'. Try not to be down on yourself about this – a little self-compassion is required here. Be assured that the way a narcissist behaves when in a narcissistic rage, borne out of narcissistic injury, would have even the Dalai Lama thinking about reaching for the Valium. You are doing just fine. Remember that anxiety is just an emotion, and that in order for it to take hold, it must be preceded by a thought. Here are some things that might help you when anxiety threatens to overwhelm you.

Using your sense of smell to bring yourself back into the present

A quick trick to jolt you out of your anxiety provoking thoughts is by using your sense of smell. Carrying a small bottle of essential oil such as lavender or tea tree oil in your bag or pocket may be useful here, to quickly whip out and sniff as soon as you feel yourself losing control. The strong fragrance can quickly bring you back into the present, and give you an opportunity to get grounded. If you don't have anything like this to hand, if perhaps you are outside, you may want to try plucking a leaf off a tree or bush and crushing this in your hand to then smell and focus on. This can be surprisingly effective.

Stimulating your parasympathetic nervous system

Your sympathetic nervous system is activated when you are in fight, flight or freeze mode, raising your heart rate, making you sweat, making your hairs stand on end and causing you to hyperventilate – the classic physical signs and symptoms of anxiety. You may also feel sick and suffer from chest pain (in the latter case, it is essential to rule out anything more serious by discussing with your doctor first). In order to counteract the sympathetic nervous system, it is possible to stimulate the parasympathetic system, which works in opposition to it. Try any of the following:

- Run your fingers back and forth over your lips. Your lips have parasympathetic nerve fibres running through them, which are stimulated by touch.

- Immerse your face in cold water (this is known as the diving reflex).

- Carry out the 'Valsalva manoeuvre'. Here you are attempting to exhale against a closed airway. You keep your mouth closed and pinch your nose closed whilst trying to breathe out. This works by increasing the pressure in your chest, which stimulates the vagus nerve, a major nerve of the parasympathetic system.

- Try box breathing. This is intentional deep breathing. The breath holding part of it allows the carbon dioxide to build up in your bloodstream which then enhances the parasympathetic nervous system stimulation, slowing your heart rate and reducing your blood pressure.

  Step 1: Sitting upright, slowly exhale through your mouth, getting all the oxygen out of your lungs.

  Step 2: Slowly inhale through your nose as deeply as you can, whilst counting slowly in your head to four. Let the air fill your lungs completely, as far as your abdomen.

  Step 3: Hold your breath over another slow count of four.

  Step 4: Exhale through your mouth, over a slow count of four, slowly and completely emptying your lungs of air.

  Step 5: Hold your breath again, over a count of four.

  Repeat the process again, a total of four times. It is normal to get dizzy to start with, but this improves with practice.

Fooling your brain

Smile

> *"Sometimes your joy is the source of your smile, but sometimes your smile can be the source of your joy." (Thich Nhat Hanh)*

Just as you smile when you are happy, smiling can actually make you happy too, by working in reverse on the brain. Smiling has been shown to speed up recovery when a short term stressor is over. The most effective type of smile is a genuine smile involving the use of the eye muscles, but even just holding a pencil sideways in your mouth to make your muscles hold your mouth in the same way as you do in a smile works to lower stress. It may be that smiling lowers the stress hormone cortisol in the body, but more research is needed to prove the exact mechanism of its effect on stress.

Tell yourself that you are excited

When we are stressed, anxious and fearful, cortisol and adrenaline are produced as a result of activation of the sympathetic nervous system. This has various effects on the body, giving the classic symptoms of anxiety. Here you are on high alert, because of the perceived danger. But think for a moment of how you feel when you are excited. Not a million miles away from how you feel when you are stressed – the racing heart, the butterflies, the narrowed focus.

Now here is the important bit – it is possible to use the energy of stress to actually tell yourself that what you are feeling is *excitement, not fear*. To deliberately change the fight or flight response into the so called 'excite and delight' response. By doing this, rather than narrowing your focus as you do in fight or flight, you actually widen it. So by simply telling yourself (whether you believe it or not) that you are excited rather than stressed, you function more effectively than if you tell yourself that you are scared, increasing your problem solving abilities and your ability to think on your feet. The brain, which is essentially just a machine, actually listens to the words you tell it and believes them. (Note that whilst *you* might not believe the words you are saying, *your brain does*, and that's how you change your physiology). This is a useful tool, particularly if you find yourself going to trial and having to be cross-examined as part of your divorce.

Exercising your chimp

We are referring here to Professor Steve Peter's excellent book, *The Chimp Paradox*, in which he describes the three parts of our minds – the computer (where we store all our experiences and memories), the human (which is the rational and logical part of the brain, located in the frontal lobe) and the chimp.

The chimp is where our emotional and irrational thinking comes from, and it's the home of our survival instincts and the fight, flight or freeze response. The amygdala and other old evolutionary brain structures make up the chimp. Whenever we come across perceived danger, the chimp kicks in and takes over from the other parts of the brain, beating its chest and running riot.

Whenever we find ourselves behaving irrationally or over emotionally (for example when we are anxious) it is because the chimp has come out, and it has overridden the human (the logical parts of the brain) and the computer. The problem is that the chimp, not being rational itself, isn't actually very good at accurately assessing the real risk of the danger we are in, so it can run the show when perhaps it shouldn't be.

When embroiled with a narcissist who is behaving badly, the chimp is on high alert and needs to be managed when it starts to run amok, as it frequently will. This is where exercising the chimp comes in.

Here you have to let the chimp run around, beating its chest and screeching wildly, in a safe place.

The best way to do this is to have a rant to an understanding friend. Crying, shouting and screaming are all fine here. The process of talking it out will calm the chimp, which will then be ready to be gently led back to its box, to go to sleep. The human is now back in charge.

Never rant to the narcissist – this will be entirely counterproductive.

If you've no one to offload on when the chimp is running wild, find another method that works for you in order to process these emotions out – scribbling furiously in your journal, writing a letter that you are never going to send, or just allowing yourself to cry, perhaps. Your chimp will always be with you, and it is not to be ignored. Accept it and work with it, now you know what it needs and that it is on your side.

Do a 'three minute breathing space'

This is effectively an emergency meditation, borrowed from Mindfulness Based Cognitive Therapy, to be used in times of acute stress. It acknowledges your thoughts, emotions and body sensations, and then allows them to be viewed from a wider perspective. Each step lasts approximately one minute.

Step 1

In order to come into the present moment quickly, and to signal to the brain that you are doing this, first take a definite posture – sit on a chair if possible, with your back straight, but not stiff, your feet planted firmly on the floor, and your shoulders back, so your chest is wide and open, in a dignified, alert pose.

Close your eyes.

Now you notice what is going on in your mind, separating out your thoughts from your emotions and your body sensations. If you haven't done this before, you might find it difficult at first – it's particularly common to confuse your thoughts with your emotions, so be aware of this and really try to classify them correctly when you get on to the next step.

First, notice your thoughts, without engaging or becoming involved with them – just notice them and mentally note them. What thoughts are present?

Then notice your emotions – what emotions are present? Give each a name, without giving in to them or trying to push them away – just acknowledge their presence. Try not to judge them or yourself for having them.

> "*Never rant to the narcissist* – **this will be entirely counterproductive.**"

Then ask yourself what body sensations you are experiencing – are there sensations of tension? Again, notice them and mentally note them.

Step 2

Now take your attention to a single focus, the movements of the breath. Focus attention on the movement of your abdominal wall as your breath naturally rises and falls. If a thought comes into your mind and distracts you, when you've noticed this has happened just let the thought go, and bring your attention back to the breathing movements of your abdomen, as you breathe in and out.

Step 3

Now allowing your awareness to expand, as well as being aware of the sensations of breathing at the abdomen, become aware of the rest of the body as whole. Notice how you are sitting. Notice any sensations. Notice any tension in the muscles of the face, in the shoulders, in the neck and back. At the same time follow your breath as if the whole body is breathing. When you have done this for around a minute, open your eyes, when you feel ready.

Waking in the night

Anxiety will often affect your sleep, and most people in your situation will find themselves waking in the small hours of the night, consumed by a feeling of fear and dread. The main thing here, rather than tossing and turning and just hoping that you will be able to get back to sleep, is to have a plan.

In addition to trying any or all of the techniques above, consider:

- Having a hypnosis mp3 or mediation mp3 downloaded on your phone ready to listen to as soon as you wake up. Keep headphones by your bed. You may wish to try an app such as Calm for this.

- Using a mental technique such as building a house from the foundations up in your mind, or cooking a meal in your mind from the beginning.

- Taking a hot bath or shower when you wake in the night. This leads to the body cooling down after the bath, and the cooling signals to the brain that it is time to sleep. A warm bath is also a signal to the pineal gland in the brain to produce melatonin, which is the body's naturally occurring sleep hormone.

- Use lavender oil. Have some ready, either to put in your middle of the night bath, on your pillow, in an aromatherapy diffuser, or on your wrists and temples. Several studies confirm the effectiveness of lavender as a natural sleep remedy.

Self-nurturing

> *"In your soul are infinitely precious things that cannot be taken from you."*
> *(Oscar Wilde)*

You have been gas-lighted, demeaned and criticised, and your thoughts, values, and feelings have invalidated. It is no wonder that your self-confidence may be low. You have prioritised the needs of the narcissist over and above your own, nurturing them at the expense of yourself. You have not received any nurturing in return. You have not been loved and you have not been cherished, although you loved and cherished them.

It's time to take a step back and look inwards at who you really are *outside* of your external duties and your relationship to the narcissist; to rediscover your sense of self. It's time to make a commitment to nurture *yourself*, as a priority. You cannot fight this fight without the strength that comes from self-confidence and self-love.

Silencing the negative self-talk

Do you recognise the critical little voice in your head that tells you that you are not good enough? Perhaps it tells you that you are fat or ugly when you look in the mirror. It calls you stupid when you make a mistake, or when things don't go right. Perhaps it tells you that you deserved all of this, that you are ridiculous.

This voice is 'the narcissist in your head', and you may have got used to allowing it to devalue you without even realising it was there.

The good news is that this is one narcissist you can control. These negative thoughts have become wired into the brain through repetition, and have become ingrained as habits. Key to breaking these neural pathways is simply noticing these thoughts when they occur, and instead of taking them to heart, denouncing them as you would, in outrage, if someone had spoken to your friend in such as way. After all, you would never let your friend be spoken to like this, let alone speak to them yourself in such a manner. It is time therefore to stand up for *yourself*. It is time to be your own best friend. Slay the narcissist in your head, and reclaim your self-esteem.

Savouring your achievements

It is likely that your self-belief and self-confidence needs a supercharge at this time in your life. If, like many victims of narcissistic abuse, you have been made to feel small, useless and insignificant, this method below might help you to remember who you actually are, and what great things you are capable of.

To do this, take yourself right back to your earliest memory and make a list of every little thing you feel you have achieved all the way up to the present. As long as the achievements meant something to you at the time, they still count – even things from childhood that you may not consider to be big now, such as a piece of work done in primary school, or the achievement of being Joseph in the school nativity play. Include all aspects of things you are proud of – having made lifelong friends, coming out of a traumatic experience with greater strength, not being put off by failure would all be very appropriate.

Once the list is complete, enjoy connecting emotionally with the memory of each achievement, and basking in them. This is a wonderfully life affirming exercise, and well worth the time spent on it. It may also be worth keeping the list and forcing yourself to look at it when sadness strikes, as it invariably will through the divorce process. As you make the list, if you find yourself getting swept up by thoughts of the narcissist, just notice that this has happened, and get back to where you were on your list. This is very definitely about you, not them.

Boost your mood by scheduling nourishing activities

In stressful situations, we humans have a tendency to cut down on the activities that nourish and energise us, eventually leaving us carrying out only the bare essentials. Unfortunately, most of these seem to be activities that deplete us of energy, and dampen mood. Of course, at times like this you aren't going to feel motivated to do the things that you enjoy, but it is important to do them anyway, regardless of whether you feel like it, as this is an essential component of taking care of yourself to prevent a further decline in mood, and a potential descent into a full scale depression.

So, write a detailed list of all the things that you do on a typical working day over a 24 hour period, breaking the activities down into small parts. For example, get out of bed, have a cup of coffee, shower, get dressed, make the children breakfast, drive to work, talk to colleagues, answer emails and so on.

Once you have this list, consider each item, and how it makes you feel. If it raises your energy and mood, mark it with an N as a nourishing activity; if it does the opposite, mark it with a D for depleting activity.

Now list the nourishing activities separately and you will notice that there are two groups. Some activities may give you a direct sense of pleasure (for example phoning a friend, having a hot bath, getting eight hours sleep), and others may not be pleasurable in themselves but give a sense of accomplishment once achieved, such as perhaps tidying a drawer, completing a tax return or working out at the gym.

The next step is to consider what other nourishing activities you could add to the list to carry out when you are feeling down.

If you get stuck, try asking yourself the following question: "If it were possible to be living five completely different other lives, what would they be?" This can give powerful insights into what you might enjoy, and reawaken passions which you may have let slide during your narcissistic relationship. Now, where possible, take elements from those other lives and incorporate them into this life. For example, if you put down famous singer, perhaps commit to learning how to sing just one of your favourite songs.

It is also important to look at the depleting activities to see if you can find a way to convert any of them into nourishing activities. For example, an unpleasant rush hour drive to work might be made more nourishing by downloading an interesting podcast to listen to. Cleaning the house may be made more pleasurable by dancing to music at the same time, or promising to reward yourself with a coffee or treat afterwards.

Once you've done this, create a 'play list' that you can refer to when you need an activity to boost your mood, and make a commitment to schedule as many nourishing activities into your day as practically possible. *Do this because you deserve it.*

Positive affirmations

Positive affirmations work, they really do, no matter how new-agey they may sound. Given that you are probably nearing the end of your tether, you may well want to give them a try. They can lift your self-belief at the same time as honing your understanding of who you want to be in your new, narcissist-free life.

Learning how to make effective affirmations are crucial to them actually working. Affirmations are essentially you speaking to your subconscious, in order to reprogram its beliefs about you (which of course, are really *your* beliefs about *yourself*).

Repetition is essential if they are to work. You will need to say them to yourself several times a day – perhaps at times associated with other things, to help you remember. For example, if you have them written on post-it notes stuck to your bathroom mirror, you can do them before you brush your teeth or shave. Perhaps stick some to your computer screen, or in your sandwich box. Changing your computer and phone password to different affirmations is also a great way to incorporate them into your day. Make doing them into a habit, and after a few weeks you may be surprised at how your view of yourself and your confidence, as a result, has changed.

Once you've successfully incorporated a belief about yourself into your mind, you will just 'know it' to be true, and you can replace it with another empowering belief that you wish to hold about yourself. This is an incredibly powerful technique, and we urge you to give it a go.

> **"Positive affirmations work, they really do. "**

Writing your affirmations

- Affirmations need to be simple, concise and clear.

- They have to be all about you.

- Affirmations need to be written in the present tense, as the subconscious doesn't understand the concept of time. So, "I will be happy" is not going to work, and nor is 'I want to be happy' – "I *am* happy" is.

- They need to be stated in the positive. In other words, "I am not afraid" will not work. Nor will any other negatives work, like "don't", "won't" or "can't". "I am fearless" or "I am courageous" is better.

- They need to be specific, so in the example above, "I am courageous", you might want to further break down into what courageous looks like to you – for example, "I calmly respond to my ex's lawyer's letters".

If you need help starting, just think back to what the critical voice in your head (the narcissist in your head) says about you, and start there. If it says, "You are ugly" then you want to change the belief to, "I am attractive". To make that more specific you may want to say something like, "I have glossy hair" or whatever is true for you. If the narcissist in your head tells you that, "No one could ever love you", then you may want to change this to, "I am loved", or perhaps more specifically, "I am treated by others with kindness", or similar.

You might want to start with around eight affirmations. The first couple should be ones that you already know are actually true about yourself, and then the others can be things that you would like. Here is an example affirmation list:

- I am organised

- I make people laugh

- I am treated with respect by others

- I am confident when dealing with my ex

- I calmly respond to my ex's lawyer's letters

- I am a patient mother to the children

- I eat healthy food

- I go to the gym on Monday, Wednesday and Friday straight after work

If making a positive affirmation list is too much for you at the moment, then perhaps try just one – "I am enough" is a great one to start with.

Learning to self-soothe

This is so important when grief washes over you, as it inevitably will at times. How you do this will be particular to you – it may be that you imagine yourself as a baby and comfort yourself by rocking yourself soothingly as you would a crying baby. You may find that something from your playlist of nourishing activities such as a hot bubble bath and candles, or your favourite movie, may help. You may allow yourself to cry yourself to sleep, or play an uplifting song to dance around to. The main thing is to have a plan so that when the grief strikes, you know what you are going to do. You may also want to remind yourself that if ever you had taken your woes to the narcissist, they most probably would have had them invalidated anyway, or stopped listening, talked over you or talked about their own problems. Don't fall into the trap of romanticising the notion of crying on their shoulder when the sadness strikes. You are much better off embracing your independence and becoming your own nurturer and friend. Be kind to yourself.

Moving forwards, letting go and forgiveness

"This, too, shall pass" (*King Solomon*).

One day this process of disentangling yourself from the narcissist will be over, and you will be able to walk into your future at last. But before you do, you will have some serious healing to do. Therapy or specialist narcissistic abuse recovery coaching may be helpful here, and you may even need to heal from PTSD. There are a variety of options that might help you process and deal with trauma, such as EMDR, EFT Tapping, or Logosynthesis, which you may wish to research.

Finding love

You may be tempted to get into another relationship quickly, particularly once you have taken on board the fact that the narcissist was never really able to re-ciprocate your love in an authentic way – but you would be wise to reconsider this. You have learnt the validity of the statement, "You find the person whose teeth fits your wounds" the hard way, through your relationship with the narcis-sist. It stands to reason that these wounds, sustained mostly in early childhood but also throughout life, need to heal over completely if you are to avoid the same thing happening again. You need to examine, in depth, what it was about *you* that drew you to the narcissist, and what vulnerabilities in you *drew them* to you. And be aware that time will not heal these wounds – only work will.

If your family of origin was also narcissistic, you may feel that you have *never* actually been loved and this can make you believe that you are completely un-lovable. We have already cautioned against diving into a relationship in the im-mediate aftermath of a narcissistic relationship in an earlier chapter, but need to emphasise it once more. Now is not the time for seeking validation or comfort in the arms of another, no matter how desperate you are to be loved. Now is the time for seeking it from yourself.

Learning to love yourself before you love another is actually the *only* way forward here. And if you find this difficult to countenance, consider the words of the African saying, "Be careful when a naked person offers you a shirt." You cannot give to others what you don't already have for yourself. As a victim of narcissistic abuse, self-love is likely to be sadly lacking. You have to fill your own cup with love. Everything in that cup is for you. Only that which overflows is for others. Here are a few strategies to help you fill your cup.

> **Now is not the time for seeking validation or comfort in the arms of another.**

Mirror work

It's surprisingly difficult to look yourself deeply in the eye in the mirror, say your name out loud and tell yourself tenderly that you love yourself. But this simple act, practiced repeatedly, can be hugely transformative in lifting your self-esteem. Mirror work was invented by the late Louise Hay, one of the founders of the self-improvement movement. Daily repetition until it becomes a habit is important, and building it into a routine (such as just before you brush your teeth) is a great way to do this. It may be simple, but it works.

Write a love letter to yourself

It's interesting that ideas that initially make us cringe or that we feel some sort of aversion to may be the very things that we need to turn towards and embrace for our own self development, and our reactions are often the messengers telling us this. So, *especially* if this one makes you feel uncomfortable, imagine receiving the perfect love letter from a lover, detailing all the reasons why they love you and what they love about you, and then address and write this letter *to yourself*. Be honest with yourself. You may find you uncover a few of your character strengths and reveal some of your values. Keep it 100% positive. You may want to keep it to refer to whenever the chips are down.

Make commitment vows to yourself

Close your eyes and imagine yourself with your ideal partner, perhaps in the context of a wedding or other type of commitment ceremony. Now try to connect with the emotions you would be experiencing in that moment, and imagine your partner looking into your eyes and making the most perfect vows for you. This process often reveals what we feel is missing in our lives, that we wish someone else could give us. Now write down these vows (I will support your dreams, I will encourage you, I will celebrate your successes, I will take care of you when you are ill, I will buy you flowers, for example). Carve out some alone time to actually say these vows out loud to yourself somewhere meaningful (perhaps on a mountaintop, or on a windy beach), and give yourself a symbolic token, such as a ring, to remind yourself on a daily basis of your vows to yourself. And then try to live by them. Treat yourself as you would wish to be treated by the love of your life, and *become* the love of your own life.

Clearing out toxic friends and family

Well, you've removed the narcissist from your world as much as you can, but it is likely that you have noticed in this process how many of your friends and family have similar traits. As we discussed earlier, narcissists exist in clusters.

You may wish to look at the limitations of some of your other narcissistic relationships and decide whether you want to remove people from your life or maintain a relationship, but within your own parameters of what you consider acceptable.

Clearing out at least some of these types to make room for new healthy people is difficult at first, but one day you will be surrounded by fewer narcissists than non-narcissists, and accepting toxic behaviours will cease to be the norm for you.

Establishing your boundaries

Giving endlessly of yourself is likely to be the way you operate, and the narcissists in your life will exploit your porous boundaries repeatedly. So be clear on what you will and will not accept. The next time someone asks you for a favour, or expects something of you, take a moment to check in with yourself and ask yourself how you are feeling about the situation, before giving in to any knee jerk reaction to say yes. Do you feel even a tinge of resentment or unwillingness? Do you feel put upon, unappreciated or used? Would helping out serve *you* in any way? Learning to say no is an important skill and self-protection tool, and it doesn't require explaining. A simple, firm, calm "I'm afraid I won't be able to help you with that" will suffice. If you feel you have to give some kind of a reason for not attending something, you can simply say, "It's not my thing." And know that you, as a human being, also *have the right to change your mind* without having to explain yourself.

Work out who you are by doing something differently

We are creatures of habit, driven on autopilots that we may not even be aware of. As a result, our experiences and therefore our worlds can shrink, without us even realising. This can have the effect of drastically limiting our lives and our potential, keeping us stuck in a sort of groundhog day. This is particularly true when one's life has revolved around another, and one's own likes and dislikes have been sidelined in favour of a narcissist's preferences.

So why not try doing something differently, to take yourself out of your normal comfort zone and expand and enrich your world? Perhaps even imagining how you would do things if you were not you, but someone completely different?

Whilst this may sound like quite a big thing to commit to, it's particularly interesting to start by experimenting with the tiny things, and make a point of noticing your reactions. You may be surprised at how simple changes such as listening to a different radio station, or substituting tea for your morning coffee can invoke quite powerful feelings, perhaps of discomfort, or even excitement. Changing the voice on your satnav, ordering a totally different wine, becoming vegetarian for a day, finding a new dog walk, taking a different route to work, having an evening bath instead of a morning shower are examples to whet your appetite.

Once you've become accustomed to carrying out such minor experiments, and noticing your accompanying feelings, you might be inspired to push a little further, perhaps going to the theatre on your own, or test-driving a car you have no intention of buying. The aim is not necessarily to commit to any particular activity long term, but to gain a wider worldview, a different perspective, a sense of how much of your life you may be living out of unconscious habit, and a feel for where the edge of your comfort zone may be. This can be a surprisingly fun endeavour too, and it may ultimately even open up a sense of new possibility and direction for your life. At the very least it will confirm your likes and dislikes, which, if you were a co-dependent, you may not have even been aware of.

Moving forwards from victimhood

Were you a 'victim' of narcissistic abuse? Yes, you were. But victimhood no longer has to define you. You have the power to step out of the drama triangle of victim, perpetrator and rescuer, and view it from the sidelines, for what it really is. It is a tragic fact that many victims of narcissistic abuse, even once divorced, never take off their black cloak of victimhood, and they wear it, with warped pride, almost as a faded battle flag, for the whole of the rest of their lives. And of course, this is their choice. But there is another choice.

Should the narcissist, who stole your love (given in such good faith), your dreams and your potential, also be allowed to steal your *future*, when they no longer are even a meaningful part of your life? Should you let your history define your destiny? Will you choose to throw it all away, this precious life, so full of possibility, because of what occurred? Because of one fateful roll of the die that turned you into the sacrificial lamb to the slaughter? Should you hold on to resentment when letting it go would serve you better? (Resentment, as they say, is like drinking poison and then hoping it will kill your enemies).

One day, unbelievable as it might seem, you may come to see this dreadful episode as a gift. This experience of narcissistic abuse can actually open your eyes to your own wounds. It can lead to profound healing, change, wisdom, evolution and personal growth. It can lead to great strength and fortitude in the face of difficulty. Surviving it can make you a leader, it can make you effective, and it can raise your conscious awareness and further your understanding of what it is to be human. It can even teach you how to be happy. Big gains, indeed.

You can, *and must, as a priority*, learn to forgive yourself for what happened to you. And then, when you are ready, try forgiving everybody else. Not because they deserve it, but because *you* deserve inner peace. And not so you can put yourself in harm's way again. Aim to forgive your notion of God, the Universe, your parents. Forgive the narcissist's enablers, your siblings, your toxic former friends, so you, *you* can move on.

But, you might ask, will I ever be able to forgive the tiny, snarling, self-piteous, self-loathing, remorseless, half-creature behind the golden mask? As full of repugnance for the idea as you might be right now, the answer is 'Probably, yes'. And *that* will be the day that you are truly set free.

The Last Word

Invictus

Out of the night that covers me,
Black as the pit from pole to pole,
I thank whatever gods may be
For my unconquerable soul.

In the fell clutch of circumstance,
I have not winced nor cried aloud.
Under the bludgeonings of chance
My head is bloody, but unbowed.

Beyond this place of wrath and tears
Looms but the Horror of the shade.
And yet the menace of the years
Finds, and shall find, me unafraid.

It matters not how strait the gate,
How charged with punishments the scroll.
I am the master of my fate:
I am the captain of my soul.

William Ernest Henley

Glossary

Term	Definition
Altruistic Narcissist	Another name for Communal Narcissist.
Arbitration	Private out of court process to resolve disputes. The couple will pay the arbitrator an agreed fee in equal shares. The arbitrator will provide an award in financial proceedings or a determination in children proceedings. This is then fast tracked as an Order by Consent with the court. A good option to consider in narcissistic divorces.
Attachment styles	The child of a narcissist could have a 'dismissive avoidant', 'fearful avoidant' or 'anxious preoccupied' attachment style, leading to difficulties forming close, stable, secure bonds with a partner.
Blameshifting	Those with narcissistic adaptations do not take the blame (except in the rare instances when doing so will give them narcissistic supply) and will pass the blame on to others with lightning speed.
Closet Narcissist	This type of narcissist (also called the 'Vulnerable', 'Introverted' or 'Covert' Narcissist) tries to feel special by association, by attaching themselves to a person, cause or object that they hold up as being special. Then, rather than asking people to admire them directly, they divert attention away to this third party, asking people to admire it instead, whilst basking in the reflected glory, soaking up its perfection, wonderfulness, uniqueness and entitlement to special treatment. They often consider themselves as 'the wind beneath the wings' of another.

Term	Definition
Co-dependents	Co-dependency is a specific relationship addiction characterised by preoccupation and extreme dependence – emotional, social and sometimes physical – on another person. Co-dependents feel extreme amounts of dependence on loved ones in their lives and they feel responsible for the feelings and actions of those loved ones. The partners of narcissists, alcoholics, substance abusers and those with chronic illnesses are often co-dependents. They characteristically put the other's needs ahead of their own.
Cognitive dissonance	Essentially, this occurs when a person is holding two or more contradictory thoughts or beliefs in their minds at the same time. This creates an uncomfortable sense of unreality and confusion, which the brain resolves by choosing one of the thoughts to believe, discarding the other as unimportant through denial, minimisation or justification.
Collaborative practice	Out of court process where the parties and their solicitors work together as a group of four to resolve disputes. A Participation Agreement will be signed confirming that the couple will not issue any form of court proceedings. In the event that proceedings are to be issued consideration must be given as to the instruction of alternative firms of solicitors to deal with the adversarial process. Avoid this method with narcissists.

Term	Definition
Communal Narcissist	Also called the Altruistic Narcissist. These are the narcissists who prop up their self-esteem and sense of specialness by giving to others. They obtain admiration, attention and a sense of specialness ('narcissistic supply') from good works and deeds, (seeing themselves as the *most* generous, the *most* caring, the *most* kind). They may start off in this vein with their significant others, but eventually their narcissism comes at the expense of those closest to them. They pride themselves on being 'nice', but quite often they give themselves away by becoming overly territorial in whatever arena they are practising their altruism.
Counsel	Another name for a barrister.
Covert Narcissist	Another name for a Closet, Vulnerable or Introverted Narcissist.
Cycle of 'idealise' and 'devalue'	The initial stage of a relationship with a narcissist is the 'idealisation' phase, also known as the 'love-bombing' phase, in romantic relationships. The next stage, the devalue stage, follows love-bombing/idealisation. It occurs as the narcissist realises that their target is not the perfect human that they had idealised and put on a pedestal during the initial phase.
Deletions	Pieces of information that the brain filters out that are not in line with your beliefs or your view of the world and those around you.
Devalue stage	The second stage of the cycle of idealise and devalue. This stage follows love-bombing/idealisation. It occurs as the narcissist realises that their target is not the perfect human that they had idealised and put on a pedestal during the initial phase. It is usually not an abrupt change, but a gradual turning up of the heat, so slowly that you may not notice. The victim becomes the proverbial frog in boiling water, and does not jump out.

Term	Definition
Devaluing Narcissist	Also called the Toxic or Malignant Narcissist. These narcissists turn on others to bring them down. They exhibit many of the other more general narcissistic behaviours too, but what is more prominent in this type of narcissist is that they devalue, criticise and demean others in order to inflate themselves.
Distortions	The brain distorts how we view reality, in line with our own personal prejudices due to former experiences, magnifying or diminishing our perceptions of things. Our perceptions of reality are therefore distorted, producing distortions.
Drama triangle	Karpman's drama triangle was first described in the 1960s as a description of conflict in social interactions. There are three roles within the triangle – victim, rescuer and perpetrator. In high conflict relationships people tend to move around the triangle taking up the different roles at different times, perpetuating the drama, so that it continues on and on.
Echoists	Echoists are essentially the polar opposites of narcissists, on the opposite end of the spectrum. They have poor interpersonal boundaries, and do not like asking for or accepting help or gifts. They feel uncomfortable having needs at all, and prefer to focus on fulfilling other's needs and wishes. They have an aversion to feeling special.

Term	Definition
Exhibitionist Narcissist	Also known as Grandiose or Overt Narcissist. They are typically the extroverted type. They are superficially charming in whatever way works best for them, and on the surface there are unlimited different outward appearances. They may present themselves as the affable buffoon, or the magnanimous entrepreneur. The altruistic pastor, with a dedicated following. The hardworking doctor, the dentist, or the strong, powerful CEO. The housewife, with over-achieving children and the perfect home. The childless housewife engaging in Twitter rants. The failed actress, or the famous actor. Many are financially successful in their chosen fields, but many are not, preferring instead to exploit others financially, as a result of the sense of entitlement which is part and parcel of the disorder.
Exploitation	One of the triple Es of pathological narcissism, the others being empathy and entitlement.
False self or false persona	Narcissists outwardly project a 'false self', which they cannot maintain without attention from others (which comes in the form of drama, conflict and adoration). This false self often appears grandiose or self-assured, and is so convincing and so at odds with the underlying emptiness that a casual onlooker would find it difficult to see what lies beneath. Many refer to this outward image as a 'mask', which can temporarily drop when the narcissist feels threatened or abandoned.
Fight, flight or freeze response	When a human brain sees a threat which it perceives as a threat to life, the old brain gets activated first, and without even thinking, the person is thrown into an instinctive fight, flight or freeze response, with the release of various stress hormones, such as cortisol and adrenaline. Blood is diverted away from the cortex (the thinking part of the brain) to other areas of the body, such as muscles, so that they can fight harder or run faster.

Term	Definition
Final hearing	Also called an adjudication, a contested hearing, or a defended hearing. The final hearing is the third hearing in the court process (after the FDA and FDRA) at which a judge will make an adjudicative decision.
Financial abuse	A type of domestic abuse, commonly employed by narcissists. Other types include emotional, physical and legal abuse.
Financial Dispute Resolution Appointment (FDRA)	The second hearing at which the judge will endeavour to assist the parties reach an agreement on a 'without prejudice' basis. The FDRA judge may not then deal with the final hearing of the case as they will be privy to the without prejudice proposals. The hearing is similar to a mediation appointment but with a judge mediating between the two sides.
First Directions Appointment (FDA)	This is the first court hearing in which the finances of the parties are considered. The judge will look at what is required in order to move the case along in the court process, including answers to questions raised (see 'questionnaire') and valuation evidence.
Flying monkey	One of the narcissist's fan club. Named after the flying monkeys in the Wizard of Oz who do the evil bidding of the wicked witch, they abuse the narcissist's victim on their behalf, spying on them and spreading lies about them to curry favour with the narcissist.
Fogging technique	A communication technique where the non-narcissist acknowledges the literal truth in what the narcissist is saying, but doesn't react to any implicit suggestions they are making, and doesn't agree to do things they may want them to do.
Gas-lighting	The act of undermining another person's reality by denying facts, the environment around them or their feelings.

Term	Definition
Generalisations	Another way in which the human brain filters out incoming information (others include deletions and distortions), by making automatic assumptions based on the person's past experiences, ignoring any exceptions that may be present.
Golden child	The child who is being idealised by the narcissist and is treated differently to the others, as if they can do no wrong.
Grandiose Narcissist	Another name for an Exhibitionist or Overt Narcissist.
Grey rock technique	A communication technique to minimise the amount of narcissistic supply one gives to a narcissist, by giving no emotional response at all – not even the merest hint. The ways in which this can be done include reducing eye contact (possibly to no eye contact at all), making the voice flat and boring, speaking slowly, ignoring completely inflammatory statements and immobilising all facial expressions.
Hoovering	The term given to the narcissist's tactic to suck the target back into the relationship, so that the narcissist can continue to use them as a source of narcissistic supply. It is another form of idealisation but specific to imminent abandonment.
Hybrid mediation	A fusion of the family and civil/commercial mediation models undertaken by specially trained mediators. Meetings will usually be held separately and may be attended by the parties' lawyers. A good option to consider with narcissists.
Idealisation phase	Also called the love-bombing phase. The idealisation phase is the initial stage of a relationship with a narcissist, during which the narcissist puts their victim on a pedestal.
Intermittent reinforcement	Technique used by narcissists to keep their victims hooked to them by giving them unpredictable, varying wins.

Term	Definition
Introverted Narcissist	Also called a Closet, Covert or Vulnerable Narcissist.
Invisible child	The child who is not seen or heard by the narcissist, whose siblings may be cast in the roles of golden child or scapegoat by the narcissistic parent.
Kubler-Ross model	A 5 stage grief process model consisting of denial, anger, bargaining, depression and finally, acceptance relevant in the loss of a relationship.
Love-bombing	Also called the 'idealisation' phase. The initial stage of a relationship with a narcissist.
Malignant Narcissist	Another name for a Devaluing or Toxic Narcissist.
Mask	The mask is the outward projection of the narcissist's false self. But when the narcissist does not get enough narcissistic supply or enough of what he or she wants from their target, the mask will drop, to reveal their true nature. See also false persona.
Mediation	The facilitation by a mediator of discussion on a 'without prejudice' basis to assist the couple in reaching their own agreement. The mediator may provide information but not legal advice. Classic mediation generally does not work where one of the couple is narcissistic.
Mediation Information and Assessment Meeting (MIAM)	Before issuing any court application it is necessary to attend a MIAM. At this appointment an accredited mediator will discuss out of court options as an alternative to a court application.
Narcissistic abuse	This is mostly covert emotional abuse but physical abuse can also be a feature of narcissistic behaviour.
Narcissistic injury	This occurs when the narcissist's outer bubble is punctured; when the protective suit of armour is penetrated by some external event. It could be a perceived personal slight which brings on the injury, or any situation in which things do not go the narcissist's way. It leads to narcissistic rage.

Term	Definition
Narcissistic Personality Disorder	Personality disorder characterised by a pattern of exaggerated feelings of self-importance, an excessive craving for admiration and low levels of empathy.
Narcissistic pseudologic	A typical narcissist's communication style which includes multiple contradictions, irrational conclusions, and loose associations between ideas.
Narcissistic rage	Intense fury as a consequence of narcissistic injury.
Narcissistic supply	Narcissists need 'feeding' attention, in some form or other, to maintain the fragile image that they present to the world. This external validation is what is termed 'narcissistic supply'. Without narcissistic supply those with NPD are forced to feel their own sense of unworthiness and shame. Almost everything a narcissist does is with the aim of securing narcissistic supply through attention, adoration, drama or conflict.
'No contact'	If at all possible, the spouse or partner of the narcissist should have no contact at all with the narcissist. However, if they share children, are still living under the same roof, or if they are involved in a joint business venture, this may not be possible. If it is possible, however, then they should block the narcissist from all methods of contact (including phone, email, social media, messaging apps, texts) and limit essential communication to taking place via solicitors. 'No contact' is the most effective way to remove narcissistic supply from a narcissist.
Object constancy	The ability to believe that a relationship is stable and intact, despite the presence of setbacks, conflict, or disagreements. Narcissists have not developed this ability, so they cannot see you as somebody they love, and someone who has angered them at the same time.
Overt Narcissist	Another name for an Exhibitionist or Grandiose Narcissist.

Term	Definition
Parallel parenting	A method of parenting to use when healthy, co-operative and empathic co-parenting is impossible, such as with a narcissistic parent. Here the parents communicate only when absolutely necessary, do not attend events relating to the children together, and allow the rules of the parent at whichever household the child is currently staying to apply. It allows the non-narcissistic parent to disengage as much as possible from the narcissist to facilitate healing, and lowers conflict and therefore damage to the children as a consequence.
Parental alienation	The process though which a child becomes estranged from a parent as a result of the psychological manipulation of the other parent.
Parental responsibility	The rights gained automatically or by application for parents and other adults to make decisions on behalf of the child.
Parenting Plan	A written plan agreed between parents after they separate to cover the practical issues of parenting. The plan can help clarify any issues which may arise during the child's minority. Also called a child arrangements plan.
Passive aggression	Examples are silent treatment, lateness, procrastinating on jobs, sabotaging other's work and name calling and insults re-framed as jokes.
Projection	A psychological defence mechanism unconsciously used by many people, but by all narcissists. Anyone who finds it difficult to accept their failures, weaknesses, poor behaviours and their own less flattering traits may unwittingly use projection as a way of feeling better about themselves, by accusing another person of exhibiting those traits or carrying out those behaviours. Essentially they are assigning those imperfect or flawed parts of themselves to other people.

Term	Definition
Projective identification	If a victim has been gas-lit for years, it is quite common for them to take on, believe and identify with whatever it is that the narcissist is projecting on to them. This is called 'projective identification'. They come to believe what the narcissist is telling them about themselves.
Questionnaire	A document which raises relevant questions in connection with financial disclosure. It should ask for provision of any missing information from the other side's Form E, and ask for clarification of any facts that are unclear regarding the other party's financial situation. A narcissist typically will give incomplete or obtuse answers to the questionnaire..
Rescuers	Rescuers need to rescue others to feel needed and to matter, and although they may think their rescuing tendencies are generous in nature, in fact, even with non-narcissists, they are dis-empowering to the recipient. A narcissist will exploit this trait time and time again, pulling the target into the drama triangle and keeping them there by playing the victim.
Scapegoat	The child of a narcissist who is blamed, shamed and can do nothing right – the golden child's opposite number.
Shamedumping	Giving away ('dumping') feelings of deep shame to others, so that they do not have to feel the shame themselves – characteristic of narcissists.
Silver separators	People who separate in later life.
Spectrum of narcissism	Narcissism exists on a spectrum. Those at the lowest end of the spectrum, who do not feel special, are the echoists. Those at the opposite end of the spectrum are the narcissists who are blind to the needs and feelings of others, concerned only with meeting their own needs to feel special. Those in the middle of the spectrum are healthy – able to stand up for themselves but not at the expense of others.

Term	Definition
Toxic Narcissist	Another name for a Devaluing or Malignant Narcissist.
Trauma bonding	The neurochemical addiction of a victim to the narcissist, as a result of their intermittent reinforcement schedule of rewards, because of the repeating cycle of idealise and devalue.
Triangulation	Where the narcissist brings a third person into the equation, playing them off the others in the triangle. That person will often be another unwitting victim of the narcissist, who is being groomed by the narcissist as another source of narcissistic supply.
Vulnerable Narcissist	Another name for a Closet, Covert or Introverted Narcissist.
Welfare Checklist	The checklist set out in Section 1 of the Children Act 1989 which will be followed as a guide in any application involving minor children.
Whole object relations	This is the capacity to integrate the liked and disliked parts of a person into a single, realistic, stable picture – as opposed to alternating between seeing the person as either all-good or all-bad, as narcissists do.
Without prejudice	Anything which is marked 'without prejudice' is privileged between the author and recipient and may not be shown to the court or referred to openly (i.e. in a different communication which is *not* marked without prejudice). Financial settlement offers (and other types of offer) are often made out of court between the parties on a without prejudice basis, and a narcissist may seek to exploit this by shifting the goalposts just as these agreements are nearly reached, or by making unreasonable offers which cannot later be brought to the court's attention. The FDRA is a without prejudice hearing, so anything said there cannot be mentioned at the final hearing.

Term	Definition
Word salad	The nonsensical style of communication from a narcissist after they have descended into narcissistic rage – illogical and ranting in nature, with very loose associations between ideas.

Further reading

Co-dependency for Dummies by Darlene Lancer

Re-thinking Narcissism: The secret to recognizing and Coping with Narcissists by Dr Craig Malkin.

The Chimp Paradox by Prof Steve Peters

Mindfulness: The Eight-Week Meditation Programme for a Frantic World by Prof Mark Williams and Dr Danny Penman

The Family Court without a Lawyer: A Handbook for Litigants in Person by Lucy Reed

Narcissism and Family law – A Practitioner's Guide by Dr Supriya McKenna and Karin Walker

Index

Made in the USA
Middletown, DE
30 July 2023

35988007R00213